I NEVER THOUGHT
I'D SEE THE DAY!

ALSO BY DR. DAVID JEREMIAH

The Coming Economic Armageddon

AVAILABLE WHEREVER BOOKS
ARE SOLD

I NEVER THOUGHT I'D SEE THE DAY!

CULTURE AT THE CROSSROADS

DR. DAVID JEREMIAH

FaithWords

New York · Boston · Nashville

FaithWords
Hachette Book Group
1290 Avenue of the Americas
New York, NY 10104
www.faithwords.com

The Author is represented by Yates & Yates, www.yates2.com.

Unless otherwise indicated, Scriptures are taken from the NEW KING JAMES VERSION. Copyright © 1979, 1980, 1982, Thomas Nelson, Inc., Publishers.

Scriptures noted KJV are taken from the King James Version of the Bible.

Scriptures noted The Message are taken from The Message. Copyright © 1993, 1994, 1995, 1996, 2000, 2001, 2002. Used by permission of NavPress Publishing Group.

Scripture taken from the HOLY BIBLE, NEW INTERNATIONAL VERSION®. Copyright © 1973, 1978, 1984 Biblica. Used by permission of Zondervan. All rights reserved.

Cover photo of Dr. Jeremiah by Alan Weissman

All rights reserved. Printed in the United States of America

RRD-C

Originally published in hardcover by Hachette Book Group.

First trade edition: October 2012
10 9 8 7 6 5 4 3 2

FaithWords is a division of Hachette Book Group, Inc.

The FaithWords name and logo are trademarks of Hachette Book Group, Inc.

The publisher is not responsible for websites (or their content) that are not owned by the publisher.

The Library of Congress has cataloged the hardcover edition as follows:
Jeremiah, David, 1941–
    I never thought I'd see the day! : culture at the crossroads / David Jeremiah. —1st ed.
        p. cm.
    Summary: "David Jeremiah highlights the decline in Western culture, especially America, and calls on his readers to reverse this downward spiral" —Provided by the publisher.
    ISBN 978-0-446-56595-0 (regular edition) —ISBN 978-1-4555-0734-4 (large print edition)
    1. United States—Church history—21st century.   2. Christianity and culture—United States.   3. United States—Social conditions—21st century.   4. United States—Civilization —21st century.   5. Social values —United States.   6. Civilization, Western.   7. Apologetics.   I. Title.
    BR526.J47 2011

    277.3'083—dc23

                                2011027141

ISBN 978-0-446-56596-7 (pbk.)

To Drs. Tim and Beverly LaHaye
You have shown our generation
what it means
to be
"Salt and Light"
Matthew 5:13–14

ACKNOWLEDGMENTS

The first person to hear my vision for a writing project, and the first person to believe in that vision is my wife Donna. She has walked with me in the writing of over thirty books. When I am overwhelmed by the pressure of writing a book while at the same time leading a large congregation and media ministry, she prays for me and encourages me.

David Michael Jeremiah is Vice President and Director of Operations at Turning Point, and he is vitally involved with each book that I write. Besides managing the day-to-day operation of the Turning Point Ministries, David is the architect and orchestrator of our book launch strategy. He also plans and directs our arena events which feature each new book we release. Father and son...best of friends...partners in ministry...it doesn't get any better than that! Thank you, David Michael!

Paul Joiner and the Turning Point Creative Department made the release of *I Never Thought I'd See the Day!* the focus of their collective efforts for the six months that preceded its release. The promotional kit and the dramatic series "The Account" is like nothing I have ever seen in the world of publishing. Paul, I never cease to be amazed at the ideas God gives to you and your ability to make them come to life. Thanks also to Martin Zambrano who designed the illustrations you will find throughout the book.

With each new book and each new radio and television release, the challenge of managing my office becomes more complex.

Diane Sutherland is my administrative assistant. Somehow she finds a way to stay ahead of everything that flows through our office. She is a consummate organizer and administrator, and wherever I go on my many journeys, people tell me "how special it is to work with Diane." Thank you, Diane, for representing us all so very well.

Barbara Boucher keeps everything running smoothly in my office at Shadow Mountain Community Church and she has been doing so faithfully for many years. Barbara, I am so grateful to you for all you do behind the scenes that enables me to fulfill my calling.

If you examine the footnote section at the end of this book, you will get a pretty clear picture of the amount of research that has gone into this project. Cathy Lord has been our research coordinator for the last several books and she began this project with us as well. When it became necessary for her to return to her home in Cincinnati, Beau Sager stepped in and led us the rest of the way home. Beau, your commitment to excellence is evident to us all and we are so thankful for your sacrificial investment in *I Never Thought I'd See the Day!*

Thanks to William Kruidenier for making this book his number one priority. Rob Morgan, you added value to this manuscript. And Tom Williams, your editorial skill is evident in every chapter. You are all a blessing to Turning Point and to me personally.

As the publishing world continues to grow more complex and challenging, I am blessed to have the council and direction that comes from the firm of Yates and Yates. For over twenty-five years, Sealy Yates has been my literary agent and my good friend.

I also want to express my gratitude to the people at Faith-Words for their commitment to this project. Publisher Rolf Zettersten and editor Joey Paul have joined hands with us at Turning Point in a shared effort to get this book into the hands and hearts of as many people as possible.

Most of all, I am thankful for another year of opportunity to serve my Lord and Savior, Jesus Christ.

David Jeremiah

San Diego, California

July 1st, 2011

CONTENTS

A Slow Drift in the Wrong Direction

"Toto, I've a feeling we're not in Kansas anymore." With that famous line from the movie version of L. Frank Baum's *The Wonderful Wizard of Oz*, Dorothy and her dog, Toto, find themselves in the strange and wonderful land of Oz—quite different from the Kansas of her childhood.

As I wake up and scan today's headlines, I am often tempted to think, *Toto, we're not in America anymore.* I'm exaggerating, of course, but only a little. When I look at the changes that have occurred in the land I love—and in the Church I love even more—just in my lifetime, I have to pinch myself to see if it's a dream gone bad. Sadly, what I see is all too real. I do a double take several times a week—sometimes several times a day—as I witness more and more changes I never thought I would see.

When I first began my vocational ministry nearly five decades ago, if someone had suggested that I would someday write a book titled *I Never Thought I'd See the Day*, I would probably have thought, *That's an unlikely idea for a book! What would it be about?* Today, I obviously think differently. In fact, I could have written this book many years ago when I first began to see things I never thought I'd see. The changes are coming so fast and furiously that I could no longer put it off.

My calling in life is neither to be an author nor to be a prophet. I am a pastor-teacher, by the grace of God, with shepherding steward-ship over a specific congregation of Christian believers in Southern California. My focus throughout my ministry has been on one thing: lifting up Jesus Christ by the faithful preaching of the Word of God through the exposition and application of the Bible to daily life.

But something has happened in recent years. There has always been a stark difference between life as the Scriptures describe it and life in our fallen world, but lately the contrast has grown even more stark. The changes we have experienced in the United States and the world have been more numerous, more consequential, and more threatening than any in my lifetime. As I have addressed these changes from a biblical perspective for the benefit of my own congre-gation, I have found there is a hunger for answers in a much wider audience. There are many, many Christians across the country and around the world who have seen, and suffered through, many of these cataclysmic events. And they want answers. They want to know what God's Word says not only about the cultural and spiritual changes themselves, but how to live faithfully in the midst of them.

So I have, over the last four years, preached on and written about these subjects to the best of my ability. I don't claim that these books are the last word on the subjects they address. But I cannot sit idly by and watch believers be "destroyed [spiritually] for lack of knowledge" (Hosea 4:6). Life is becoming more challenging in our world, and fol-lowers of Christ are going to have to be at their strongest (*His* stron-gest) in order to continue standing firm in wisdom and in hope.

These unprecedented times demand unprecedented discernment

from Christians. I don't know what the future holds, but my commitment to God is to do whatever I can to bring biblical light to bear on these challenging times. My prayerful goal is to have the same discerning spirit as did "the sons of Issachar who had understanding of the times, to know what [the people of God] ought to do" (1 Chronicles 12:32).

This is actually the fourth in a series of books I never dreamed of writing. The scope of the first three books was the present and the future—prophetic clues and trends and how to live in light of them.[1] The scope of this book is the present as compared with the past—the dramatic changes I have seen in recent years and how they are shaping the world we find ourselves in today. These are large subjects, the kind of trends that develop over years. They move at a glacial pace compared to the frenetic lifestyle most Americans live, which makes them easy to miss.

But no one misses the effects of these changes. They contribute to the deteriorating moral and spiritual culture in which we live. We have this feeling that we're not in Kansas anymore. America today is not the America we thought it was, but we're not sure why. I believe some of the subjects I tackle in this book will help connect the dots between this feeling and what we see happening around us. And, it will help us evaluate the changes we're experiencing from a biblical point of view.

I have chosen to address nine developments that I never thought I would see in my lifetime, all of which have significant implications for the Church of Jesus Christ. The first is the rise of angry atheists. Atheists used to be relatively passive, but we now have a spate of emboldened nonbelievers who are angry and proactive and determined to intimidate believers in God.

Next I address the intensifying of spiritual warfare. The more the Gospel progresses and the closer we get to the end of the age, the more aggressive the enemy becomes. Sadly, many Christians are unaware that a battle is raging all around them, and they have not reported for duty.

No subject in this book grieves me more than the dethroning of Jesus Christ. In today's America He has moved from the central figure of world history to source material for late-night comics and pundits who would not dare treat other religious leaders with such disrespect.

Next I address the redefining of marriage. The heterosexual union of a man and a woman in marriage is no longer considered the norm upon which nations build their cultures. Marriage itself has become an option, with an alarming number of unmarried couples living together and having children. Following marriage I address America's loss of its moral compass—its inability to be shocked or shamed by gross immorality. Moral failures, public and private, have become part of the fabric of life.

Intertwined with this free fall in morality is the growing marginalization of the Bible, which has moved from the center of political and cultural discourse to the far edges—from providing the founding principles of our nation to becoming a resource for token verses as ornamental platitudes. Sadly, many Christians and a growing number of churches have followed the lead of the culture and pushed the Word of God away from the center of their lives.

This leads us to the growing irrelevance of the Christian Church in the eyes of our society. While society may be biased, the Church needs to ask itself whether it has lost, by its impassivity and lack of zeal, the right to be heard or to exercise its former civil, social, and spiritual roles concerning the major issues of the day.

Moving from internal deterioration to external concerns, I address the growing influence of rogue nations. Iran's increasing power and radical Muslim theocratic mission have created a whole new level of instability in an already fragile Middle East and destabilized the rest of the world.

Last I address the erosion of America's loyalty to Israel. Since America's founding she has been a friend to the Jews, which has resulted in God's blessing on our nation (Genesis 12:3). But America's current trend toward reduced loyalty to Israel in an attempt to appease Palestinians or ensure access to oil resources puts her on a collision course with God.

These are serious subjects and I have treated them as such. Every chapter is filled with cultural and biblical information to illustrate God's standard and how America and the world have departed from it. I believe one of our biggest problems is that America's departure from God's standard has occurred so slowly that many of us do not realize just how far we have drifted. To illustrate how this can happen, let me tell you a true story.

Sir William Edward Parry (1790–1855) was an English naval officer and record-setting explorer of the Arctic—and an Evangelical Christian. He made one of the very first attempts to reach the North Pole and, in doing so, penetrated farther north than any previous explorer—a record that stood for nearly fifty years. On one of his trips to the Arctic, Parry and his men were pushing hard, trekking across the ice toward the Pole. At one point he stopped and recalculated his position by the stars, then continued pushing north. Hours later they stopped, exhausted. Again Admiral Parry calculated his position and discovered something unbelievable: They were actually farther south than when they made their previous calculation! Parry was an expert in astronomical observations and calculations (he wrote a book on the subject), so a mistake on his part was not likely. He eventually discovered the problem: He and his team had been on a gigantic ice floe that was moving south faster than they were trekking north. It was a classic example of the old "one step forward, two steps backward" routine.

The ice floe was so big and moving so slowly that Parry's loss of position was imperceptible until he recalculated. While he thought he was gaining ground, he was losing.

This is what has happened in America. When we calculated our position back in the 1950s, we thought we knew where we were. We had just defeated Nazism and the Axis powers in World War II, we had a world-famous Army general for a president (Eisenhower), the economy was booming, churches were full, and it seemed that most everybody loved God, Mom, Chevrolet, and apple pie. So we marched on. But in the first decade of the twenty-first century, many of us began to sense that we had long ago veered off course. A new set of calculations—nine of which I describe in this book—have revealed something I never thought I'd live to see: We've been losing spiritual and moral ground in America.

America is big, multicultural, and ever-changing. We are like that giant ice floe Admiral Parry was on—so big that changes over the last fifty years have seemed of little concern on a day-to-day basis. But on a century-to-century basis, these changes stand out like a flashing neon warning sign. Fifty years ago, standards of marriage and morality and respect for Jesus Christ, the Church, and the Bible were widespread. Iran was never in the headlines, and in 1948 President Harry Truman was the first head of state to openly declare his nation's support for the newly formed political State of Israel. When you examine these and other areas of our national life, it is all too obvious that we have lost, not gained, ground in the last half century.

Now we come to the big question Christians are asking: What do we do in light of the devolution of society around us? When we ask the question in that way, we betray a misunderstanding of the problem. We mistakenly think the problem is outside us—that it originates with the non-Christian population. We sometimes adopt the attitude of the Pharisee who prayed, "God, I thank You that I am not like other men—extortioners, unjust, adulterers, or even as this tax collector" (Luke 18:11).

The truth is, we can echo the words of Pogo in the old Walt Kelly comic strip: "We have met the enemy and he is us!" All too often we Christians are like "other men." We have allowed the world to *conform* us to its image instead of allowing the Holy Spirit and the Word of God to *transform* us into the image of Christ (Romans 8:29). Our records on faithfulness to marriage, standards of morality, support and involvement in our local churches, honoring the testimony of Scripture, and other critical areas of life are too often similar to those of the world. We who profess to believe in Christ often make no more difference in the world than those who profess no such belief.

So when it comes to answering the question, "What do we do?" the first thing we do is let judgment "begin at the house of God" (1 Peter 4:17). We must remove the beams from our own eyes before we point out the speck in the world's eye (Matthew 7:3–5). Christ declared us as Christians, not the world, to be salt and light (Matthew 5:13–16). In prerefrigeration days, if a slab of salt-cured pork went bad, nobody blamed the pork. They blamed the quality, amount, or application of the salt! And the Church of Jesus Christ is the salt of the earth.

Therefore, in the final chapter of the book I have addressed the

"What now?" question by focusing on Christians instead of the world. In Romans 12:1 the apostle Paul uses two words that represent essentially opposite conditions: *conformed* and *transformed*. We live our lives on a mountain peak, always standing at a tipping point. If we allow the world to conform us to its image, we slide into the world's valley. But if we allow ourselves to be transformed into the image of Christ, we live in the opposite valley. Because we stand balanced at that tipping point, it is critical for two reasons that we address the issues I raise in this book from a Christian perspective.

First, we are to be a means of preservation. Even if we live the best and brightest life possible for Christ, the world may continue to decline. But we do not have to be pulled down into the valley with it. Only by renewing our minds with God's truth can we defend ourselves against the conforming power that the world constantly exerts against us. If you or I were the last Christian on earth, God would still expect us to live a life that is pleasing to Him, not yielding to the world, the flesh, and the devil even though they are all around us.

Second, we are to be a source of inspiration. We can make a difference in this world! Salt and light radically impact everything they touch. Every time the world comes in contact with a Christian, a transference of hope, love, and relevancy should occur. But we will not change the world by living like the world. Jesus did not change the world in His day by embracing the values of the culture around Him. People were attracted to Christ because He was different. In Him they saw something that neither the Romans nor the established Jewish religion had to offer. And if we are being transformed by that same Christ, the One who lives in us (Galatians 2:20), people will be attracted to Him through our manifestation of His righteousness, His purpose, His love, and His unchanging ways.

If we will allow our minds to be renewed continually by the Word of God, we will spot immediately when we, or the world, have gone off course and need correction. We will not drift slowly, carried along by the winds of change. Rather, we will implement corrections in our course countless times each day—for preservation and inspiration.

I recently read that the world has changed more in the last two or three decades than in the previous twenty or thirty centuries. And unless some cataclysmic event throws the entire world into a decades-long black hole, change is going to occur only faster. Therefore, the potential is great for Christians to be overcome by the world and to lose their voice in the world. But neither has to be true.

To prevent these failures we must learn from history by measuring the past against the present. Then we must commit to a different future by measuring our power to be transformed by Christ against the pressure to be conformed to the world. I pray this book will help with both sets of measurements: that we may stand firmly and faithfully until we see our Lord face-to-face.

I NEVER THOUGHT I'D SEE THE DAY!

CHAPTER 1

When Atheists Would Be Angry

On May 15, 2007, Jerry Falwell, one of our generation's leading Evangelicals, died. That same day, CNN anchor Anderson Cooper asked the outspoken atheist Christopher Hitchens for his reaction:

COOPER: I'm not sure if you believe in heaven, but, if you do, do you think Jerry Falwell is in it?

HITCHENS: No. And I think it's a pity there isn't a hell for him to go to.

COOPER: What is it about him that brings up such vitriol?

HITCHENS: The empty life of this ugly little charlatan proves only one thing, that you can get away with the most extraordinary offenses to morality and to truth in this country if you will just get yourself called reverend.

COOPER: Whether you agree or not with his reading of the Bible, you don't think he was sincere in what he spoke?

HITCHENS: No. I think he was a conscious charlatan and bully and fraud. And I think, if he read the Bible at all—and I would doubt that he could actually read any long book...that he did so only in the most hucksterish, as we say, Bible-pounding way.[1]

Because Jerry Falwell and his family have been personal friends of mine for more than thirty years, I found Hitchens's words to be cruel and insensitive, and most of all inaccurate. But I am sure Hitchens would argue that he was not singling out Falwell for any special treatment. He and his atheist friends have mounted an aggressive offensive against all Evangelicals. As Christian apologist Dinesh D'Souza has written, "A group of prominent atheists—many of them evolutionary biologists—has launched a public attack on religion in general and Christianity in particular; they have no interest in being nice."[2]

It's not hard to find evidence to support D'Souza's assertion. Richard Dawkins, in his book *The God Delusion*, spews out his anger at God: "The God of the Old Testament is arguably the most unpleasant character in all fiction: jealous and proud of it; a petty, unjust, unforgiving control-freak; a vindictive, bloodthirsty ethnic cleanser; a misogynistic, homophobic, racist, infanticidal, genocidal, filicidal, pestilential, megalomaniacal, sadomasochistic, capriciously malevolent bully."[3]

Dawkins is no longer content to argue about God—he's angry *at* God. A *Christianity Today* editorial attempts to explain this new level of vitriol:

> You can also tell that atheism is in trouble because it is becoming increasingly intolerant. In the past, atheists... were often condescendingly tolerant of their less-enlightened fellow citizens. While they disdained religion, they treated their religious neighbors as good-hearted, if misguided. But now key activists are urging a less civil approach. At a recent forum sponsored by the Science Network at the Salk Institute in La Jolla, California, the tone of intolerance reached such a peak that anthropologist Melvin J. Konner commented: "The viewpoints have run the gamut from A to B. Should we bash religion with a crowbar or only with a baseball bat?"[4]

One former atheist, Antony Flew, called this a "look-back-in-anger, take-no-prisoners type of atheism."[5] The irony of the New Atheists' anger is captured in editor/professor Joe Carter's article "When Atheists Are Angry at God":

> I've shaken my fist in anger at stalled cars, storm clouds, and incompetent meteorologists. I've even, on one terrible day that included a dead alternator, a blaring tornado-warning siren, and a horribly wrong weather forecast, cursed all three at once.

I've fumed at furniture, cursed at crossing guards, and held a grudge against Gun Barrel City, Texas. I've been mad at just about anything you can imagine.

Except unicorns. I've never been angry at unicorns.

It's unlikely you've ever been angry at unicorns either. We can become incensed by objects and creations both animate and inanimate. We can even, in a limited sense, be bothered by the fanciful characters in books and dreams. But creatures like unicorns that don't exist—that we truly believe not to exist—tend not to raise our ire. We certainly don't blame the one-horned creatures for our problems.

The one social group that takes exception to this rule is atheists. They claim to believe that God does not exist and yet, according to empirical studies, tend to be the people most angry at him.[6]

When I write of the anger of the atheists, I am not primarily referring to the classic atheists such as Bertrand Russell, Jean-Paul Sartre, Karl Marx, and Sigmund Freud. The atheists I am writing about are the "New Atheists." The term "new atheism" was first used by *Wired* magazine in November 2006 to describe the atheism espoused in books like Daniel Dennett's *Breaking the Spell*, Richard Dawkins's *The God Delusion*, Lewis Wolpert's *Six Impossible Things Before Breakfast*, Victor Stenger's *The Comprehensible Cosmos*, Sam Harris's *The End of Faith*, and Christopher Hitchens's *God Is Not Great*.[7]

As Antony Flew observed,

What was significant about these books was not their level of argument—which was modest, to put it mildly—but the level of visibility they received both as best sellers and as a "new" story discovered by the media.

The chief target of these books is, without question, organized religion of any kind, time, or place. Paradoxically, the books themselves read like fundamentalist sermons. The authors, for the most part, sound like hellfire-and-brimstone preachers warning us of dire retribution, even of apocalypse, if we do not repent of our wayward beliefs and associated practices.[8]

Why such anger? How can people be so angry with God if they do not even believe in His existence? And why would the most angry among them feel so compelled to preach their anti-God religion with such evangelistic zeal?

It would be presumptuous, if not impossible, to state categorically why the New Atheists are angry at God. Is it because the number of Christians is increasing while the number of atheists is decreasing? Is it because they are not swaying the mainstream with their arguments? Is it an example of Santayana's definition of *fanaticism*: "redoubling your effort when you have forgotten your aim"?[9] Is it the anger of rebellion that often comes from the conviction of sin—sin that one does not want to give up (John 16:8)?

I cannot answer these questions because I cannot know the hearts of these angry atheists. But I do know this: Today's vocal crop of atheists has ramped up the volume, if not the substance, of the modern attack on religion that we see going on in several quarters. We've always had atheists, and we always will until the Lord comes again. But the shrill scream of today's atheists is nothing like the more respectful opposition to belief we've seen in the past. I never thought I'd see the day when atheists would so openly and viciously attack us, abandoning rational argument and descending into toxic vitriol and groundless accusation. But that day has come, and in this chapter we will explore this new atheism, what it means, and how we can respond.

What's So New About "New Atheism"?

While the proactivism, "evangelistic" fervor, and militant spirit of the New Atheists are new, atheism itself is not.[10] The English words *atheist* and *atheism* do not appear in modern translations of the Bible. But the ideas they represent certainly do. Our English word *atheist* is derived from the Greek word *atheos*, which occurs once in the New Testament (Ephesians 2:12). In the Greek the prefix *a–* is a negative, meaning "no," while *theos* is the word for God. So *a* + *theos* = *atheos*, which means, literally, "no god." It could also mean "without God," which is how Paul used it in Ephesians 2:12: "having no hope and without God in the world."

Atheos can be understood in at least three ways:

First, people can be without God due to circumstance. In Ephesians 2:12, Paul describes Gentiles as being "without God" because they were "aliens from the commonwealth of Israel and strangers from the covenants of promise." It wasn't that Gentiles were opposed to the existence of God (Acts 17:22–23), yet they were without God because they had not received specific information about Him—information Paul was delivering to them through his evangelistic efforts. There are unreached peoples in the world today who are without God because the biblical Gospel has not yet reached them. But they are not atheists in the sense we use the word today. People who have not heard of God cannot be characterized as rejecting Him by choice.

The second way *atheos* can be used is to designate people who are without God by choice. This is the sense in which *atheos* is used today, incorporating both meanings of the word: "no God" and "without God." Modern atheists are "without God" because they believe there is "no God." They have the same evidence for God that theists have—in nature and in the Bible—but they have chosen to reject it and are therefore *atheists*. They do not believe God exists. This is likely what is described in Psalms 14:1 and 53:1: "The fool has said in his heart, 'There is no God.'" In the Old Testament, especially in the book of Proverbs, a fool is someone who rejects counsel, wisdom, and evidence and goes his own way. The fool is often contrasted with the wise or prudent person, who receives counsel and correction and adjusts his way accordingly (Proverbs 10:8; 12:15; 15:5). There is even a hint of "New Atheism" in Proverbs 14:16: "A fool rages and is self-confident."

A third way to understand *atheos* is "without God by callousness." This is sometimes referred to as "practical atheism": being a *theist* in mind but an *atheist* in heart and action. I'll have more to say on this later.

Obviously, in this chapter I am focusing on number two in the list above: atheists by choice. In spite of their energy and marketing efforts, we can be thankful that their aggressiveness is not serving their cause very well. Let's explore the several ways in which atheists are hurting themselves.

Their Arrogance Is Disgracing Them

At the launch in 2010 of her satirical book *The Loser Letters*, Hoover Institution fellow Mary Eberstadt explained why she takes on the New Atheists: "Their movement has repeatedly assailed religious people as self-righteous, ignorant of history, and humorless, all the while remaining self-righteous, ignorant of history, and humorless itself to a quite remarkable degree."[11]

It's hard to read their books or watch their interviews without concluding that the New Atheists think they are a lot smarter than the rest of us, and especially the rest of us who happen to be Christians. In the past, atheists attempted to mask this arrogance; now it is flaunted. The change occurred in 2003 when Daniel Dennett and Richard Dawkins decided that atheists needed a less offensive name. The term chosen to spruce up atheism was "bright." A "Bright" was defined as someone who holds "a naturalistic worldview," which is "free of supernatural and mystical elements."[12]

In a 2003 article in England's the *Guardian*, Richard Dawkins explains why a new word was needed to raise consciousness about atheism: "Those of us who subscribe to no religion; those of us whose view of the universe is natural rather than supernatural; those of us who rejoice in the real and scorn the false comfort of the unreal, we need a word of our own, a word like 'gay.' You can say 'I am an atheist' but at best it sounds stuffy (like 'I am a homosexual') and at worst it inflames prejudice (like 'I am a homosexual')."[13]

Shortly after the term "Brights" was introduced, Steven Waldman responded with an NPR commentary:

I'm not sure what the image buffers were aiming for, but the name "The Brights" succinctly conveys the sense that this group thinks it's more intelligent than everyone else. The rest of us would be "The Dims," I suppose. Daniel C. Dennett wrote, in a recent *New York Times* op-ed, "We Brights don't believe in ghosts, or elves, or the Easter Bunny, or God."

Let's put aside the questionable intelligence of trying to improve your image by choosing a title that makes everyone hate you; they might as well have chosen "The Smugs" or "The Smartypants." Let's instead, examine the substance of their platform...

What about their bolder assertion, or implication, that people who believe in god [*sic*] or the supernatural are just not as, well, bright. In fact, two surveys earlier this year—one from Harris, and one from Gallup—indicate that even supernatural religious beliefs are held not only by most Americans, but by the majority of well-educated Americans.

Listen to these numbers—55% of people with post-graduate degrees (lawyers, doctors, dentists, and the like) believe in the Devil. 53% believe in Hell. 72% believe in miracles. Remember these are people with post-graduate educations. 78% of them believe in the survival of the soul after death. 60% believe in the virgin birth. And 64% believe in the resurrection of Christ.[14]

While the Brights themselves vigorously assert that "bright" carries no connotation of superior intelligence, it's hard to deny the conclusion reached by Waldman—that within their own circles, they surely view their intellects as capable of more rational and realistic conclusions, which makes them superior to those who believe in supposedly nonrational spiritual truths.

It is important to note in this connection that, from a biblical perspective, "irrational" is not the only alternative to "rational." There is a third category called *transrational*—a level of thinking that is not irrational though it is beyond human rationality. For example, God says, "My thoughts are not your thoughts, nor are your ways My

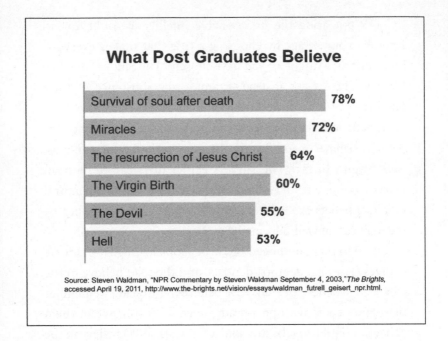

What Post Graduates Believe

Belief	Percentage
Survival of soul after death	78%
Miracles	72%
The resurrection of Jesus Christ	64%
The Virgin Birth	60%
The Devil	55%
Hell	53%

Source: Steven Waldman, "NPR Commentary by Steven Waldman September 4, 2003," *The Brights*, accessed April 19, 2011, http://www.the-brights.net/vision/essays/waldman_futrell_geisert_npr.html.

ways... For as the heavens are higher than the earth, so are My ways higher than your ways, and My thoughts than your thoughts" (Isaiah 55:8–9). This passage refers to thoughts and ways that are beyond (*trans-*) human thoughts and ways, beyond human comprehension. Therefore, while belief in an unseen God may appear humanly irrational because it is beyond the limited reach of the human mind, it is perfectly rational from God's perspective, which we embrace as Christians.

Peter expresses this transrational perspective when he writes, "Jesus Christ, whom having not seen you love. Though now you do not see Him, yet believing, you rejoice with joy inexpressible and full of glory" (1 Peter 1:7–8). The Brights find such belief irrational;

but Christians find no conflict in believing and loving beyond what human rationality would confirm.

Dinesh D'Souza agrees with this perspective: "While the atheist arrogantly persists in the delusion that his reason is fully capable of figuring out all that there is, the religious believer lives in the humble acknowledgment of the limits of human knowledge, knowing that there is a reality greater than, and beyond, that which our senses and minds can ever apprehend."[15]

While we rightly place great emphasis on faith in our approach to the transrational, I don't want to leave readers with the impression that it's a blind faith devoid of rational thinking or empirical evidence. The existence of matter, life, and reason demands an explanation that cannot be satisfied rationally by the Brights' subrational claim that everything sprang from nothing or is self-existent.

One of the clear messages of the Bible is the danger of pride. We see pride exhibited when men place their own reasoning powers above the revelation of God and depend on their own finite minds to determine infinite truths. Pride was the original sin and has its place on God's hate list (Proverbs 6:16–19). King Solomon warns, "Pride goes before destruction, and a haughty spirit before a fall" (Proverbs 16:18). Indeed, God resists the proud in all their endeavors (James 4:6).

Their Advocates Are Deserting Them

One hardly ever hears of a leading Evangelical denouncing his Evangelical faith so that he can become an atheist. But throughout history many prominent atheists have found their way to belief in God. Here are a few examples:

Antony Flew

Philosopher and former atheist Antony Flew set the agenda for modern atheism with his 1950 essay, "Theology and Falsification," which became the most widely reprinted philosophical publication of the last half-century.[16] Flew has published more than thirty books, including *God and Philosophy*, *The Presumption of Atheism*, and *How to Think Straight*.

A 2004 Associated Press story describing Flew's transformation carried this headline: "Famous Atheist Now Believes in God." The story went on to say, "A British philosophy professor who has been a leading champion of atheism for more than a half-century has changed his mind. He now believes in God."[17] Flew was adamant in maintaining that he had not become a Christian, but rather a "deist like Thomas Jefferson."[18] But simply changing from "no God" to "God" was enough to send shock waves through atheist camps.

In his 2007 book, *There Is a God*, Flew discloses how his commitment to "follow the argument wherever it leads" led him to a belief in God as Creator. One reviewer described the book as "a most uncomfortable jolt to those who were once his fellow atheists."[19]

The cover of Flew's book tells the whole story. The title, *There Is No God*, has the word *No* crossed out and the word *A* inserted. While Flew did not come to believe in the God of the Bible, he concluded that atheism is not logically sustainable.

A. N. Wilson

Once thought to be the next C. S. Lewis, A. N. Wilson renounced his faith and spent years mocking Christianity. He recently returned to faith. The reason, he said in an interview with the British magazine *New Statesman*, was that atheists "are missing out on some very basic experiences of life."[20]

While writing his biography of C. S. Lewis, he noticed similarities between himself and his subject, such as a happy childhood shading into miserable boarding-school years and a rejection of boyhood faith on reaching maturity. But another parallel slowly dawned on him: Just as Lewis gradually became aware that his favorite authors were Christians, Wilson noticed a difference between the skeptical and the devout. Attractive and amusing as David Hume was, did he confront the complexities of human existence as deeply as his contemporary Samuel Johnson? The perception of his atheist friends seemed rather "parochial and flat."[21] Listening to Bach and reading the works of religious authors, he realized that their "perception of life was deeper, wiser, and more rounded than my own."[22]

Matthew Parris

Parris, a well-known British atheist, made the mistake of visiting Christian aid workers in Malawi, where he saw the power of the Gospel transforming them and others. Concerned with what he saw, he wrote that it "confounds my ideological beliefs, stubbornly refuses to fit my worldview, and has embarrassed my growing belief that there is no God." Parris went on to pay Christian evangelism a glowing compliment that utterly confounds and contradicts the ragings against faith spewed by the New Atheists: "I've become convinced of the enormous contribution that Christian evangelism makes in Africa: sharply distinct from the work of secular NGOs, government projects and international aid efforts. These alone will not do. Education and training alone will not do. In Africa Christianity changes people's hearts. It brings a spiritual transformation. The rebirth is real. The change is good."[23]

While Parris is unwilling to follow spiritually where his observations lead intellectually, he is obviously wrestling with how Christianity makes better sense of the world than other worldviews, and he has the honesty to say it openly.

Peter Hitchens

While Peter Hitchens was never an outspoken advocate for the New Atheists, he was formerly an atheist and is the brother of the outspoken New Atheist Christopher Hitchens. Peter Hitchens is a British journalist and author of the 2010 book *The Rage Against God*. At the age of fifteen, he set fire to his Bible on the playing field of his Cambridge boarding school and set out on a life of denying the existence of God.

He attributes his return to faith to seeing socialism in practice during his years as a correspondent in Eastern Europe and in Moscow during the collapse of the Soviet Union. In his book, he describes what it was like for the Russian people who were living under the tyranny of godless Communism:

> Soviet citizens...knew the daily drudgery of finding anything decent to eat. They knew all the sugar had disappeared from the shops because the official anti-alcohol campaign had impelled millions to make their own vodka in the bathtub. They knew that if they wanted anesthetics at the dentist, or antibiotics at the hospital, or co-operation from their child's teacher, or a holiday by the sea, they would need to bribe someone to get

them. Even in Moscow, the show city of the Evil Empire, they knew that they dwelt in the suburbs of hell, that in mile after mile of mass-produced housing you would be hard put to find a single family untouched by divorce, that no mother reared her own children, that the schools taught lies, that secret government establishments leaked radiation into air and water. Fresh eggs were an event. "No" meant "How much will you pay me?" Rats were commonplace and played merrily among the trashcans of apartment blocks and in the entrances of railway terminals. Windows were filthy as a matter of course; I never saw a clean one.

While most struggled to survive, a secret elite enjoyed great privileges—special living spaces, special hospitals with Western drugs and equipment, special schools in which their children were well taught in English, special waiting rooms in stations and airports, and special lanes (one ran down the middle of the street on which I lived) along which the Politburo's giant armored limousines roared at 90 miles an hour, shouldering aside anyone who dared get in the way. The elite had privileged access to good food, foreign travel and books, and the groveling servility of the organs of the state, which oppressed the common people and extorted money from them. This society, promoted by its leaders as an egalitarian utopia, was in truth one of the most unequal societies on earth.[24]

Peter Hitchens describes life in Russia in the early nineties as harsh and dangerous. In 1990 there were 6.46 million abortions in the USSR and only 4.85 million live births. For the average citizen, life was "lived at a dismally low level materially, ethically, and culturally."[25]

This Russia of the 1990s was simply the result of the 1917 Bolshevik Revolution that led to the formation of the Soviet Union. Alister McGrath describes it this way:

> When the Bolsheviks seized power in 1917, the elimination of religious belief was a core element of their revolutionary program. This was not accidental or incidental; it was seen as an essential aspect of the new state that was to come into being... Churches were closed; priests were imprisoned, exiled or executed. On the eve of the Second World War there were only 6,376 clergy remaining in the Russian Orthodox Church, compared with the prerevolutionary figure of 66,140... In 1917, there were 39,500 churches in Russia; in 1940, only 950 remained functional. The remainder had been closed, converted for secular use or destroyed.[26]

Peter Hitchens describes the final experience that brought him back to belief in God. He was in Dallas, Texas, with a few hours to spare before catching his plane back to Washington, DC, and he decided to visit the city's Museum of Art. He found himself standing speechless in front of a painting called *The Prodigal Son* by American painter Thomas Hart Benton. Benton's portrayal of the story told a far more bitter ending than the joyful reunion of father and son in Jesus' version (Luke 15:11–32):

> [The son] has come home too late. Nobody has seen him from afar off and run joyfully to meet him. There will be no forgiveness, no best robe, no ring, no "music and dancing." He stands in his shabby clothes with his poor, roped suitcase. A

beaten-up car—the last trace of his squandered wealth—is parked in the background. He is gaping, with his hand to his mouth, at the ruin of the family homestead, ruin caused by his own greed and wastefulness. He looks as if it is just dawning on him that he is stupid and cruel and without hope. The light is failing in a chilly sky beneath wind-ripped, twisted clouds. Instead of a fatted calf, there is a stark, white animal skeleton, the skull horned, lying in the untended grass. We can guess at the grief, resignation, and failure that have overtaken the family and its home during his heedless absence. Who can he blame for it but himself? The desolation is infinite. And as I surveyed the melancholy remnants of my own church, out of which I had reluctantly stomped, I felt the same. It was terrible and wrong, but what was I to say? Where had I been when I was needed?[27]

Standing before the painting, Hitchens knew he was the prodigal, knew the Christian church in his homeland of England was the run-down, decrepit homeplace in Benton's picture. Where had he been when he was needed? Running from God, pursuing his own intellectual pleasures. The experience was a turning point for him—he "threw [himself] ... into an effort to halt or reverse the destruction" that had occurred in his absence from Christianity.[28]

Many influential Christians have turned from atheism to belief, such as C. S. Lewis, Malcolm Muggeridge, Josh McDowell, Francis Collins, Alister McGrath, Aleksandr Solzhenitsyn, and Lee Strobel, to name a few. As Jesus promised, those who honestly search for truth will find it: "Ask, and it will be given to you; seek, and you will find; knock, and it will be opened to you" (Luke 11:9).

Their Arguments Are Dividing Them

One of the New Atheists' favorite arguments against Christianity is that religion is responsible for the majority of the evil and pain in the world. That argument was popularized by Christopher Hitchens's book *God Is Not Great: How Religion Poisons Everything*. Alister McGrath summarizes the argument: "The faults of the world are to be laid at the door of backward-looking superstitions, which hold the world back from its rational and scientific destiny. Eliminate religion and the world will be a better place. Religion has led only to violence, intellectual dishonesty, oppression and social division."[29]

In his book *How the Mind Works*, Steven Pinker echoes Hitchens: "Religions have given us stonings, witch-burnings, crusades, inquisitions, jihads, fatwas, suicide bombers, abortion-clinic gunmen, and mothers who drown their sons so they can be happily reunited in heaven. As Blaise Pascal wrote, 'Men never do evil so completely and cheerfully as when they do it from religious conviction.' "[30]

While there can be no doubt that some horrible things have been done in the name of religion—and one death that arises from a religious motivation is one death too many—the atheist argument that religion poisons everything is nothing less than revisionist history. In his book *What's So Great About Christianity*, Dinesh D'Souza cites real facts to counter the atheists' accusations. He concentrates specifically on the Crusades, the Inquisition, and the Salem witch trials.

D'Souza's voluminous research begins with the Crusades, which, according to the atheists, were supposedly responsible for the massacre of thousands. D'Souza reminds his readers that the Crusades were an attempt on the part of Christians to recover territory that had been taken from them by Islamic armies. "In the context of the history of warfare, there is no warrant for considering the Crusades a world historical crime of any sort. The Christians fought to defend themselves from foreign conquest, while the Muslims fought to continue conquering Christian lands."[31] European Christians had good reason to be concerned about foreign conquest. Islamic armies had been turned back from conquering what is now modern France in AD 732 at the Battle of Tours. Had Islamic armies won that battle, the entire history of Western civilization would have been radically altered.

When it comes to the Spanish Inquisition, D'Souza discovered that "the horrific images of the Inquisition are largely a myth concocted first by the political enemies of Spain—mainly English writers who shaped our American understanding of that event—and later by the political enemies of religion."[32] Citing Henry Kamen's book *The Spanish Inquisition: A Historical Revision*, D'Souza points out that the total number of people who were executed by Roman Catholic inquisitors for heresy was approximately two thousand. While this is not an insignificant number, it is important to remember that these deaths occurred over a period of 350 years.[33]

The Salem witch trials are the New Atheists' best example of religiously motivated violence in America. Again, D'Souza's research provides correctives to the accepted critical view: "How many people were killed in those trials? Thousands? Hundreds? Actually, fewer than twenty-five. Nineteen were sentenced to death, and a few others died in captivity."[34]

In a written debate on the subject, "Is Christianity Good for the World?" Christopher Hitchens sets forth the claim that religion in general and Christianity in particular are responsible for most of the evils of the world. And theist Douglas Wilson responds:

You say that if "Christianity is to claim credit for the work of outstanding Christians or for the labors of famous charities, then it must in all honesty accept responsibility for the opposite." In short, if we point to our saints, you are going to demand that we point also to our charlatans, persecutors, shysters, slave-traders, inquisitors, hucksters, televangelists, and so on. Now allow me the privilege of pointing out the structure of your argument here. If a professor takes credit for the student who mastered the material, aced his finals, and went on to a career that was a benefit to himself and the university he graduated from, the professor must (fairness dictates) be upbraided for the dope-smoking slacker that he kicked out of class in the second week. They were both formally enrolled, is that not correct? They were both *students*, were they not?

What you are doing is saying that Christianity must be judged not only on the basis of those who believe the gospel in truth and live accordingly but also on the basis of those baptized Christians who cannot listen to the Sermon on the Mount without a horse laugh and a life to match. You are saying that those who excel in the course and those who flunk out of it are all the same. This seems to me to be a curious way of proceeding.[35]

So the New Atheists' characterizations of Christian evils err in two significant ways: The first is an error of proportion in claiming that the historical deaths inflicted in the name of Christianity come anywhere close to matching the massive deaths of scores of millions inflicted by godless regimes headed by men such as Hitler, Stalin, and Mao. The atheists' second error is in even attributing those deaths to the practice of valid Christianity. They were inflicted in the name of Christianity, but by people who had departed from Christian principles and teachings.

Their Adversaries Are Defeating Them

In his book *There Is a God*, Antony Flew tells how impressed he was with Israeli scientist Gerald Schroeder's point-by-point refutation of what Flew called the "monkey theorem." This theorem asserts that life could have arisen by chance, using the analogy of a multitude of monkeys banging away on computer keyboards until they eventually write a Shakespearean sonnet. Schroeder cites an experiment conducted by the British National Council of Arts: "A computer was placed in a cage with six monkeys. After one month of hammering away at it...the monkeys produced fifty typed pages—but not a single word...even though the shortest word in the English language is one letter (*a* or *I*). A is a word only if there is a space on either side of it."[36]

So what are the chances of getting a Shakespearean sonnet? Schroeder answered conclusively:

> If you took the entire universe and converted it to computer chips—forget the monkeys—each one weighing a millionth of a gram and had each computer chip able to spin out 488 trials at, say, a million times a second; if you turn the entire universe into these microcomputer chips and these chips were spinning a million times a second [producing] random letters...You will never get a sonnet by chance...Yet the world just thinks the monkeys can do it every time.[37]

This is but one example of how the New Atheists must rely on unproven or unprovable theorems to buttress their claim that the universe, life, matter, and intelligence arose from nothing. As C. S. Lewis wrote, any assertion that the universe came about without the agency of an intelligent first cause is flawed at its base. He calls it a myth and marvels at the credulity and denial of common sense on the part of those who believe it: "To those brought up on the Myth nothing seems more normal, more natural, more plausible, than that chaos should turn into order, death into life, ignorance into knowledge."[38]

Surprisingly, this denial of common sense is frankly acknowledged by no less than atheist and famed evolutionary biologist Richard Lewontin, who wrote,

> Our willingness to accept scientific claims that are against common sense is the key to an understanding of the real struggle between science and the supernatural. We take the side of science *in spite* of the patent absurdity of some of its constructs, *in spite* of its failure to fulfill many of its extravagant promises of health and life, *in spite* of the tolerance of the scientific community for unsubstantiated just-so stories, because we have a prior commitment, a commitment to materialism. It is not that the methods and institutions of science somehow compel us to accept a material explanation of the phenomenal world, but, on the contrary, that we are forced by our *a priori* adherence to material causes to create an apparatus of investigation and a set of concepts that produce material explanations, no matter how counter-intuitive, no matter how mystifying to the uninitiated.

Moreover, that materialism is absolute, for we cannot allow a Divine Foot in the door.[39]

And it's people who think like this who are claiming we are the ones who are irrational! It's easy to see why the New Atheists' claims are being so readily refuted.

Their Amnesia Is Discrediting Them

In his book *The God Delusion*, Richard Dawkins writes, "There is not the smallest evidence...that atheism systematically influences people to do bad things...Individual atheists may do evil things but they don't do evil things in the name of atheism."[40]

Can a man of Dawkins's intelligence really believe what he has written? Somewhere in the core of his being he has to know that history will not support his assertions. Alister McGrath puts my question in a different way when he writes, "What rational soul would sign up to such a secular myth, which is obliged to treat such human-created catastrophes as Hiroshima, Auschwitz and apartheid as 'a few local hiccups' which in no way discredit or disrupt the steady upward progress of history?"[41]

Once again, I appeal to the research of Dinesh D'Souza, who gives an excellent analysis of the evils of atheism:

In the past hundred years or so, the most powerful atheist regimes—Communist Russia, Communist China, and Nazi Germany—have wiped out people in astronomical numbers. Stalin was responsible for around twenty million deaths...

Mao Zedong's regime a staggering seventy million deaths...
Hitler comes in a distant third with around ten million murders, six million of them Jews...We have to realize that atheist
regimes have in a single century murdered more than one hundred million people...

Whatever the cause for why atheist regimes do what they
do, the indisputable fact is that the religions of the world put
together have in three thousand years not managed to kill
anywhere near the number of people killed in the name of
atheism in the past few decades. It's time to abandon the mind-
lessly repeated mantra that religious belief has been the main
source of human conflict and violence. Atheism, not religion, is
responsible for the worst mass murders in history.[42]

Alistair McGrath says the idea that religion poisons everything is
"simply childish. Of course religion can lead to violence and evil. But
so can politics, race and ethnicity—and an aggressive and dismissive
atheist worldview."[43]

Their Attrition Is Diminishing Them

Lest one think that British universities are a stronghold solely of atheistic scholars (for example, Richard Dawkins), it should be noted that
equally proficient British scholars are firm defenders of theism and,
more specifically, of Christianity. One of the most capable and prolific is Alister McGrath, who holds earned doctorates from Oxford in
molecular biophysics and divinity and who has authored more than
two dozen books on scientific and theological subjects. As a former
atheist, McGrath is "respectful yet critical of the movement."[44]

According to McGrath, "Atheism is in trouble. Its future seems increasingly to lie in the private beliefs of individuals rather than in the great public domain it once regarded as its natural habitat... Atheist thinkers are more than happy to appear on the nation's chat shows to promote their latest book. But they have failed to communicate a compelling vision of atheism that is capable of drawing and holding large numbers of people."[45]

A *Christianity Today* magazine editorial, written two years after McGrath's observations, noted that the "trouble" in atheism continues: "The new atheistic rhetoric betrays panic, another sign of weakness. Atheism knows that it is losing both arguments and the global tide. Stories of the global vibrancy of religion are everywhere trumping the grand narrative of evolutionary progress. And the best philosophers are still taking the God-hypothesis seriously."[46]

Dinesh D'Souza begins the first chapter of his book *What's So Great About Christianity* by announcing that "God has come back to life."[47] And he concludes the chapter by saying that "Christianity is winning, and secularism is losing. The future is always unpredictable, but one trend seems clear. God is the future, and atheism is on its way out."[48] The late Tony Snow, broadcast journalist and former press secretary to President George W. Bush, agreed: "Atheists may be selling books, but they're not making converts. Christianity is [making converts], especially in places and congregations that take Scripture seriously—and joyously."[49]

For the last twenty-seven years, the *International Bulletin of Missionary Research* has issued a "Status of Global Mission" report that presents the state of Christianity worldwide compared to other major religions. Commenting on the 2011 report, author and social activist George Weigel writes,

Compared to the world's 2.3 billion Christians, there are 1.6 billion Muslims, 951 million Hindus, 486 million Buddhists, 458 million Chinese folk-religionists, and 137 million atheists, whose numbers have actually dropped over the past decade, despite the caterwauling of Richard Dawkins, Christopher Hitchens, and Co. One cluster of comparative growth statistics is striking: As of mid-2011, there will be an average of 80,000 new Christians per day (of whom 31,000 will be Catholics) and 79,000 new Muslims per day, but *300 fewer atheists* every 24 hours [italics added].

The big lesson of the 2011 Status of Global Mission report can be borrowed from Mark Twain's famous crack about his alleged death: Reports of Christianity's demise have been greatly exaggerated. Christianity may be waning in Western Europe, but it's on an impressive growth curve in other parts of the world, including that toughest of regions for Christian evangelism, Asia. Indeed, the continuing growth of Christianity as compared to the decline of atheism (in absolute numbers, and considering atheists as a percentage of total world population) suggests the possibility that the vitriolic character of the New Atheism—displayed in all its crudity prior to Pope Benedict's September 2010 visit to Great Britain—may have something to do with the shrewder atheists' fear that they're losing, and the clock is running. That's something you're unlikely to hear reported in the mainstream media. The numbers are there, however, and the numbers are suggestive.[50]

Their Aggressiveness Is Defining Them

Timothy Larsen is a professor of Christian thought at Wheaton College and author of *Crisis of Doubt: Honest Faith in Nineteenth-Century England*—a study of leading intellectuals in Victorian England who abandoned their Christian faith and then rediscovered it. Their "crisis of faith" was followed by a "crisis of doubt" in which their atheism was abandoned and faith again embraced. This shows us it's a mistake to think that atheism is necessarily a permanently settled belief. In fact, one factor driving C. S. Lewis out of atheism was the discovery that an unbelieving friend, whom Lewis described as "the hardest boiled of all the atheists I ever knew," was assailed by fears that the evidence for God was so good that He might actually exist. Lewis wrote that if this man, "the cynic of cynics, the toughest of toughs, were not—as I would still have put it—'safe,' where could I turn? Was there no escape?"[51]

Larsen suggests that the screaming voice of the New Atheists may indicate the presence of a conflict within themselves between an untenable belief and real truth: "Some actually are really trying to answer questions. That's why they sound so angry...They're in a struggle for their own soul."[52]

There is probably a lot more soul-searching going on among atheists than they would like us to know about. The daughter of one of the most famous modern atheists, Bertrand Russell, wrote openly about her father in her 1975 book, *My Father, Bertrand Russell*:

I could not even talk to him about religion...I would have liked to convince my father that I had found what he had been looking for, the ineffable something he had longed for all his life.

I would have liked to persuade him that the search for God does not have to be vain. But it was hopeless. He had known too many blind Christians, bleak moralists who sucked the joy from life and persecuted their opponents; he would never have been able to see the truth they were hiding...I believe myself that his whole life was a search for God...Somewhere at the back of my father's mind, at the bottom of his heart, in the depths of his soul, there was an empty space that had once been filled by God, and he never found anything else to put in it...Nevertheless, I picked up the yearning from him, together with his ghostlike feeling of not belonging, of having no home in this world.[53]

Betrand Russell himself is reported to have said, "Nothing can penetrate the loneliness of the human heart except the highest intensity of the sort of love the religious teachers have preached."[54] His heart recognized the kind of love he needed and wanted, yet he could not bring himself to receive it.

A more intellectually honest atheist, John D. Steinrucken, wrote a 2010 article for *American Thinker* titled, "Secularism's Ongoing Debt to Christianity." In his article he made this remarkable admission:

It is rational to conclude that religious faith has made possible the advancement of Western civilization. That is, the glue that has held Western civilization together over the centuries is the Judeo-Christian tradition. To the extent that the West loses its religious faith in favor of non-judgmental secularism, then to the same extent, it loses that which holds all else together...

Although I am a secularist (atheist, if you will), I accept that the great majority of people would be morally and spiritually lost without religion. Can anyone seriously argue that crime and debauchery are not held in check by religion? Is it not comforting to live in a community where the rule of law and fairness are respected? Would such be likely if Christianity were not there to provide a moral compass to the great majority? Do we secularists not benefit out of all proportion from a morally responsible society?

An orderly society is dependent on a generally accepted morality. There can be no such morality without religion. Has there ever been a more perfect and concise moral code than the one Moses brought down from the mountain?

Those who doubt the effect of religion on morality should seriously ask the question: Just what are the immutable moral laws of secularism? Be prepared to answer, if you are honest, that such laws simply do not exist! The best answer we can ever hear from secularists to this question is a hodgepodge of strained relativist talk of situational ethics. They can cite no overriding authority other than that of fashion. For the great majority in the West, it is the Judeo-Christian tradition which offers a template assuring a life of inner peace toward the world at large—a peace which translates to a workable liberal society.[55]

In spite of his belief that "most men do have a need for God,"[56] Steinrucken doesn't count himself among them. But he issues a warning to his fellow nonbelieving "elitists":

If the elitists of our Western civilization want to survive, then it is incumbent upon them to see to the preservation of the hoary, time-honored faith of the great majority of the people. This means that our elitists should see that their most valued vested interest is the preservation within our culture of Christianity and Judaism. It is not critical that they themselves believe, only that they should publicly hold in high esteem the institutions of Christianity and Judaism, and to respect those who do believe and to encourage and to give leeway to those who, in truth, will be foremost in the trenches defending us against those who would have us all bow down to a different and unaccommodating faith.[57]

One has to admire John Steinrucken's powers of honest observation. He does not have a negative opinion of religion—indeed, he is a firm believer in the power of religion to build and preserve stable societies in which the irreligious can safely function. Yet he is atheistic about God. While I appreciate his honesty and his generous analysis, I am baffled by the inconsistency of his thinking: How could a religion that he believes to have at its center a fundamental flaw (belief in the existence of God) have the power to serve as the foundation for Western civilization? It was Jesus who said that houses built on unbelief will eventually crumble (Matthew 7:24–27). If there really is no God, could a religion built on a lie sustain Western civilization as Christianity has done for a thousand years without being exposed as a sham?

A Challenge to Practicing and Practical Atheists

Earlier I noted that some people declare themselves to be *theists* (believers in God), even *Christian theists* (believers in the deity of the Lord Jesus Christ), yet they live as if they don't believe. They live as practical atheists. Practical atheists run the gamut from people who believe they will somehow escape God's notice and their accountability to Him (Psalm 10:4, 6, 11, 13) to people who profess to be followers of Christ yet do not honor Him in their lives. Any time we callously fail to live up to what we believe, we declare ourselves to be practical atheists. By living as if God does not care about what we think and choose is, by our actions, to deny ample evidence to the contrary.

Which brings me to my challenge for atheists of any stripe. Whether an atheist by choice (practicing) or by callousness (practical), it takes a lot of energy to maintain atheism. It takes energy to suppress evidence that is abundantly available—energy that might be used in far more fruitful and satisfying ways. In Romans 1 the apostle Paul writes about people who "suppress the truth" about God (v. 18). They have to continually work to suppress the truth "because what may be known of God is manifest in them, for God has shown it to them. For since the creation of the world His invisible attributes are clearly seen, being understood by the things that are made, even His eternal power and Godhead, so that they are without excuse" (vv. 19–20).

Anyone who has ever told a lie knows the spiritual, emotional, and intellectual energy required to suppress the truth initially and to keep it suppressed continually. Truth about God is everywhere—even the heavens declare it (Psalm 19:1–6). It's one thing to lie ("There is no God; God doesn't care what I do"), but it's another thing to actively suppress the truth—to deny God's existence and role in the face of overwhelming evidence. As I have already noted, the Bible labels that person a fool.

My challenge to you is to accept the same challenge as the one given by Jesus to some who doubted who He was: "If anyone wills to do His will, he shall know concerning the doctrine, whether it is from God or whether I speak on My own authority" (John 7:17). Whether you are an atheist or a Christian living as if you don't believe, apply your spiritual energy in a different direction. I challenge you to make a daring experiment: Instead of suppressing the truth, try opening yourself to it. If, in spite of all the evidence, you have trouble believing, act as if it is true. The stakes are high enough that it's worth the effort to set aside your tendency to disbelieve and try living like a Christian for a while.

In the George MacDonald story "The Golden Key," the young heroine Tangle is on a quest to find the country from whence the shadows fall. Her long journey has been filled with signposts and directions, and it finally leads her to the Old Man of the Earth. When she asks him the way, he points to a black hole in the ground. "That is the way," he says. "But there are no stairs," Tangle replies. "You must throw yourself in," the Old Man answers. "There is no other way."[58]

We have overwhelming evidence for the existence of God, the veracity of the Bible, and the historical life of Jesus on earth. Yet all this evidence leaves in our hearts a place that requires faith in order to come to full belief. The evidence will lead us on a long journey toward belief, but we will come to the place where the evidence points to a mystery into which we must plunge. Often people stop at the edge and insist on yet another piece of evidence as a stairway into the unknown. That is the point at which we must exercise the step of faith that forces us to trust in God and throw ourselves in. As George MacDonald said, "There is no other way."

Use your spiritual energy to seek after God, and then watch as God's will becomes clear to you. "And you shall know the truth, and the truth shall make you free" (John 8:32).

CHAPTER 2

When Christians Wouldn't Know They Were in a War

Sir William Slim knew war as well as any man. As a distinguished commander he served in the British army, fighting in both World Wars and being wounded three times.

Blessed with a humble upbringing and a common demeanor, he had none of the self-serving flair of a MacArthur or Montgomery. He was a brilliant strategist who wrested victory from near-certain defeat more than once. He was beloved by his men and is revered in history.

When asked where he learned his greatest lesson as a soldier, Lieutenant General Slim told a story so simple yet effective that to this day it's repeated in the training manuals of the United States Marine Corps.

"'Many years ago,' he said, 'as a cadet hoping some day to be an officer, I was pouring [sic] over the 'Principles of War,' listed in the old Field Service Regulations, when the Sergeant-Major came up to me. He surveyed me with kindly amusement. 'Don't bother your head about all them things, me lad,' he said. 'There's only one principle of war and that's this. Hit the other fellow, as quick as you can, and as hard as you can, where it hurts him most, when he ain't lookin!'"[1]

That is war in its simplest form.

From the beginning of time, war has been easy to define. Opposing armies had names; each represented its own nation or leaders; each wore identifying uniforms and used similar kinds of weapons. The armies met on identifiable battlefields, and the wars had beginnings and endings—even if they lasted decades, like the Hundred Years' War in fourteenth- and fifteenth-century France.

Because armies were sponsored by states or nations, they had political leaders who sanctioned the army's participation in a war. And those leaders were available to sit down at the end of a war, sign a treaty, and agree that the war was over.

One of the first signs that the nature of modern military engagement was changing appeared during the Vietnam War. A new kind of military conflict emerged. "Guerrilla warfare" is a Spanish-derived term that has been in use since the eighteenth century. It means "little war." Guerrilla warfare resorts to hit-and-run, surprise, sabotage, booby traps, ambushes, and disguises to render the enemy unidentifiable. Guerrilla tactics create random "little wars" inside the big war. These tactics were employed in Vietnam and forever changed our perception of war. War became more confusing, less definable, and harder to execute.

If that was true in Vietnam in the 1960s, it is doubly true in today's "War on Terror." Perhaps the most significant difference in the War on Terror is that it is not a war against a nation; it is a war against an ideology—religiously fueled and intent on replacing all other ideologies with militant, fundamentalist Islam.

Yes, the Nazi idea of "Aryan supremacy" was an ideology, but at least Hitler's armies fought on battlefields and wore uniforms. Today the terrorists' battlefield is the entire world, and the enemy may be a shopper in a mall or a fellow passenger on a plane. Their chief weapons are fear and intimidation. Today's wars are not like your grandfather's and certainly not like wars in centuries past.

The term "War on Terror" was formally introduced in the post-9/11 environment. During the presidency of George W. Bush, "War on Terror" became part of the cultural conversation. The enemy was any person or nation that threatened or carried out violent acts against the American people.

Unfortunately, the subsequent administration discontinued the term "War on Terror" and replaced it with "Overseas Contingency Operation."[2] But if we fail to call offensive and defensive military actions "war," what exactly are they? And how do we execute such nonwar activity? How do we identify the enemy and understand his strategy against us?

We need to raise these same questions about a similar kind of warfare with which I have far more experience.

Biblically and practically speaking, we are in a spiritual war. The Christian's spiritual enemy is not in uniform, and he doesn't meet us on an identifiable battlefield. He uses ruthless and unconventional tactics, such as deceit, deflection, and disguise. As the Obama administration has done with the War on Terror, a large number of pastors and teachers ignore or downplay spiritual warfare to the point that many professing Christians don't even know they're in a war. This puts Christians in serious danger. The Church of Jesus Christ needs to know its enemy and his strategies. And above all, Christians need to know how to gain victory over this enemy.

Two things are happening today that I never thought I would live to see. First, spiritual warfare is getting much more intense and Satan is becoming much more real. Second, as mentioned above, too many Christians are not taking spiritual warfare seriously or even believing such a war is going on. These two factors taken together mean we have a crisis on our hands. When the danger increases and awareness decreases, an alarm needs to be sounded to prevent disaster. In this chapter I intend to sound that alarm.

The Rise of Satanism and Demonic Activity

We have strong evidence that demonic activity is increasing today. This was predicted in the Bible. The apostle Paul warned his protégé Timothy that as the end of the present age approached, satanic activity would increase: "The Spirit expressly says that in latter times some will depart from the faith, giving heed to deceiving spirits and doctrines of demons" (1 Timothy 4:1).

The book of Revelation tells us that demonic activity will become fully manifested during the seven years of tribulation. In the ninth chapter, the apostle John describes the visible presence of demons during this period:

They had hair like women's hair, and their teeth were like lions' teeth. And they had breastplates like breastplates of iron, and the sound of their wings was like the sound of chariots with many horses running into battle. They had tails like scorpions, and there were stings in their tails. Their power was to hurt men five months. And they had as king over them the angel of the bottomless pit, whose name in Hebrew is Abaddon, but in Greek he has the name Apollyon. (vv. 8–11)

Later in the book of Revelation, we are told that "the spirits of demons" will be employed to gather the nations to the Battle of Armageddon (16:14).

Today, as we move ever closer to the appearing of Christ for His Church and the subsequent Tribulation period, we are witnessing this predicted increase in occurrences of demonic activity all around the world. In Italy, according to CBS News commentator Mark Phillips, there are now 350 trained exorcists working. Ten years ago, there were only twenty. "Even in the United States... one-in-ten Catholics, according to a recent survey, now say they've either submitted to or witnessed an exorcism."[3]

Father Thomas Williams, Dean of Theology at the Regina Apostolorum Pontifical University in Rome, reports: "There's increased interest in the occult, even in Satanism. Where I live in Italy, Satanic worship is actually on the rise. And this is true in a lot of places in Europe."[4]

In the United States, a November 2010 conference sponsored by the nation's Roman Catholic bishops garnered a wave of media attention. The conference, held in Baltimore, attracted more than fifty bishops and sixty priests who learned how to detect and defeat demons. The conference was created to address the lack of trained exorcists and an increase in demand for them.

Laurie Goodstein of the *New York Times* wrote: "There are only a handful of priests in the country trained as exorcists, but they say they are overwhelmed with requests from people who fear they are possessed by the Devil."[5] Later in this chapter I'll have more to say about the role of exorcism in the life of a Christian. But for now, these statistics serve to inform us that demonic activity is accelerating all around the world.

Knowing Our Enemy

There is a book on military strategy that is required reading for all Central Intelligence Agency officers and recommended reading for U.S. Military Intelligence personnel. It is also listed in the U.S. Marine Corps Professional Reading Program. The book was brought to the attention of U.S. military leaders during the Vietnam War because the North Vietnamese leader of tactics against American forces was a student of the book. Today, leaders in business, entertainment, education, law, politics, government, sports, and many other fields are reading the book.

Sound like something fresh off the Harvard Business School presses? Think again. This book was written twenty-six hundred years ago in China: *The Art of War* by Sun Tzu. Each of the thirteen chapters contains a list of principles. It is principle number eighteen, the last principle in chapter 3, that we must take to heart in our consideration of spiritual warfare. Sun Tzu wrote,

> Hence the saying: If you know the enemy and know yourself, you need not fear the result of a hundred battles. If you know yourself but not the enemy, for every victory gained you will also suffer a defeat. If you know neither the enemy nor yourself, you will succumb in every battle.[6]

Based on that paragraph, Sun Tzu is often credited with originating the phrase "Know your enemy." But this commonsense idea is even older than Sun Tzu. Moses sent the twelve spies from Kadesh into Canaan to "see...whether the people who dwell in it are strong or weak, few or many" (Numbers 13:18). Joshua did the same from the east bank of the Jordan River before entering Canaan, sending spies to assess the strength of Jericho (Joshua 2:1). Even Jesus Christ recommended such knowledge: "What king, going to make war against another king, does not sit down first and consider whether he is able with ten thousand to meet him who comes against him with twenty thousand?" (Luke 14:31).

If the idea of knowing one's enemy makes military sense and common sense, it makes even more spiritual sense because the enemy is stronger and the stakes are higher. The biblical writers spared no effort in giving us intelligence on the nature of our spiritual enemy, Satan himself. Indeed, they covered both of Sun Tzu's requirements for victory: Know yourself and know your enemy. Our task is to embrace what the Bible tells us and be prepared for the battle we most certainly will face.

In Ephesians 6:12, the apostle Paul gives a detailed analysis of our foes: "We do not wrestle against flesh and blood, but against principalities, against powers, against the rulers of the darkness of this age, against spiritual hosts of wickedness in the heavenly places."

John Phillips, formerly of Moody Bible Institute, notes how these dark, invisible forces operate in the tangible world:

> Our enemies are not people. We must see beyond people. Satan may use people to persecute us, lie to us, cheat us, hurt us, or even kill us. But our real enemy lurks in the shadows of the unseen world, moving people as pawns on the chessboard of time. As long as we see people as enemies and wrestle against them, we will spend our strength in vain.[7]

In order to know our enemy, we must understand how Satan goes about accomplishing his purposes. I paged through the Bible, writing down the verbs describing his activity: Satan beguiles, seduces, opposes, resists, deceives, sows terror, hinders, buffets, tempts, persecutes, blasphemes—and more. There are no edifying verbs associated with Satan. His determined goal is to diminish and deface the glory of God. And in pursuit of that goal he is utterly deceitful, divisive, and destructive. Let's look at what the Bible tells us about those three characteristics.

Satan Is the Great Deceiver

John 8:44 records Jesus' reply to a group of Jews who were resisting His message. Jesus boldly told them that they were children of their father the devil, and that they were not hearing the truth because their father's native language was lies. A person's native language is what he converses in most easily. And Satan speaks the language of deception most fluently.

Revelation 12:9 refers to Satan as the one "who deceives the whole world," which he does by imitating the work of God with counterfeit and camouflage. In fact, Satan's last and greatest deception will be to bring the Antichrist to the world at the end of the age. The Antichrist will initially be a peacemaker who uses persuasive speech and manifests supernatural powers much as the real Christ did. But once people fall for this counterfeit, the Antichrist will lead people not to God, but away from Him.

Pastor and theologian R. Kent Hughes explains one of the reasons for Satan's effectiveness as a deceiver and manipulator:

> I am no genius at mathematics, but even with my limited capabilities I could be terrific at math if I worked on it for 100 years (maybe!). If I labored at it for 1,000 years and read all the learned theories, I would be a Newton or an Einstein. Or what if I had 10,000 years? Given that time, any of us could become the world's greatest philosopher or psychologist or theologian or linguist...Satan has had multiple millennia to study and master the human disciplines, and when it comes to human subversion, he is the ultimate manipulator.[8]

Spiritual deception may be Satan's most insidious weapon in his guerrilla warfare against us. Jesus and the apostles speak of it nearly thirty times in the New Testament. One of Satan's greatest deceptions today is leading people, even Christians, to believe he does not really exist or that he isn't as bad as he's made out to be. The problem is, deceived people don't know they're being deceived! Undetected deception makes us extremely vulnerable because we do not know the enemy is even there, which means we neither watch for nor erect defenses against him. The continual deception of the great deceiver requires constant vigilance and dependence on the Word of God and the Holy Spirit.

Satan Is the Great Divider

The ancient Romans had a saying: *Divide et impera*—meaning "Divide and rule," or "Divide and conquer," as it is most often rendered today. This strategy enabled Rome to conquer their world for two reasons: First, smaller areas were easier to conquer; and second, once conquered, they were easier to control.

Satan has always been a divider. When he was cast out of heaven he divided the angels, taking a third into rebellion with him (Revelation 12:4). He divided the first couple, bringing sin and disharmony between Adam and Eve. He divided the first family, pitting Cain against Abel (Genesis 4:8). In the early Church, Satan influenced the heart of Ananias, dividing his loyalty between God and money (Acts 5:3).

Today Satan continues his strategy of division. He injects into humanity the poisons of suspicion, intolerance, hatred, jealousy, and criticism. That poison seeks an outlet and finds it in the human tongue.

James describes the result in his letter: "The tongue is a fire, a world of iniquity. The tongue is so set among our members that it defiles the whole body, and sets on fire the course of nature; and it is set on fire by hell...It is an unruly evil, full of deadly poison" (3:6, 8).

This poison ejected through the tongue is one of Satan's most divisive strategies. It divides husband from wife, brother from brother, friend from friend, family from family, church from church, and even nation from nation. All these divisions are steps toward Satan's ultimate goal: to divide the soul from the body, bringing us down into the state of being divided eternally from God. Only our utter dependence on the unifying sacrifice of Christ can prevent this from happening.

Satan Is the Great Destroyer

The Bible likens Satan to five different animals:

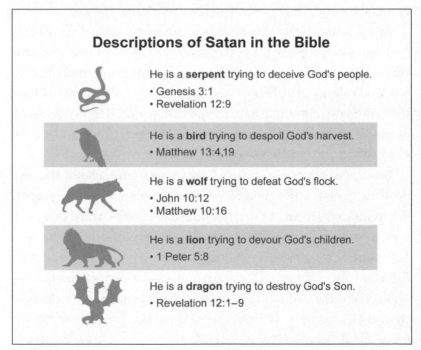

Descriptions of Satan in the Bible

He is a **serpent** trying to deceive God's people.
- Genesis 3:1
- Revelation 12:9

He is a **bird** trying to despoil God's harvest.
- Matthew 13:4,19

He is a **wolf** trying to defeat God's flock.
- John 10:12
- Matthew 10:16

He is a **lion** trying to devour God's children.
- 1 Peter 5:8

He is a **dragon** trying to destroy God's Son.
- Revelation 12:1–9

Satan is consumed by his obsession to destroy the work of God in the universe, and specifically on Planet Earth. He will delay, deflect, demolish, or dismantle any part of creation into which he can get his claws. When God allowed Satan access to Job's life, what did the devil do? He destroyed everything—Job's livestock, his family, his health, and his property, all in an attempt to embitter Job against God (Job 1–2). Though he failed in that attempt, the story illustrates that there is nothing halfhearted about Satan's methods: Use a hammer, and if that fails, get a bigger hammer! Destroy. Wreck. Ruin. Kill. Inflict grief, disease, pain, and anguish. And then cause the victim to blame it all on God. Satan will do anything to make God look bad in the eyes of the world, and especially in the eyes of God's people.

The sad thing is that this strategy so often works. How many times have we heard people in the grip of severe loss, grief, or tragedy blame God: "How could a good God allow this to happen to me?" But it's not God's doing. All the evil and destruction inflicted on us have their ultimate source in Satan, the great destroyer. His evil presence in our world is not God's doing; it is ours. We open the door to him by yielding to his temptation.

Satan does not have a creative bone in his spiritual body. His only power is in destruction, and he wields that power with a vengeance. Yet, as much mayhem as Satan has inflicted, we are warned that there is even worse to come. Earlier I mentioned the conflagration that is to occur during the Great Tribulation. A demonic horde will be released from hell for a five-month rampage of killing and destruction on earth. Guess the name of the "angel of the bottomless pit" who is in charge: His "name in Hebrew is Abaddon, but in Greek he has the name Apollyon" (Revelation 9:11). Both names, in their respective languages, mean "Destroyer."

Satan's Strategies

Based on Scripture and my own observations during four decades of ministry, there are five key words that summarize Satan's strategy to deceive, divide, and destroy God's people.

Indifference

Satan's cleverest ruse in the modern world is to make us think he doesn't exist. He seduces us into believing that he is just a metaphor—a harmless symbol for what's bad in the world. And if Satan doesn't exist, the need to resist doesn't exist!

His strategy seems to be working. Today even many self-professed Christians fail to take seriously the Bible's teaching about Satan and spiritual warfare. On April 10, 2009, the Barna Group issued the following insightful results of a survey of 1,871 self-described Christians regarding this statement: "Satan is not a living being but is a symbol of evil":

- 40 percent of respondents agreed with the statement.
- 19 percent agreed "somewhat."
- 26 percent disagreed with the statement.
- 9 percent disagreed "somewhat."
- 8 percent were not sure what they believe about Satan.[9] (all figures rounded)

You can see the confusion in the minds of Christians about Satan and evil. Only 35 percent believed Satan is a real being (the 26 percent and 9 percent that disagreed with the statement). And another 8 percent were not sure what they believe.

Two factors enable Satan to remain so undetected. First, he is a spirit being. We cannot apprehend him with our physical senses; and in today's climate of empiricism, people have trouble believing in a spirit world. Second, he clothes himself in the images of this world that people perceive as good, noble, attractive, or uplifting—art, literature, entertainment, education, and scholarship. How many impressionable students have lost their faith under the influence of a learned college professor who mocked the idea of God? How much indecency do we tolerate in the name of art, which elevates creativity above the rules of morality? How many Christians are passively lulled into accepting perversions as normal when they are presented hour after hour on television? Satan's influence has become pervasive in many of the institutions we want to look to as noble, enlightening, or entertaining. Until we see through this deception and wake up to its insidious effects on us, we are in danger. And few of us even seem to notice.

The apostle Paul warned of false apostles in his day who masqueraded as apostles of light. They were empowered by Satan, who himself is able to appear as an angel of light (2 Corinthians 11:13–15).

We do not see Satan himself or his demonic minions, but the *effects* of their presence are clearly visible. We see those effects daily as we survey the chaotic and painful terrain of Planet Earth. Never forget: "The whole world lies *under the sway* of the wicked one" (1 John 5:19; italics added). You would shudder to know how many times he has passed near you as he roams "to and fro on the earth...walking back and forth on it" (Job 2:2).

When I hear individuals who profess to be Christians express disbelief in the reality of Satan and demons, I wonder about the source of their beliefs. The Bible could not be more clear about the existence of the devil and the reality of the spiritual conflict going on all around us. Let's look once again at Ephesians 6:10–12:

> My brethren, be strong in the Lord and in the power of His might. Put on the whole armor of God, that you may be able to stand against the wiles of the devil. For we do not wrestle against flesh and blood, but against principalities, against powers, against the rulers of the darkness of this age, against spiritual hosts of wickedness in the heavenly places.

Each time Paul mentions another class of spiritual beings, he reaffirms that we wrestle *against* them. The word *against* appears six times in these three verses. Think of an oarsman rowing his boat *against* the current. He is trying to make progress in one direction while the current seeks to take him the opposite way. We are trying to make progress toward the kingdom of God, and Satan turns the current of the world in the opposite direction, resisting us with every stroke of the oar.

Satan's war against us is organized and complete with strategies. The word *principalities* (Ephesians 6:12) refers to his head officers, while the word *wiles* (v. 11) refers to clever plans, crafty deceptions, and cunning methods. Like a military general, Satan plans his attacks and directs his demonic forces.

So, the more unsuspecting or unbelieving a person is concerning the reality of spiritual warfare, the more easily he or she becomes prey. More than a century ago, the Evangelical Anglican J. C. Ryle wrote:

> The saddest symptom about many so-called Christians is the utter absence of anything like conflict and fight in their

Christianity. They eat, they drink, they dress, they work, they amuse themselves, they get money, they spend money, they go through a scanty round of formal religious services once or twice every week. But the great spiritual warfare—its watchings and strugglings, its agonies and anxieties, its battles and contests—of all this they appear to know nothing at all.[10]

In his book *This World: Playground or Battleground?* the late A. W. Tozer wrote about the disappearance of the concept of spiritual conflict in the modern church:

In the early days, when Christianity exercised a dominant influence over American thinking, men conceived the world to be a battleground. Our fathers believed in sin and the devil and hell as constituting one force, and they believed in God and righteousness and heaven as the other...Man...had to choose sides—he could not be neutral. For him it must be life or death, heaven or hell, and if he chose to come out on God's side, he could expect open war with God's enemies. The fight would be real and deadly and would last as long as life continued here below...The Christian soldier...never forgot what kind of world he lived in—it was a battleground, and many were wounded and slain.

How different today. The fact remains the same, but the interpretation has changed completely. Men think of the world not as a battleground, but as a playground.[11]

Many Christians have lost sight of the fact that they are in a war—a war for the ages and a war for the souls of men. Yes, God wins in the end, and we Christians win with Him. But that does not take into account the casualties along the way that could be prevented if we were "sober" and "vigilant" instead of indifferent.

Ignorance

Missionary and professor Paul Hiebert caused a stir in conservative theological circles in January 1982 when his article "The Flaw of the Excluded Middle" was published in a leading scholarly missionary journal. Hiebert recounted his confusion and lack of resources as a missionary in India when confronted with the spirit world that native Indians took for granted. Trained in Western schools, he knew nothing of what he came to call "the excluded middle"—the unseen realm of spiritual activity between heaven and earth in which the Indians believed. He explains:

> The reasons for my uneasiness with the biblical and Indian world views should be clear. I had excluded the middle level of supernatural but this-worldly beings and forces from my own world view. As a scientist I had been trained to deal with the empirical world in naturalistic terms. As a theologian, I was taught to answer ultimate questions in theistic terms. For me the middle zone did not really exist. Unlike Indian villagers, I had given little thought to spirits of this world, to local ancestors and ghosts, or to the souls of animals. For me these belonged to the realm of fairies, trolls, and other mythical beings. Consequently, I had no answers to the questions they raised.[12]

He explained that Westerners have a two-tiered worldview: Religion is the upper tier—the domain of faith, miracles, otherworldly concerns, and sacred matters. Science is the lower tier—the world of sight, experience, the natural order, and secular matters. He discovered that the Indians he was trying to reach with the Gospel had a third tier—a middle tier between heaven and earth, between religion and the material world. This tier intersected heavenly activity with earthly activity; it was the tier Hiebert found missing from his own worldview. It was a biblical tier, profusely evident in Scripture, but missing in many Western missionaries' worldview.

> How did this two-tiered world view emerge in the West? Belief in the middle level began to die in the 17th and 18th centuries...The result was the secularization of science and the mystification of religion...It should be apparent why many missionaries trained in the West had no answers to the problems of the middle level—they often did not even see it. When tribal people spoke of fear of evil spirits, [missionaries] denied the existence of the spirits rather than claim the power of Christ over them.[13]

The same graduate schools and seminaries that trained those Western missionaries also train the pastors that fill the pulpits of our land. It is no surprise, then, that so many Christians don't know the enemy against whom they struggle. The "middle tier" of reality has been excluded from their worldview—the realm that allows Satan and his demons to walk to and fro on the earth, seeking whom they might devour. Before we can know our enemy, we must believe there *is* an enemy to know. We must stop looking at life only as the culture conditions us to do, through the lens of science, and begin looking at it through the lens of Scripture—through which we will see the realm in which biblical spiritual warfare is fought.

We must not make the mistake of thinking that because this middle tier is "spiritual," it does not have the reality that our material world has. It's a common mistake to believe the word *spirit* means something ethereal, wispy, insubstantial, or less than solid. We assume that the invisible spirit world is somehow less real, less solid, and has little effect on the "real" world we perceive with our senses. The opposite is true. The spirit world may be more solid, more substantial than our material world. Jesus showed us the nature of the spiritual body after His resurrection. He could pass through walls, not because His body was less substantial than the walls, but because the walls were less substantial than His body and could not hold Him back. It is through this overlooked middle tier—this solid, powerful, and highly active spirit world—that Satan attacks us and influences our behavior.

We can see the persistence of Satan's attacks throughout the course of biblical history. The most pointed evidence of Satan's activity was in his efforts to keep the Savior of the world from being born in Bethlehem and carrying out His mission on earth. He has tried everything he could to thwart God's step-by-step plan to bring this to fruition. Satan tried to keep the Hebrews enslaved in Egypt and to keep them from entering the Promised Land. He tempted them to worship false gods, causing God to send them into exile. He tried to disrupt the rebuilding of the temple and the wall around Jerusalem when the remnant returned from Babylon. He tried to kill the infant Jesus by destroying all the baby boys of Bethlehem. He tried to keep Jesus from completely obeying the Father during the forty days in the wilderness. He tried to destroy Jesus at the hands of His opponents, and prompted Judas to betray Jesus into the hands of men who would execute Him under the false charges of blasphemy and sedition.

The one thing Satan could not prevent was the resurrection of Christ from the grave. But even after that, he tried to use Saul of Tarsus to disrupt the growth of the early Church and keep it from spreading the message of the resurrected Christ. (In a beautiful bit of irony, Christ called that same Saul to be His chief evangelist to the Gentile world.) Satan never gave up in opposing the will and work of God, and he has not given up today. Every person who confesses Jesus Christ as Lord is a threat to Satan and therefore a target for his attacks.

When Jesus Christ came into the world, He came as a light into darkness (John 1:5; 3:19; 8:12; 12:46), invading the territory of Satan. The Bible says God "has rescued us from the dominion of darkness and brought us into the kingdom of the Son he loves" (Colossians 1:13 NIV). We were taken from Satan, taken out of darkness, and made disciples of Jesus in His kingdom of light. Satan was none too happy about this invasion into his domain. Thus, he continues to attack Christians, trying to cause them to bring shame upon the name of Christ and woo them back to the darkness of sin from which they were rescued.

If you belong to Jesus, you are living and breathing in that unseen "middle tier" of reality where you are subject to attack at any moment. Failure to know your enemy can be fatal. In his second letter to the Corinthian church, Paul warns that the first step in keeping Satan from taking advantage of us is to be knowledgeable about his strategies (2 Corinthians 2:11).

Infiltration

If Satan cannot defeat us through indifference or ignorance, he will try to infiltrate our lives. When we willingly tolerate sin in our lives, we "give place to the devil" (Ephesians 4:27). We have been infiltrated. We have given him a foothold, and we run the risk of being overtaken by his power. As Proverbs 6:27 asks us, "Can a man take fire to his bosom, and his clothes not be burned?"

Many modern Christians build this fire in their bosoms with their thought lives, their lifestyle choices, their tenacious clinging to pet sins, and their dabbling in dark practices like astrology and fortune-telling. And then they wonder why their Christian lives keep crashing and burning.

A pastor in Haiti created the following parable to illustrate for his people the fatal danger of making even the tiniest compromise with Satan:

A certain man wanted to sell his house for $2,000. Another man wanted very badly to buy it, but because he was poor, he couldn't afford the full price. After much bargaining, the owner agreed to sell the house for half the original price with just one stipulation: he would retain ownership of one small nail protruding from just over the door.

After several years, the original owner wanted the house back, but the new owner was unwilling to sell. So first the [original] owner went out, found the carcass of a dead dog, and hung it from the nail he still owned. Soon the house became unlivable, and the family was forced to sell the house to the owner of the nail.[14]

The Haitian pastor told his congregation: "If we leave the Devil with even one small peg in our life, he will return to hang his rotting garbage on it, making it unfit for Christ's habitation."[15] That's infiltration.

That is the kind of ruthless enemy we're up against. Do not give him the tiniest toehold in your life. Do not open the door to your heart even a crack. Do not rationalize or excuse any failure to obey the true Lord of your life. And when failures or missteps occur, as they will, confess them immediately and be cleansed "from all unrighteousness" (1 John 1:9).

The only way to protect oneself from Satan's infiltration is to be on the side of the One who is more powerful than he is: "because He who is in you is greater than he who is in the world" (1 John 4:4).

Intervention

Webster's Unabridged Dictionary defines *intervention* as the "interference of one state in the affairs of another." Satan has his own "intervention" program. He loves to intervene in the lives of Christians so he can cause them to do his will instead of the will of God.

Blaise Pascal is reported to have said, "All human evil comes from a single cause, man's inability to sit still in a room." I am convinced that part of Satan's intervention plan is to keep God's people so frenetically busy, so occupied with the things of this world, that they will have no time or energy left to devote to their spiritual lives.

As I was writing this chapter, a friend sent me a devotional that reminded me of the subtlety of this strategy. The devotional imagines Satan addressing a worldwide convention of demons and promising them victory in believers' lives if they will faithfully do the following twelve things:

1. Keep them busy with nonessentials.
2. Tempt them to overspend and go into debt.
3. Make them work long hours to maintain empty lifestyles.
4. Discourage them from spending family time, for when homes disintegrate there's no refuge from work.
5. Overstimulate their minds with television and computers so that they can't hear God speaking to them.
6. Fill their coffee tables and nightstands with newspapers and magazines so they've no time for Bible reading.
7. Flood their mailboxes with sweepstakes, promotions and get-rich-quick schemes; keep them chasing material things.
8. Put glamorous models on TV and on magazine covers to keep them focused on outward appearances; that way they'll be dissatisfied with themselves and their mates.
9. Make sure couples are too exhausted for physical intimacy; that way they'll be tempted to look elsewhere.
10. Emphasize Santa and the Easter bunny; that way you'll divert them from the real meaning of the holidays.
11. Involve them in "good" causes so they won't have time for "eternal" ones.
12. Make them self-sufficient. Keep them so busy working in their own strength that they'll never know the joy of God's power working through them.[16]

The devotional concludes, "Have you figured out the difference between being busy and being successful in what God's called you to do? Sometimes being B-U-S-Y just means Being Under Satan's Yoke!"[17]

Satan prods us to clutter our lives with a frenzy of programs,

hobbies, activities, entertainment, sports, and useless Internet trivia—
not to mention the accumulation of things that keep us occupied with
maintenance and payments. The devil's fiery darts come in all shapes
and sizes, not the least of which are the darts of distraction. And he
fires them relentlessly with the ultimate goal of destroying God's
people.

Intimidation

Yes, we must be knowledgeable about Satan and his determination to
destroy us. But that does not mean we should fear him or be intimidated. Randy Alcorn reminds us of Satan's limitations: "When asked
to name the opposite of God, people often answer, 'Satan.' But that's
false. Michael, the righteous archangel, is Satan's opposite. Satan is
finite; God is infinite. God has no equal."[18]

What this tells us is that we need not fear Satan. If we have God in
our lives, we have within us more power and more protection than
any evil can overcome.

With that in mind, let's revisit the question of exorcism. Earlier
I cited statistics showing the rise in the number of exorcisms in the
Roman Catholic Church. Those statistics were presented simply to
demonstrate the increase of demonism around the world. But they
also raise the question: What role should exorcism have in the life of
a Christ follower? Albert Mohler, president of the Southern Baptist
Theological Seminary, offers these wise words:

> Evangelicals do not need a rite of exorcism, because to adopt
> such an invention would be to surrender the high ground of
> the Gospel. We are engaged in spiritual warfare every minute
> of every day, whether we recognize it or not. There is nothing

the demons fear or hate more than evangelism and missions, where the Gospel pushes back with supernatural power against their possessions, rendering them impotent and powerless. Every time a believer shares the Gospel and declares the name of Jesus, the demons and the Devil lose their power.

So we should respect the power of the Devil and his demons, but never fear them. We do not need a rite of exorcism, only the name of Jesus. We are not given a priesthood of exorcists—for every believer is armed with the full promise of the Gospel, united with Christ by faith, and indwelt by the Holy Spirit.[19]

When you're out for a walk or a jog and you suddenly see a large, barking dog tearing across a yard toward you, you know what fear feels like. You whisper a prayer, close your eyes, and brace yourself for the worst.

Squinting your eyes open just a fraction, you find that the dog has stopped just at the edge of the yard. He is pacing back and forth, barking like mad, frustrated that he can't make the leap to get to you. Suddenly you realize that you have been saved by the invisible fence—an electric wire buried in the ground around the perimeter of the property. When the dog gets too close to the wire, it sends a shock to a device on the dog's collar. The dog has learned it can go just so far without being painfully reined in.

Within its domain, that dog has the power to hurt you. But when it is on a leash or contained within an invisible electric fence, you can stand within a couple feet of it without fear of harm.

Christians need to have a healthy respect for the power of Satan. It would be the height of naïveté and presumption to have a flippant attitude toward him. But Satan is on a leash. He can go no further than our sovereign God allows. The story of Job demonstrates that lesson clearly. It was only by permission that Satan was allowed to trouble Job. Just as God knew when to end Satan's troubling of Job, one day He will put an end to Satan's troubling of us.

The Bible says, "The Son of God was manifested, that He might destroy the works of the devil" (1 John 3:8). The book of Revelation reveals Satan's ultimate fate: eternal torment in "the lake of fire and brimstone" where, along with the Antichrist and the False Prophet, he will be "tormented day and night forever and ever" (20:10). We are currently in the interim period between Satan's death sentence and his execution. When Christ was raised from the dead, Satan's defeat was made certain. When he is cast into the lake of fire, his eternal death sentence will be carried out.

In the meantime, God calls every believer to stand strong, going to battle in a war that has already been won. We have been called to "fight the good fight" (1 Timothy 6:12), to "endure hardship as a good soldier" (2 Timothy 2:3). We must take to heart the advice Paul gave to Timothy: "No one engaged in warfare entangles himself with the affairs of this life, that he may please him who enlisted him as a soldier" (2 Timothy 2:4). We are to "watch, stand fast in the faith, be brave, be strong" (1 Corinthians 16:13) and "wage the good warfare" (1 Timothy 1:18).

Commenting on these passages, J. C. Ryle writes, "Words such as these appear to me clear, plain, and unmistakable. They all teach one and the same great lesson, if we are willing to receive it. That lesson is, that true Christianity is a struggle, a fight and a warfare."[20]

Knowing Our Armor

Now that we know the nature of our adversary, we need to get acquainted with the nature of our armor. In Ephesians chapter 6 we are told that God has given us the girdle of truth, the breastplate of righteousness, the shoes of the preparation of the Gospel of peace, the shield of faith, the helmet of salvation, and the sword of the Spirit, which is the word of God (vv. 14–17). If we add to this list the weapon of "all prayer," which is mentioned in Ephesians 6:18, we discover that we have been given five pieces of defensive armor and two powerful weapons with which to fight the spiritual battle.

Although space will not permit me to deal with each of these implements of spiritual warfare, I can summarize their effectiveness by pointing out that, taken together, they represent nothing less than Christ Himself. The armor is Christ. This becomes clear when we compare Paul's words in two passages: In Ephesians 6 Paul tells us to put on the whole armor of God. In Romans 13:14 he says something too similar to be coincidental: "Put on the Lord Jesus Christ."

Paul is telling us to wear Christ as we wear a suit of spiritual armor—"the armor of light" as he calls it in Romans 13:12. The verses in Ephesians describe seven pieces of armor and give us a commentary on the words I've quoted from Romans. When we put on the armor, we are putting on Christ and going forward in His strength to do the battle.

In his wonderful paraphrase of Ephesians 6:10–18, international conference speaker Jack Taylor writes about the armor of the Lord and explains how he puts on the armor every morning with this declaration:

I choose now to be strong in the Lord and in the power of His might. I confess that I am in the Lord and thus, am located in the power of His might.

I choose to put on the whole armor that God has provided me, in order that I might stand against the methods of the enemy. I know that the battle is not with flesh and blood but against principalities, powers, rulers of darkness, and spiritual wickedness in high places.[21]

He writes that when he gets to that place, he actually stands up:

Therefore I stand to accept the armor, which is mine in Jesus... I put on the breastplate of righteousness, the Lord Jesus Christ. He is made unto me righteousness. I am made righteous in Him.

I put on the girdle of truth. I accept the fact that Jesus is Truth and that Truth has made me free. I refuse deception and I accept the truth.

I slip into the footwear of preparation in the Gospel. I am now ready to walk with Him.

I put on the helmet of salvation. The certainty of my salvation covers and protects my mind and my outlook. I stand in that certainty now!

I take up the shield of faith. I now trust in the trustworthiness of God! I am covered from head to toe so that Satan's fiery darts cannot touch me...

I now take my offensive weapon, the Word of God...declaring it to be true without error, reliable, powerful, and alive—God's word to me!

And now I am dressed from head to foot for battle. On my head is the helmet of salvation, on my body is the breastplate of righteousness and the girdle of truth. On my feet is the footwear of preparation of the Gospel of peace. In my left hand is the shield of faith. In my right hand is the Word of God. I am now ready for the engagement of prayer.[22]

The late Swiss theologian Oscar Cullman has noted that every military campaign in history turned on the outcome of a single, decisive battle. Waterloo decided Napoleon's fate; and the Battle of Gettysburg turned the American Civil War in the North's favor. The D-day invasion of Allied forces into France sealed the doom of the Axis powers and ensured the outcome of World War II.[23]

In the same way, the death and resurrection of Jesus Christ was the turning point in the war between Satan and God.

It is said of Napoleon Bonaparte that as he attempted to conquer all the kingdoms of the known world, he spread out a map on a table, pointed to a specific place, and said to his lieutenants, "Sirs, if it were not for that red spot, I could conquer the world." The spot to which he pointed was the British Isles—the very nation that met Napoleon at Waterloo in Belgium and defeated him in league with a group of allied nations.

I have no doubt that when Satan talks with his minions about conquering the world, he says the same thing about the red hilltop of Calvary where Christ's blood was spilled: "If it were not for that red spot, I could rule the world!" But that red spot is what makes all the difference in our spiritual battle. We do not have to live in fear of the devil. We need enter only the spiritual battle to which we have been called, aware of its reality and its subtlety, and armed with the truth that the ultimate victory against Satan has already been achieved. Therefore, right now at this present moment we are "more than conquerors through Him who loved us" (Romans 8:37). "Thanks be to God, who gives us the victory through our Lord Jesus Christ" (1 Corinthians 15:57).

CHAPTER 3

When Jesus Would Be So Profaned

In 2010 the makers of Doritos corn chips created a contest to choose a video commercial to be shown during the 2011 Super Bowl. One entry that was not chosen, aired, or sanctioned by Doritos was nevertheless picked up by various websites and viewed by thousands.

In the commercial, a priest is worried about how to boost attendance in his church. As he is praying for ideas, heaven reveals the solution: Replace the bread or wafers in the Communion service with Doritos. Catholics found the commercial especially insensitive because, according to their doctrine of transubstantiation, the bread or wafer in the Eucharist actually becomes the literal body of Jesus Christ.

But that's not the worst of it. On January 13, 2011, Stephen Colbert, host of Comedy Central's *The Colbert Report*, raised the level of insensitivity to new heights when he spoofed the controversial Doritos ad on his show. Following is a partial transcript of Colbert's spoof after the commercial was played for the audience:

COLBERT: Now folks, I may be [a] devout Catholic but I am also a devout corporate whore. [*Audience laughter and cheers. Colbert pulls a bag of Doritos Nacho Chips from beneath his desk.*] I know the Eucharist is usually bread, but through transubstantiation it becomes the body of Christ. So I honestly don't understand, Why can't Jesus be a Dorito? [*Audience laughter. Traditional image of Jesus appears on screen.*] They're unleavened, and after all, He did "snackrifice" Himself for our sins. [*Audience laughter.*] And remember, at the Last Supper, according to Mark 14:20, Jesus says that He would be betrayed by one of the twelve "who dips with Me in the bowl." [*Audience laughter. Image of Bible and text of Mark 14:20 appears on screen.*] They had dip! Therefore, Jesus was a chip! [*Audience laughter.*] Everybody knows the Catholic Church can use a little extra scratch right now. What better way than product placement? Next Ash Wednesday we can all get our foreheads marked with Cheetos dust. [*Audience laughter. Image of man in church with the sign of the cross on his forehead in orange "dust."*][1]

Unless you saw Colbert's spoof of the commercial, you probably didn't hear much, if anything, about his equating Jesus with a corn chip or saying He "snackrificed" Himself for our sins. Indeed, incorporating Jesus Christ into profane and demeaning situations is now so common in America that it garners little attention.

In a 2010 interview, Elton John provocatively stated that Jesus was "a compassionate, super-intelligent gay man who understood human problems."[2] Renowned atheist Richard Dawkins suggested that a "reborn" Jesus would be compelled to wear a "Jesus for Atheists" T-shirt today.[3] He also said, "We owe Jesus the honor of separating his genuinely original and radical ethics from the supernatural nonsense which he inevitably espoused as a man of his time."[4]

Biblical Christians draw no distinction between secular and sacred—*all* of life is sacred. Most cultures around the world have been essentially secular but have acknowledged a sacred dimension to life. But in America that respectful recognition has slipped. When people in the public eye take sacred objects—like images of Jesus Christ—and use them in profane ways, the message is, "Nothing is sacred anymore—and if anything is, it shouldn't be. Get over it." When Jesus is featured in profane ways on television shows like *The Simpsons* and *South Park*, He is reduced from His biblical stature of divine and holy to a cultural characterization of crude and common. When people watch such shows or view similar representations of Jesus at the national level—and millions do—the national religious and spiritual psyche is changed.

At the personal level—and here I am speaking to professing

Christians—these images can have a radical desensitizing effect. It can be a challenge to live in a culture where "anything goes" while trying to remember that not everything "should go." Christians seem to forget Paul's words in 1 Corinthians 10:23: "All things are lawful for me, but not all things are helpful; all things are lawful for me, but not all things edify." Or said another way, "Possibility is not permission." Just because it's possible to equate Jesus with a Dorito doesn't mean such acts have value or that Christians should tolerate them. We should not. But in refusing to tolerate these acts I do *not* mean that we should offer hurtful or violent responses to the perpetrators, but rather that we must not tolerate them in our lives lest we lose the ability to be offended or shocked. Sitting alone in front of a television or computer screen, it has become all too easy for Christians to watch unmoved as the Savior who died for them is reduced to another common object to be used in any way one wants until He becomes just a piece of furniture in the nation's increasingly unkempt living room.

As Christians we are personally obligated to censor what we approve, what we call entertainment, what we say and think, and what we tolerate in a supposedly civil and moral culture. The apostle Paul wrote, "Finally, brethren, whatever things are true, whatever things are noble, whatever things are just, whatever things are pure, whatever things are lovely, whatever things are of good report, if there is any virtue and if there is anything praiseworthy—meditate on these things" (Philippians 4:8).

In *The Message*, Eugene Peterson's paraphrase of the Bible, the first few words of that verse read: "Summing it all up, friends, I'd say you'll do best by filling your minds and meditating on..." Those words suggest censorship and deliberate choice—filling your mind with *this* and not with *that*. And just because something is not profanity-laced and crude doesn't mean it is "noble" and "lovely." Stephen Colbert used no profanity or crude language as he employed Jesus Christ as a source of laughs. He calls himself a "devoted Catholic," yet he finds no harm in debasing to the level of a corn chip the very Savior who suffered to save him from his sins.

I never thought I'd see the day in America when Jesus Christ would be fair game for comedians, spoofers, and commercial entrepreneurs—especially those who profess to believe in Him like the "devout Roman Catholic" Stephen Colbert.

I have focused on Colbert not because he's the worst offender out there, but rather because his spoof is actually one of the more quotable examples of the current degradation of the sacred. Some of the material my research has uncovered is so vile that I could never speak of it in public. But Colbert serves to show how easy it is for Christians to get squeezed into the mold of this world if we do not constantly filter out the profane from what we find entertaining.

Jesus Among Scholars

As bad as this demeaning of Jesus and Christianity is, it would be comforting to think that at least it occurs only among entertainers and nonbelievers from whom we've learned to expect a disrespectful attitude toward the sacred. But unfortunately, it doesn't stop there. Some of the worst undermining of Jesus comes from sources you would least expect: biblical scholars. How can such a thing happen? The answer is as old as Adam and Eve—the tendency of fallen humans to trust their own minds instead of God. In the case of many biblical scholars, this takes the form of elevating human reason over biblical revelation.

In 1985, two biblical scholars—Robert Funk and John Dominic Crossan—created what came to be known as the Jesus Seminar to advance "religious literacy" among the general public. Their feeling was that, generally speaking, religious studies had been conducted too long behind the closed doors of academia, excluding laymen from access to research and new developments. Their goal was to research, publish, teach, and hold public gatherings where no inquiry about religion—"including biblical and dogmatic traditions"—would be considered out of bounds.[5]

As many as two hundred scholars have participated in the Jesus Seminar at various times with the goal of analyzing the sayings of Jesus and events surrounding His life as recorded in the four Gospels. An ongoing, ever-changing translation of the four Gospels and other early Christian texts (the "Scholars Version") is one of the main tools of the Jesus Seminar for recording the consensus of the members as to what is believable about Jesus and what is not.

The approach of the Jesus Seminar is epitomized by the interesting way they have devised for arriving at decisions about the sayings and events of Jesus. At meetings, the members vote on the words and acts of Jesus by submitting a bead in one of four colors, each expressing his or her view of the saying or event:

- Red bead: an authentic saying or event
- Pink bead: a somewhat likely saying or event
- Gray bead: a somewhat unlikely saying or event
- Black bead: a nonauthentic saying or event

The resulting Scholars Version is published in a book called *The Complete Gospels*—now in its fourth edition—which is a collection of sayings and events of Jesus collated from more than twenty "Gospel" records from antiquity. These records include the four biblical Gospels as well as fifteen other accounts of the life of Jesus, all of which have been rejected as nonauthoritative by non-Catholic Christendom for centuries (like the Gospel of Thomas, the Secret Book of James, the Gospel of Mary, the Gospel of Peter, and others). Obviously, the Scholars Version of the life of Jesus is radically different from that contained in the New Testament of the Bible.

The work of the Jesus Seminar has been widely criticized by a broad range of conservative biblical scholars[6] because the seminar members base their work on two presumptions: Jesus of Nazareth is a human being like all others, and the Bible is a book like all others. There is nothing supernatural about either. It is up to the combined wisdom of a couple hundred self-appointed experts (some of whom have no scholarly standings or academic research credentials in biblical studies) to pronounce, two thousand years after the fact, what is true about Jesus and what is not.

This would not be so alarming if these people met solely for their own mutual entertainment. But they are proliferating their radical beliefs about Jesus to a broad, naive, and untaught audience that is attracted to Jesus and impressed with their so-called scholarship, and that audience is being tragically misled.

Jesus made humble submission to God's authority the prerequisite for knowing and understanding His words: "If anyone wills to do His will, he shall know concerning the doctrine, whether it is from God or whether I speak on My own authority" (John 7:17). Casting a pink, gray, or black bead may be an easy way to deny the authenticity of those words and exempt oneself from submission to God's authority. But it doesn't exempt one from the judgment Jesus foresaw for those who lead God's people astray (Matthew 18:6; 23:14).

Does this mean we Christians should stop studying the historical Jesus for fear of finding a Jesus less divine than Scripture leads us to believe? No, we must study the New Testament with a prior commitment to the true revelation of God: the written Word concerning the Living Word. N. T. Wright, recently retired Anglican bishop of Durham (England) and prolific New Testament scholar, reminds us from history what can happen if we don't maintain a rigorous commitment to the study of the biblical Jesus: "When German scholars gave up historical Jesus research in the 1920s, they left a vacuum into which the 'German [Nazi] Christians' inserted their non-Jewish Jesus, with appalling results...How will we ward off the next generation's dangerous follies (not just Dan Brown [author of *The Da Vinci Code*], though he matters too) if we don't do history?"[7]

Unfortunately, as the Jesus Seminar shows us, we don't need to wait for the "next generation's dangerous follies" to appear. We have them in our midst today.

Jesus in the Church

Christians who have a strong belief in a divine Jesus may feel reasonably safe from the distortions, caricatures, and demeaning of Him that we see among entertainers and postmodern scholars. But there are more subtle traps within the Church itself that snare many because they are set by preachers and teachers whom many trust.

You do not have to go far on television or the Internet—or perhaps in your own community—to find a Christian preacher who will tell you that Jesus wants you well and wealthy. This unorthodox version of Jesus' Gospel is referred to as "prosperity theology" or the "health and wealth" gospel. There is nothing inherently wrong with being well and wealthy. But as a basis for theology, it is far from the good news of the Gospel that Jesus preached.

Prosperity preachers usually have no trouble attracting a large following since they appeal to the basest of human instincts: the desire to avoid suffering (be healthy) and the desire for gratification (be wealthy).

Jesus' own life on earth is far from being an example of the health and wealth gospel. It's true that there is no record of Him ever being sick. And, as the Son of God it could be argued that He had the wealth of heaven at His disposal. But when He came to earth, He emptied Himself of His divine prerogatives and took upon Himself "the form of a bondservant, and [came] in the likeness of men" (Philippians 2:7). He came as a humble servant, identifying with the weakness and travail of the human condition (Mark 10:45; Philippians 2:8; Hebrews 2:17–18; 4:15; 5:8).

As for wealth, Jesus said of Himself, "Foxes have holes and birds of the air have nests, but the Son of Man has nowhere to lay His head" (Matthew 8:20). Jesus came to earth as a servant and lived like a servant, unconcerned with material comfort. And His apostles lived the same way. The apostle Paul interrupted his missionary work to make tents to provide for his own livelihood (Acts 18:3). It seems that if Jesus' Gospel had included wealth, He would have demonstrated that fact in His life and the lives of His apostles.

As for health, Jesus certainly reversed the effects of sickness and disease. But He did so not primarily to relieve suffering but to demonstrate the power of the kingdom of God over the kingdom of darkness (Acts 10:38). Jesus did not heal everyone who was suffering. Indeed, at one "hospital," the Pool of Bethesda in Jerusalem, He healed only one person of the many sick who gathered there (John 5:1–9).

The picture of Jesus painted by prosperity preachers bears little resemblance to the Jesus of the New Testament.

I could cite other examples of how Jesus is being misrepresented in our culture. It's true that various church teachings have deviated from Scripture for two thousand years. But never in my lifetime have I seen them to be as subtle and widespread as they are today. The challenge for every Christian is to know the truth of Scripture so well that errors are immediately apparent—not if, but when, they are encountered.

We are all familiar with Muzak, or "elevator music"—the ubiquitous background music that plays in elevators, shopping malls, department stores, airports, and other venues. Muzak may be the reason a song sometimes pops unbidden into your consciousness. Because elevator music is always there, we pay little conscious attention to it, yet our subconscious minds are taking it all in.

Cultural messages can be like this background music—always on, always being absorbed into the brain, consciously or not. And religious messages—including messages about Jesus Christ—are part of that background cultural noise. If you search YouTube.com using the key word *Jesus*, you'll find there are approximately 2.7 million videos on the subject. Many are devoted to Bible teaching, worship, or honoring Jesus in some way. But many ridicule and abase Him.

Apparently, Jesus is a popular subject today. But is the Jesus we see on television, at the movies, and over the Internet the real Jesus? If we are not careful, those messages, like a song subconsciously absorbed in an elevator, will become part of our lives, part of our thinking, part of our beliefs. If what the New Testament says about Jesus is true, these cultural images can be deadly. That means nothing could be more important than separating fact from fiction as we encounter these alternative, ridiculing, or demeaning portrayals of the God who came to redeem the human race.

Reclaiming the Real Jesus

In the midst of these sordid representations of Jesus Christ in our culture, we have the Bible. And in the Bible we have the New Testament. And in the New Testament we have the book of Hebrews, which contains more about the life of Jesus than any other book in the Bible except the four Gospels. The book of Hebrews is boldly upfront about its purpose, as the first verse of the eighth chapter tells us precisely: "This is the main point of the things we are saying: We have such a High Priest, who is seated at the right hand of the throne of the Majesty in the heavens."

Hebrews is about the superiority of Jesus. In it we learn that Jesus is better than everyone and everything. He is better than the angels. He is better than Moses. He is better than Joshua. He is better than the old covenant. He is better than the priests. In fact, the word *better* is used thirteen times in Hebrews. Jesus is better than the best.

Hebrews was written to a group of first-century Christians who were under great pressure, being ridiculed and persecuted by their families and friends for having turned from Judaism to Jesus Christ. Many had accepted this adversity joyfully, but others were so disheartened they were ready to quit. The Letter to the Hebrews appeals to these believers to keep their faith anchored in truth by remaining confident in Christ. And the writer, whose identity we do not know, teaches us that no believer can cope with adversity unless Christ fills his horizons, sharpens his priorities, and dominates his experience.

Did you know that Hebrews is the only book in the English Bible that begins with the word *God*? For some reason God caused the book to be translated into English in such a way that it would open with this word. Most other books begin with the name of the human writer— Paul or Peter or John. We don't know the human writer of Hebrews, but we do know the divine Author: His identity is revealed in the first word of the letter.

When it comes to knowing Jesus, we can't find a better authority than God the Father. In order to clarify the identity of the true Jesus, let's focus our attention on seven descriptions of Him found in Hebrews, chapters 1 and 2.

Jesus Is the Final Word from God

The book of Hebrews opens with: "God, who at various times and in various ways spoke in time past to the fathers by the prophets, has in these last days spoken to us by His Son" (1:1–2).

These verses explain how God revealed Himself in the Old Testament era: He spoke in various ways and in various times. He spoke to Adam a little bit. He spoke to Moses a little bit. He spoke to Abraham a little bit. He spoke to David and to Solomon a little bit. He revealed parts of His message in various seasons, beginning with Moses in the Pentateuch, continuing through the Prophets, and ending with the prophet Malachi. But He never spoke everything to any one person or at any one time.

We are blessed to have the collection of books recording what God said to the prophets of old, but there was never a time in the Old Testament where God gave mankind His final word. Then we come to the New Testament, where we are told, "But in these last days he has spoken to us by his Son" (1:2 NIV).

Did you know that one of the titles for Jesus is "the Word"? "In the beginning was the Word, and the Word was with God, and the Word was God" (John 1:1). When Jesus came to this earth, He was simply God walking around in a body. When God wanted to communicate who He is to us, He took deity and poured it into humanity.

God's revelation to us is no longer a mystery as it was in the past. We do not have to look for another word from God because He has spoken to us with finality in the person of His Son, Jesus Christ. In his commentary on the book of Hebrews, R. Kent Hughes uses the following story to illustrate this wonderful truth:

> Ingmar Bergman, the celebrated Swedish filmmaker, recounts that one day while he was listening to Stravinsky, he had a vision of a nineteenth-century cathedral. In the vision Bergman found himself wandering about a great building and finally coming before a picture of Christ. Realizing its importance, Bergman said to the picture, "Speak to me! I will not leave this cathedral until you speak to me!" But of course the picture did not speak. That same year he produced *The Silence,* a film about characters who despair of ever finding God.
>
> Bergman's problem was, he was looking at the wrong picture. Rather, he needed to listen to the massive eloquence of the Christ of Scripture—"in these last days he has spoken to us by his Son." He needs to see the eloquence of Christ's character and speech and actions and, above all, the sublime eloquence of the cross, for there he speaks salvation.[8]

Jesus Is the First Cause of Creation

Many people read "In the beginning God created the heavens and the earth" (Genesis 1:1) and assume that God the Father is solely responsible for creating everything that exists. But the last phrase of Hebrews 1:2 tells us that Jesus Christ is the Creator God: "through whom also He made the worlds." It was through Jesus Christ that the worlds were created.

The New Testament language could not be more precise about Jesus' work in creation. Consider these two clear passages found in the Gospel of John and Colossians:

In the beginning was the Word, and the Word was with God, and the Word was God. He was in the beginning with God. All things were made through Him, and without Him nothing was made that was made. (John 1:1–3)

He is the image of the invisible God, the firstborn over all creation. For by Him all things were created that are in heaven and that are on earth, visible and invisible, whether thrones or dominions or principalities or powers. All things were created through Him and for Him. (Colossians 1:15–16)

Hebrews is painting an accurate picture of Jesus; and even after two verses, we can see that it looks much different than the distorted portrait of Him painted by the culture at large. As we read on, the true portrait will come into even sharper focus.

Jesus Is the Fullness of the Godhead

Jesus is "the brightness of His glory and the express image of His person" (Hebrews 1:3). This is one of the clearest statements in the Bible concerning the deity of Jesus Christ.

While we cannot see God the Father because He is Spirit, we can see Jesus in the pages of the New Testament. And in seeing Jesus, the Bible says we see God. In fact, the mission of Jesus was to make God known: "No one has seen God at any time. The only begotten Son, who is in the bosom of the Father, He has declared Him" (John 1:18).

Jesus Himself said, "He who has seen Me has seen the Father" (John 14:9). In his First Letter to Timothy, Paul seems in awe of the deity of Jesus Christ. He said, "Without controversy great is the mystery of godliness: God was manifest in the flesh" (3:16 KJV).

One of the great theological debates today is about whether Jesus Christ is the God-man or just a good man. Christ's deity is so important to the writer of Hebrews that he revisits the subject a few verses later in the same chapter: "To the Son He says: 'Your throne, O God, is forever and ever; a scepter of righteousness is the scepter of Your kingdom'" (1:8). In this verse we hear God the Father calling Jesus, His Son, God. If you say, "I don't believe Jesus is God," then you disagree with God. God says Jesus is God.

From the first century to now, many people who have otherwise admired Christ and His teachings have strongly resisted His deity. Some who did not want to reject Him outright went to great lengths to separate His moral and ethical wisdom from His divinity in a strained attempt to create a Christ they could believe in while avoiding His authority.

One such person was Thomas Jefferson. Fortunately, much of what

Jefferson accomplished, writing the Declaration of Independence, for example, remains with us today. Also fortunately, some of what he accomplished survives only as a footnote in history, an example being *The Jefferson Bible: The Life and Morals of Jesus of Nazareth Extracted Textually from the Gospels.*

Jefferson liked Jesus' moral teachings in the four Gospels but not the references to His deity. He therefore saw the need to produce a version of the New Testament that extracted Jesus' teachings from the religious context in which they had been recorded. In a letter to John Adams (October 12, 1813), Jefferson wrote of isolating Jesus' moral teachings:

> There will be found remaining the most sublime and benevolent code of morals which has ever been offered to man. I have performed this operation for my own use, by cutting verse by verse out of the printed [Bible], and arranging the matter which is evidently [Jesus'], and which is as easily distinguished as diamonds in a dung-hill. The result is an octavo of forty-six pages.[9]

With a razor blade, Jefferson cut the verses of Jesus' teachings he admired from Matthew, Mark, Luke, and John and then pasted them together in chronological order. Jefferson omitted as superfluous any references to genealogy, miracles, angels, prophecy, the Trinity, deity, resurrection, and the like—anything suggesting that Jesus was anything more than a great moral teacher who lived a brief life but made a great impact on the world.

The Jefferson Bible ended with a sealed tomb. That was Jefferson's Jesus—the life, death, and burial of a good man and great teacher; a life cut short in its prime. No resurrection from the dead, no second coming in power and glory. Jefferson didn't allow his Bible to be published in his lifetime, but it was published in 1895 by his grandson. It was republished in 1904 by an act of the United States Congress, and for many years copies were given to new members. We can be thankful that this practice did not last long.[10]

Marilyn Mellowes, writing for the PBS show *Frontline*, provides an excellent summary of what Jefferson accomplished by his editing of Jesus:

> Jefferson discovered a Jesus who was a great Teacher of Common Sense. His message was the morality of absolute love and service. Its authenticity was not dependent upon the dogma of the Trinity or even the claim that Jesus was uniquely inspired by God. Jefferson saw Jesus as [Jefferson's words], "a man, of illegitimate birth, of a benevolent heart, (and an) enthusiastic mind, who set out without pretensions of divinity, ended in believing them, and was punished capitally for sedition by being gibbeted according to the Roman law."
>
> In short, Mr. Jefferson's Jesus, modeled on the ideals of the Enlightenment thinkers of his day, bore a striking resemblance to Jefferson himself.[11]

Ms. Mellowes's last observation is profound. The diluting and caricaturing of Jesus in the modern era has been a process of decreasing His deity and increasing His humanity—a process of creating Jesus in our own image. The easiest way to feel less accountable to and intimidated by the Son of God is to do what Thomas Jefferson did: strip Him of His deity so He begins to resemble us.

Another biblical scholar, Scot McKnight, confirms the Jesus-in-our-image tendency by taking his students through an exercise at the beginning of his classes on Jesus:

> On the opening day of my class on Jesus of Nazareth, I give a standardized psychological test divided into two parts. The results are nothing short of astounding.
>
> The first part is about Jesus. It asks students to imagine Jesus' personality, with questions such as, "Does he prefer to go his own way rather than act by the rules?" and "Is he a worrier?" The second part asks the same questions of the students, but instead of "Is he a worrier?" it asks, "Are *you* a worrier?" The test is not about right or wrong answers, nor is it designed to help students understand Jesus. Instead, if given to enough people, the test will reveal that *we all think Jesus is like us* [italics added]. Introverts think Jesus is introverted, for example, and, on the basis of the same questions, extroverts think Jesus is extroverted.
>
> Spiritual formation experts would love to hear that students in my Jesus class are becoming like Jesus, but the test actually reveals the reverse: *Students are fashioning Jesus to be more like themselves* [italics added]. If the test were given to a random sample of adults, the results would be measurably similar. To one degree or another, *we all conform Jesus to our own image* [italics added].[12]

Jesus Is the Facilitator of All Things

Even as you are reading these words, Jesus is "upholding all things by the word of His power" (Hebrews 1:3). We may rest confidently in the fact that the Jesus who is before history, at the beginning of history, and at the end of history has everything under control. He is the sustainer and upholder of this world.

This is what Paul communicated in his Letter to the Colossians when he said: "He is before all things, and in Him all things consist" (1:17). It is not ultimately magnetic force fields or the tendency of certain atoms to combine with others that holds the universe together. It is the active and continuing power of Jesus Christ. Were He to abandon this function, the universe would disintegrate into chaos. There has never been a moment from the dawn of creation that Jesus Christ has failed to perform this mighty work. He is the facilitator of all things.

Jesus Is the Forgiveness of Our Sins

"He . . . by Himself purged our sins" (Hebrews 1:3).

When we are told that Christ has purged our sins, it means He has cleansed us. It is no accident that this phrase appears in the context of what the writer of Hebrews has already told us about Jesus: He who is before all things and in whom all things are summed up—the One who is the Father's delight and glory; the One of infinite power in the universe—He is the One who purged our sins.

Jesus accomplished this purging by taking our sins to Himself and bearing the punishment for them, which is death. As we learn later in the book of Hebrews, Jesus came to taste death for every man (2:9). This was His purpose in coming to earth; as we see in the familiar words, He came to seek and to save those who are lost (Luke 19:10). None of the magnificent attributes we have discovered about Jesus would have meaning to us were He not our Redeemer.

Think of it and rejoice in your heart! He who created the universe is the One who died for you. The only one who could have done that work of purging our sins on the cross was Jesus Christ.

Remember that the book of Hebrews was written to Jewish Christians who had a historical understanding of the importance of the purging of sins. They had been raised in Judaism, and they knew that the blood of bulls and goats prefigured the forgiveness of sins in advance of the cross. In the Old Testament, the purging of sins was never finished. Sacrifices had to be offered annually in anticipation of the perfect sacrifice that would perform the task once and for all: "not that He should offer Himself often, as the high priest enters the Most Holy Place every year with blood of another—He then would have had to suffer often since the foundation of the world; but now, once at the end of the ages, He has appeared to put away sin by the sacrifice of Himself" (Hebrews 9:25–26).

This Jesus who is the final word from God and the first cause of creation and the fullness of the Godhead and the facilitator of the universe; this same Jesus is the forgiveness of our sins.

Jesus Is the Finisher of Our Faith

The Old Testament tabernacle was filled with all kinds of extraordinary furniture. There was a lampstand, a laver, and an altar. But there was no chair. If you were an Old Testament high priest, you could never sit down in the tabernacle because your work was never done.

But after Christ accomplished His work on the cross and entered the Holy of Holies in the heavens, the Bible says He "sat down at the right hand of the Majesty on high" (Hebrews 1:3). He didn't sit down because He was tired; He sat down because He was finished!

When Jesus was dying on the cross, He cried out, "It is finished!" (John 19:30). With this cry He declared that the price for all our sins had been paid. And when He went back to heaven and sat down at the right hand of the Father, He sat down to signify that nothing else ever needs to be done for sin! Hebrews 12:2 says, "looking unto Jesus, the author and finisher of our faith, who for the joy that was set before Him endured the cross, despising the shame, and has sat down at the right hand of the throne of God."

In their book *Dethroning Jesus: Exposing Popular Culture's Quest to Unseat the Biblical Christ,* scholars Darrell Bock and Daniel Wallace explain that the popular view of Jesus today is not biblical Christianity but a "Jesusanity" in which Christ has no throne:

> *Jesusanity* is a coined term for the alternative story about Jesus. Here the center of the story is still Jesus, but Jesus as either a prophet or a teacher of religious wisdom…His role is primarily one of teacher, guide, and example. Jesus' special status involves his insight into the human condition and the enlightenment he brings to it. There is no enthronement of Jesus at God's side, only the power of his teaching and example. In this story, the key is that Jesus inspires others, but there is no throne for him.[13]

You may be thinking, *Is there something I need to do for my sins to be forgiven?* No, there is nothing you need to do or can do because Jesus did it all. He did it all so well that when He finished His work, He sat down. You don't need to do anything but receive what He has already done for you.

Jesus Is Our Faithful High Priest

"In all things He had to be made like His brethren, that He might be a merciful and faithful High Priest in things pertaining to God, to make propitiation for the sins of the people. For in that He Himself has suffered, being tempted, He is able to aid those who are tempted" (Hebrews 2:17–18).

Twelve times in the book of Hebrews, Jesus is referred to as our High Priest. Here we are told that He is "a merciful and faithful High Priest." He is merciful in that He understands man, and He is faithful in that as God He can be approached with absolute confidence that His mercy is available for all who request it.

When we have problems and face challenges, it is so encouraging to know that we can go to someone who has been where we are and understands what we are facing. As the Hebrews writer tells us, that is one reason why Jesus Christ became a man: "We do not have a High Priest who cannot sympathize with our weaknesses" (4:15).

Raymond Brown writes, "When Christ assumed our humanity he became like us, exposed to all the hazardous perils of our life and death. He was not protected from trouble and adversity. When we find ourselves immersed in the harsh realities of human experience, he knows exactly how we feel."[14]

The word *sympathize* is made up of two Greek words that mean "with" and "suffer." This word expresses not simply the compassion of one who sees suffering from the outside, but the intimate identification of one who enters into the suffering and makes it his own. To sympathize means to share the experience of another. Our High Priest shares our suffering.

The Greek word for *weakness* that is used in Hebrews 4:15 often means "without strength." In the Bible it is also used to describe physical illness (Philippians 2:26), or financial need (Acts 20:35). It can refer to any of the limitations of humanity. Jesus experienced human weariness, disappointment, abandonment, and intense pain. There is nothing we experience that He has not experienced at the deepest level.

The Bible teaches that one of the reasons for the incarnation was that we might have someone like us who has firsthand knowledge of our experiences and knows how to help us in our time of need.

But the writer of Hebrews gives us a second reason to rejoice in the high priestly ministry of Jesus Christ. He not only sympathizes with us in our weaknesses, He strengthens us in our temptations: "In that He Himself has suffered, being tempted, He is able to aid those who are tempted... For we do not have a High Priest who cannot sympathize with our weaknesses, but was in all points tempted as we are, yet without sin" (2:18; 4:15).

Some people encounter a theological dilemma in the idea of Jesus' being tempted. Throughout the centuries theologians have debated the question: "Was Jesus able not to sin or was He not able to sin?" I believe Jesus was not able to sin. He is the sinless Son of God whose holiness is absolute, and this means it is impossible for Him to be anything other than perfect. You might respond by asking, "Well, then how could He have been tempted as we are?"

Here is C. S. Lewis's explanation:

A silly idea is current that good people do not know what temptation means. This is an obvious lie. Only those who try to resist temptation know how strong it is. After all, you find out the strength of the German army by fighting against it, not by giving in. You find out the strength of a wind by trying to walk against it, not by lying down. A man who gives in to temptation after five minutes simply does not know what it would have been like an hour later. That is why bad people, in one sense, know very little about badness. They have lived a sheltered life by always giving in. We never find out the strength of the evil impulse inside us until we try to fight it; and Christ, because He was the only man who never yielded to temptation, is also the only man who knows to the full what temptation means—the only complete realist.[15]

Jesus was tempted to the fullest extent, yet He never sinned. That is why you and I can go to Jesus with our troubles, confident that He knows what it's like to be a human. He became like us, and He exposed Himself to all the hazards and perils of life and death. He was not protected from trouble and adversity.

The Urgency of Today

I've written a great deal about Jesus. Some of you may have learned more about Him in the last few pages than you ever knew before. That's great! But it's not enough to know about Him; we must know Him personally. The Bible says we must receive Him. We must be careful that we do not harden our hearts against Him. In fact, four times in Hebrews chapters 3 and 4 we are warned against hardening our hearts.

Recently, while reading through the first chapters of Hebrews in my Bible, I found the word *today* mentioned four times. I've come to this conclusion: *Today* is God's word; *tomorrow* is Satan's word.

When we hear God clearly telling us to do something, the period of time between understanding what He says and doing what He says does not belong to God. It belongs to the enemy. The enemy says,

"You can do that tomorrow. You don't have to respond to God's voice today."

Between God's command and our obedience is the wasteland of Satan. When we hear what God tells us to do, we should say, "I will obey today." If we don't say that, we will hear "tomorrow" ringing in our ears. And one of these days our tomorrow will be gone!

When D. L. Moody first started to preach the Gospel in Chicago, he would say at the end of each service, "I want you to go home tonight and think about what I've said and come back tomorrow night ready to make a decision." For years that was his standard procedure.

On the night of the Great Chicago Fire, he gave the same instruction. And many of the people who were in his congregation that night perished in the fire, never having responded to Moody's message.

From that day until he died, Moody never again said those closing words.[16] He learned the power of today. He realized that the message of the Gospel usually comes home to our hearts when we first hear it. Maybe a light goes on. Maybe we realize, *I've known about Jesus, but I've never trusted Him as my Savior.* When that happens and you know God is speaking to you, the time to do something about it is not tomorrow, not the next time you meet with God's people, but today.

Living in a Culture of Denial

The challenge for Christians is to stop being surprised at what the non-Christian world says about Jesus and become more concerned about our own response to who He is and what He requires of those who follow Him.

We must also stop expecting America to protect Jesus. Our

Founding Fathers were sympathetic toward Jesus Christ and His Gospel, but America has changed since then. Jesus is no longer given most-favored-religious-leader status. That should neither surprise us nor unravel our commitment. The growing hostility toward Jesus only makes our day more similar to the day in which Jesus and His earliest followers set the world on fire with the power of the Gospel.

We may see that fire rekindled in our day if we allow the power of Christ in us to show itself by resisting the cultural dismissal of Christianity. It is high time for the modern church in the West to decide who it is going to serve: the Jesus of the four Gospels—Son of God and Son of Man, Savior and Lord, and coming King and Judge—or the Jesus of the comedians, critics, and cultural "Christians" who opt for the tolerant Jesus—meek and mild and meaningless.

As someone has aptly said, "If Jesus isn't Lord *of* all, He isn't Lord *at* all." Jesus is Lord over entertainment, religion, creation, scholarship, and especially over the life of the Church. We don't get to choose the kind of Jesus we want. The only Jesus we have is the one whose life is recorded in the inspired pages of the New Testament.

As this chapter has shown, great damage is being done to the cause of Christ by non-Christians and pseudo-Christians living as if He isn't Lord of anything. But I'm convinced that far greater damage is done by Christians not living as if Jesus is Lord of everything.

In his book *The Case for the Real Jesus*, journalist and former atheist Lee Strobel gives us a perceptive summation of why people resist the real Jesus and search desperately for substitutes:

The one Jesus that skeptics refuse to tolerate is a uniquely divine, miraculous, prophecy-fulfilling, and resurrected Jesus—even if the evidence points persuasively in that direction. After all, that would put them in the place of being beholden to him. Their personal sovereignty and moral independence would be at risk. The problem is: *that's* the real Jesus.

We are not his equals. We don't occupy the same stratum or possess the same status. He is God, and we're not. For many people that's the crux of their predicament: if Jesus is God incarnate, then he could demand too much. And in fact, he does demand everything...

That kind of surrender sounds scary for many people. But if Jesus really is God—if he really did sacrifice himself so that we could be forgiven and set free to experience his love forever— then why should we hesitate to give all of ourselves to him? Who could be more trustworthy than someone who lays down his life so that others might live?[17]

Given all that Jesus Christ has done for us; given the great love He has shown for us in coming down from the glory of heaven to live and suffer among us and willingly submit to torture and death for our sins, I never thought I'd see the day when Jesus would be treated the way He is in our time. Given who Jesus is and all He means to us, it seems incredible that such demeaning, demoting, and devaluing of our Lord could possibly happen. But it has happened. It is happening, and we have no reason to believe that it will not continue to happen. As those days increase, I can only hope to see the day when His true Church fully and obediently embraces Him for who He is: Lord of all.

CHAPTER 4

When Marriage Would Be Obsolete

"Royal Shack-Up: Kate and William Moved in Months Ago."[1] Thus blared MSNBC's headline, using old-fashioned but universally understood language to reveal the cohabitation of England's Prince William and Kate Middleton.

Flying under the radar, the couple had been living together for eight months before announcing their engagement. Perhaps the most telling line in the news report was this: "If Her Majesty's royal subjects are aghast at the disclosure that William and Kate have been cohabiting, they haven't shown it. But then again, it is 2010."[2]

Yes, it was 2010, and attitudes toward marriage had changed drastically in the queen's lifetime. And that change is self-perpetuating. If the following hasn't happened already, it will: A young, unmarried couple in England or the United States will defend their decision to live together against the objections of their morally traditional parents. The couple's litany of defenses will include this argument: "Prince William and Kate lived together without being married! If it's okay for the future king and queen of England, why isn't it okay for us?"

That is a better question than we Americans may realize because, by implication, the royal couple had the approval of the church. You see, the reigning monarch in Britain is also the supreme governor of the Church of England. The canon law of that church states, "We acknowledge that the Queen's excellent Majesty, acting according to the laws of the realm, is the highest power under God in this kingdom, and has supreme authority over all persons in all causes, *as well ecclesiastical as civil*"[3] (italics added).

So if the queen, who attends church faithfully, listens to the teaching of Scripture, and has supreme authority over the Church of England, implicitly approves of her grandson's cohabiting with his fiancée, who are we to condemn the practice? What right have loyal British parents to challenge their child's decision to do something that the queen, as well as the next two kings—Prince Charles and Prince William—apparently approves? Given their future authority as heads of the Church of England, they must know what the Bible says about love, marriage, and sex, yet they choose to ignore it. So we of the English-speaking world are led to assume that living together before marriage is not quite the sin we've been led to believe it is. Why shouldn't we feel free to do as they have done?

It's not my intention to single out Prince William and Kate Middleton for special condemnation. I cite them only because of their visibility and stature on the world stage. They are a "modern couple" who chose to do what an increasing number of modern couples are doing: live together outside of marriage. But I also cite them because of their unbreakable link to Christian teachings through the Church of England and their apparent ease at ignoring what the Bible teaches about the sanctity of marriage. The actions of British royalty, with their high visibility and ecclesiastical connections, merely give people one more argument for flouting traditional marriage—an institution that's already reeling in today's freewheeling climate.

Is Marriage Becoming Obsolete?

Let's at least give the prince and his future bride credit for planning to marry. Given the state of marriage in the West, that decision makes them seem almost old-fashioned. I never thought I'd see the day when marriage was deemed obsolete. But that day seems to have arrived in the minds of many.

When a 2010 Pew Research Center/*Time* magazine survey asked the American public if marriage was becoming obsolete, nearly 40 percent said yes. Among those in the traditional marrying age range (18–29), the number was four points higher, at 44 percent. That survey, titled "The Decline of Marriage and Rise of New Families," recorded a number of other shocking statistics about the deteriorating state of marriage and the family in our nation. For example, in 1960, 72 percent of all adults and 68 percent of people in their twenties were married. By 2008, those numbers had dropped to 52 percent and 26 percent respectively.[4]

The present concept of marriage and family in America stands in *stark contrast to God's design for marriage*. The Pew report recognized the watershed impact on society of the attitudes revealed in their study, saying, "It's no small thing when nearly four-in-ten (39%) Americans agree that the world's most enduring social institution is becoming obsolete."[5]

We will explore God's design for marriage later in this chapter, showing clearly that America has drifted far from the safe harbor of God's intent for marriage and family. I will also show that stable marriages and families are the basic building blocks of society, and that part of our moral and spiritual confusion can be tied to the breakdown of marriage. It's mere common sense: If the building blocks crumble, it is inevitable that the entire structure of society will also crumble.

Why is marriage becoming obsolete in America? Let's look at some of the underlying causes.

Causes of Today's Deconstruction of Marriage

Prosperity

National affluence is a blessing from God that is the natural result of a people building their society on His laws. This was true of ancient Israel (2 Chronicles 20:20), and it has also been true of the United

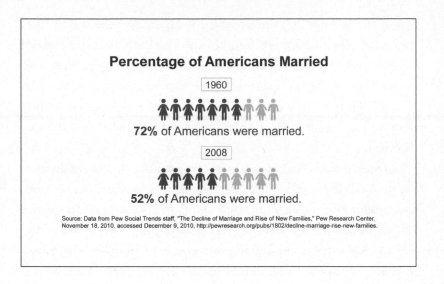

Percentage of Americans Married

1960

72% of Americans were married.

2008

52% of Americans were married.

Source: Data from Pew Social Trends staff, "The Decline of Marriage and Rise of New Families," Pew Research Center, November 18, 2010, accessed December 9, 2010, http://pewresearch.org/pubs/1802/decline-marriage-rise-new-families.

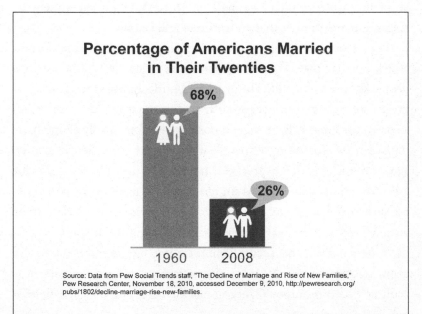

Percentage of Americans Married in Their Twenties

68%

26%

1960   2008

Source: Data from Pew Social Trends staff, "The Decline of Marriage and Rise of New Families," Pew Research Center, November 18, 2010, accessed December 9, 2010, http://pewresearch.org/pubs/1802/decline-marriage-rise-new-families.

States, which owes its unprecedented prosperity to the solid Christian principles built into its founding. But as the Lord often warned Israel, prosperity can lead to apostasy: "When I fed them, they were satisfied; when they were satisfied, they became proud; then they forgot me" (Hosea 13:6 NIV). This was the path Israel followed to their destruction, and it is clear that our nation is headed in the same direction.

Prosperity allows us to rely on our own resources instead of depending on God. It allows us to gratify our desires for pleasure, comfort, and freedom from constraints that we might have kept under control had we lacked the resources to pursue indulgence. When you add to this the influence of prevailing postmodern philosophy, which says, in effect, "The only standard for behavior is what seems right for you at the moment," you have a volatile mixture that threatens to destroy restraining institutions that ensure order and stability.

This, I believe, is one of the underlying reasons for the current attack on marriage. We see evidence everywhere we look. Why do people choose to cohabit? The prevailing philosophy—that pleasure is the greatest good—means sex without commitment no longer bears a societal stigma. Why is there a push to redefine family as the pairing of any two (or group of) people who consent, regardless of gender, age, or mode of sexual expression? It all comes down to the desire for an autonomous self—the old sin of Adam and Eve. A common viewpoint seems to be, "Why should I be bound by societal restrictions or ancient, outdated mores? I want to rule my own life." But as God tells us, "There is a way that seems right to a man, but its end is the way of death" (Proverbs 16:25). Or, as aptly summarized by the nineteenth-century Scottish author George MacDonald, "The one principle of hell is, 'I am my own.'"[6]

At its essence, the changing views on marriage in our culture reflect a fundamental shift in the foundation of our values—from being based on God's Word to being established by societal consensus.

Reinterpretation of the Bible

A second cause for the deconstruction of marriage is attacks by modern theologians. Two new books, both written by biblical scholars (one at Boston University, the other at Stonehill College), have recently appeared.[7] Both purport to give an accurate portrayal of what the Bible says about God and sex, yet both reinterpret relevant Scriptures to debunk the idea that the Bible supports sex only within the confines of heterosexual marriage. They assume that passages describing violations of God's sexual code are actually accepted norms and needlessly interpret innocent relationships, such as David's brotherly love for Jonathan, in the most sensational and decadent way possible. They find creative ways to debunk the Bible's straightforward condemnation of homosexuality.

Modern attempts to reinterpret the Bible are not new, of course. But apart from redefining the identity of Jesus Christ or the authority of Scripture, nothing will have a more profound impact on the health of American society than attacking the biblical definition of marriage as these books do. They ignore the divine model for marriage that God communicated to mankind for health and happiness and His glory. Extensive and subtly positive reviews of books such as these, appearing in widely read magazines such as *Newsweek*, lend credence to such writings in the minds of people who may make little effort to discern on their own what is or is not true.

Government Laws

Another attack on biblical marriage comes from a surprising but powerful source: the United States government. On February 23, 2011, the attorney general of the United States, at the direction of President Obama, announced that the administration would no longer defend the Defense of Marriage Act (DOMA) when it is challenged in U.S. courts. Long an opponent of DOMA, the president turned his back on the ideal of traditional marriage in America. I never thought I'd see the day when such a thing could happen. DOMA is a United States law, passed overwhelmingly by both houses of Congress and signed into law by President Bill Clinton in 1996. Under the law, no state is required to recognize a same-sex marriage that was made legal in any other state. The law also explicitly defined *marriage* as "a legal union between one man and one woman as husband and wife." Yet the president of the United States, who at his inauguration swore to defend and protect the laws of this country, has, contrary to that oath, decided not to defend or enforce this particular law.

These factors have consigned biblical marriage to obsolescence. Today, we are witnessing the alarming rise of two practices—cohabitation and divorce—now so widespread and accepted as to be considered "normal." This reality would have been unthinkable only a couple of generations ago.

Cohabitation Without Marriage

Perhaps the most prevalent evidence of marriage becoming obsolete in our society is the fast-rising incidence of cohabitation—couples living together without choosing to be married. These couples are sometimes referred to as "friends with benefits." They want the benefits of marriage without tying themselves down to a lifetime commitment or risking the hassle of divorce.

Sharon Jayson, a *USA Today* reporter who frequently writes about cultural trends, observed, "Living together has become so mainstream that growing numbers of Americans view it as an alternative to marriage."[8] She quotes the author of a recent book on cohabitation who says, "[Cohabitation is] what's happening in the world of dating, and it's not necessarily a path to anywhere."[9] In other words, cohabiting couples do not necessarily see living together as a "marriage test" to see whether they want to take the next step and tie the knot. They accept the arrangement on its own terms, simply for the momentary benefits it gives without concern for long-term goals or commitments.

Cohabiting without marriage has become so common that in a mere thirty years it has effected a complete inversion of America's attitude toward a practice that the Bible unambiguously labels *sin*. A 1969 Gallup poll showed that 66 percent of Americans believed premarital sex was wrong. At that time "shacking up," as it was termed, was considered "living in sin." By 2009, the percentage had almost reversed: a CBS/*New York Times* poll indicated that 60 percent of the population then believed that premarital sex was *not* wrong.[10]

This attitude was reflected in a video interview about the cohabitation of Prince William and Kate. Robert Jobson, the royal editor at *News of the World*, said, "Luckily we live in the twenty-first century and a lot of people live together before they marry."[11]

Jobson is right: More and more couples are choosing to treat marriage as optional. In 1977, fewer than one million American

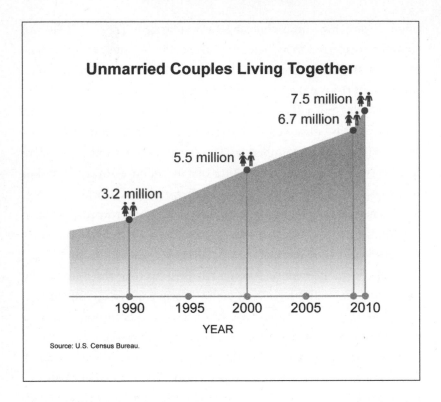

Unmarried Couples Living Together

7.5 million

6.7 million

5.5 million

3.2 million

1990   1995   2000   2005   2010

YEAR

Source: U.S. Census Bureau.

opposite-sex couples living together were unmarried. In 2007, that number rose to 6.4 million—almost 10 percent of all opposite-sex couples living together in America.[12]

As Sharon Jayson noted above, not all couples even have marriage in mind when they enter a cohabiting relationship. For example, in a 2008 *Newsweek* article titled "Yes to Love, No to Marriage," journalist Bonnie Eslinger wrote,

I am a 42-year-old woman who has lived life mostly on my own terms. I have never sought a husband and have still experienced intense, affirming love. I have explored the world and myself and sought understanding, knowledge and a sense of how I can best contribute. Ten years ago I left a New York career to return to California and pursue a writer's life. Shortly thereafter I met an intelligent teenager, also determined to live life on her own terms, who is now my fabulous foster daughter.

Meeting Jeff—an intelligent, creative, thoughtful man— became the icing on the rich cake of a life not wasted cruising singles bars and pining over lost loves.

Last year Jeff asked me to marry him, and I willingly gave my heart to the intent of his question. We are committed to spending our future together, pursuing our dreams and facing life's challenges in partnership.

Yet I do not need a piece of paper from the state to strengthen my commitment to Jeff. I do not believe in a religion that says romantic, committed love is moral only if couples pledge joint allegiance to God.

I don't need a white dress to feel pretty, and I have no desire to pretend I'm virginal. I don't need to have Jeff propose to me as if he's chosen me. I don't need a ring as a daily reminder to myself or others that I am loved. And I don't need Jeff to say publicly that he loves me, because he says it privately, not just in words but in daily actions.[13]

Ms. Eslinger's twenty-five uses of first-person singular pronouns (*I, me, my*) pretty well sum up the modern attitude that contributes so much to the destruction of marriage: the raising of personal autonomy to the highest priority in life. It's not about what communities or societies need, what a spouse needs, what children need in terms of public statements of commitment—and certainly not about what God expects. The prevailing modern attitude is about arranging life on autonomous terms—in this case, choosing a nonbinding union over a commitment in marriage. And yet Ms. Eslinger admitted the innate need to "[hold] some sort of celebration of our relationship,"[14] all the while retaining a wistful hope in the face of her realistic doubts that their families will come to celebrate something so ill-defined:

> We've begun planning a daylong event near the ocean that would allow time for us to enjoy the company of friends and family without wasting time on obligatory cake cutting and flower tosses...
>
> While I know the word "married" would mean something to them, something tangible they could use when describing our life together, I can't do it...The terms "husband" and "wife" wouldn't even begin to describe our relationship.
>
> We've set a date for July to hold our big event. No, we won't get married. But I hope our friends and family still come.[15]

Aside from the autonomy of the self, I can imagine two other reasons why Ms. Eslinger, and increasing numbers of people like her, is unwilling to take the route of legal marriage: (1) a resistance to conformity to convention, or (2) to avoid the complications of ending the union should they fall out of love. Such reasons smack more of cynicism and lack of purpose than they do of careful consideration and commitment.

The root of our problems is found in the statement so often made when someone decides to get married: "I've found someone to make me happy." Marriage is not about making ourselves happy. It's about making someone else happy. It's about finding someone you can devote your life to serving. This corresponds to the biblical view of love as expressed in Philippians 2: looking not on your own interests but the interests of the other. The genius of marriage is that when both partners are engaged in this, each is making the other happy.

Larry King interviewed Art Linkletter on his ninetieth birthday. Larry asked Art to explain the secret of longevity in marriage. I thought it was an appropriate question because Larry King has famously been married many times; and Art had been married to the same woman for nearly seventy years. So Art had a very simple answer to Larry's question.

He said, "I always say yes to anything she says."

Larry asked, "So how do you stay happy?"

"Oh, that's happy," said Art. "She's happy—when she's happy, I'm happy."[16]

There's a lot of truth in that little bit of folk wisdom.

The Scourge of Rampant Divorce

Cohabitation is only one indicator that marriage may be becoming obsolete. Another is the high rate of divorce in America. From the beginning God has required that the bond between a male and a female be one of lifetime permanence (Genesis 2:24; Matthew 19:6). Because of the high importance of this bond, it is formalized before witnesses with a vow of permanent commitment. In Ecclesiastes, Solomon stresses the great importance God places on the keeping of vows:

Do not be rash with your mouth, and let not your heart utter anything hastily before God...When you make a vow to God, do not delay to pay it...Better not to vow than to vow and not pay. Do not let your mouth cause your flesh to sin, nor say before the messenger of God that it was an error. (Ecclesiastes 5:2, 4–6)

Jesus, who had a way of boiling the Old Testament down to its essence, said this about vows: "Let your 'Yes' be 'Yes,' and your 'No,' 'No'" (Matthew 5:37). In other words, say what you mean and mean what you say.

Every day in America, thousands of people ignore these Scriptures and take back the marriage vows they spoke before God, their spouses, and their friends: "It was a mistake. I thought I loved [him or her], but I was wrong. I know I said 'I do,' but now I don't." Many people end their marriages with regret, but many do not. Far too many decide to break their marriage vows on the basis of convenience or preference.

Bertrand Russell was a brilliant mathematician and scholar, and he lived for almost ninety-eight years, allowing him to impact an entire century. But he rejected any notion of a personal God and throughout his life professed to be an atheist.

Russell, who was orphaned in childhood, found his need for love satisfied by a relationship with an American Quaker named Alys Pearsall Smith. He was seventeen and she was twenty-two. His grandmother objected, so the couple put off marriage for several years. They were married in 1894. In 1901, Russell was riding his bicycle when he decided he didn't love his wife anymore. He wrote: "I went out bicycling one afternoon, and suddenly, as I was riding along a country road, I realized that I no longer loved Alys. I had no idea until this moment that my love for her was even lessening."[17] Alys was devastated and did all she could to cling to her husband, but there was no backpedaling. In 1911 they separated, and they were divorced in 1921. Russell's subsequent romantic life was lurid and littered with marriages, breakups, divorces, infidelities, and affairs.[18]

There are prices to pay when marriages end—economically, emotionally, spiritually, and societally—for both adults and children. The high cost of marriage failures is not lost on cultural observers. In a recent *Time* magazine article, author Caitlin Flanagan wrote, "There is no other single force causing as much measurable hardship and human misery in this country as the collapse of marriage."[19]

Her claim is all the more significant because it was written in the middle of 2009 when the nation was reeling from the economic collapse that began a year earlier. Not even the dire financial straits we are in, she concluded, are causing as many hardship as the "collapse of marriage." Those hardships are many—economic, emotional, and psychological. And when children are involved the results can be even more devastating, leaving scars of rejection, behavioral problems, lifelong insecurities, and confusion due to the lack of a parental role model. The sad thing is, the collapse of marriage adds even more misery to other hardships. Think of all the divorced single mothers who lost their jobs in the economic downturn. Think of all the divorced men who lost their jobs and couldn't pay child support to help their ex-wives and children.

I want to end this section by sounding a small but hopeful note concerning divorce statistics. The rate, while alarmingly high, may not be as high as has been traditionally reported.

The "50 percent" divorce rate we often read—one divorce for every two marriages—has long been touted as the norm in America. But in 2005, the *New York Times* pointed out that a flawed method had led to this inflated statistic.[20] Social scientists have since moved to a more accurate method that simply compares the number of people who ever married with the number of those same people who divorced.[21] Counted in this way, "the [divorce] rate has never exceeded 41 percent,"[22] and will likely never reach 50 percent since it has not reached that level in any demographic of the population at large.

Divorce rates among Christians have recently been reported to mirror the general population. But that, too, appears to be an inaccurate statistic. Committed Christian couples, as opposed to those who are Christian in name only, who seriously pursue Christian disciplines such as church attendance, reading the Bible and spiritual materials, and praying together, "enjoy significantly lower divorce rates than mere church members, the general public and unbelievers."[23] They are 35 percent less likely to divorce than couples who have no church affiliation.[24]

Defending a Meaningful Marriage

Above I cited a Pew report revealing that the percentage of married Americans plummeted twenty points from 72 percent in 1960 to only 52 percent in 2008. Yet 46 percent of the unmarried people interviewed expressed a desire to be married at some point in their lives. As Steven E. Rhoads, a professor in the Woodrow Wilson Department of Government and Foreign Affairs at the University of Virginia, has written, "The marital ideal—one man and one woman bound in body and soul, sharing, comforting, communicating through good times and bad—is very appealing even, or perhaps particularly, in a cynical age."[25]

While the spirit of our age has led people to believe that happiness is achieved by satisfying the urges of the self, people still have deep within them a longing for the bonded love and security provided by a stable marriage. God created us in this way, and we cannot reinvent our basic nature. This is a universal and undeniable truth, as Maggie Gallagher, president of the Institute for Marriage and Public Policy and chairwoman of the National Organization for Marriage, has said:

I think it's important to recognize that marriage is a virtually universal human social institution. It exists in just about every known human society…yet it has a certain basic and recognizable shape. Marriage as a universal human idea is always a public union, not just a private and personal one. It's a sexual union…between a man and a woman…in which the rights and the responsibilities of the man and the woman towards each other and towards their children are publicly defined and supported. We don't just leave it up to a bunch of adolescents in the middle of romantic, erotic, emotional drama to work out on their own what this whole big dimension of human experience means…There aren't that many human universals…and you have to ask yourself, "Why?" Why is it that human beings, over and over again in all these wildly diverse societies—in the steppes of Asia and the jungles of the Amazon and the deserts of Africa, completely disconnected by religion, by economy, by culture, by history—why do human beings keep coming up with this same basic marriage idea?[26]

It's because, as the Bible affirms in Genesis 1:27, human beings are the image bearers of God who were created to reflect His design. Today there is much confusion about God's design for marriage. Dr. Robert George, Princeton law professor and coeditor of *The Meaning of Marriage*,[27] laments this fact and encourages us to remember the origin and meaning of marriage:

> You would think that it would be a given, but it's not any longer a given. We've lost our sense of exactly what marriage is; why marriage exists; why public law and public policy recognize marriage; why the church is so centrally concerned with marriage; what the norms that give shape and meaning to marriage are—norms like monogamy, exclusivity, permanence of commitment. So, given the erosion of the marriage culture and with it the loss of a sound grip on what marriage is, on the meaning of marriage—yes, we need to remind ourselves of what marriage is. We need to think again about the reasons that such a thing as marriage came into existence as a cultural phenomenon in the first place.[28]

Although space does not permit me to provide a comprehensive theology of marriage, I would like to take up Dr. George's challenge by reminding us of the simple, crystal clear picture of marriage and family as ordained by God and revealed in the Bible. Here is a concise, biblical definition of *marriage*:

> One man and one woman united spiritually, emotionally, physically, publicly, and legally, in a lifetime bond of loyal love, for

procreation, channeling sexual and emotional energy, and serving as a civilizing and stabilizing factor in society.

This biblical ideal for marriage goes back to the creation of the world, when fundamental natural and human order was established. God created humans, both male and female, to be bearers of His image and stewards of all creation.

In the beginning, God did not create a social group of multiple humans and then pair the males with females as a way of bringing order to society. Marriage does bring order, but it has a far deeper purpose: It is fundamental to the very design of life on earth. Marriage is a male and female coming together to function as "one flesh." It is a united pair whose synergistic potential is greater together than if they remained single and simply lived together without permanent commitment. Something stable and immovable happens when two individuals unite as one in a permanent bond. The permanence enables them to build for the future, passing on to their progeny material security, education, ethics, and knowledge of God—all of which form building blocks for a stable society. This is fundamental to the way couples are to use their paired identity to act as stewards of creation and bear the image of God to the rest of creation.

As we look back at the history of marriage, as we examine its current status, there is one central truth that stands unchanged: The design for marriage originates with God and rests on His eternal principles.

God Designed Marriage as a Partnership Between One Man and One Woman

Marriage is not the union of multiple partners or same-sex partners. It is the union of one man with one woman. All the debate in recent decades about the definition of marriage is based on a rejection of this creation model. From God's perspective, what constitutes a marriage is absolutely clear.

God made a man—a male. And then He designed another human being who was the same as him, but different—a woman, a female. The man and the woman corresponded to each other in a unique way, both in terms of their bodies and their personalities. And God brought them together and gave them to each other in a special relationship. This was the first marriage, and it was the pattern for marriage. From the very beginning, it was designed by God as a gift to humanity and as the foundation of social order.

It's important to notice that the union God established in Genesis 2 was characterized by the relationship words of *husband* and *wife*. The word *wife* appears in Genesis 2:24: "A man shall leave his father and mother and be joined to his wife." And the word *husband* appears seven verses later: "She also gave to her husband" (Genesis 3:6).

Marriage, then, is a covenant partnership between one man and one woman who unite in an exclusive relationship as husband and wife.

We cannot reinvent our fundamental institutions without going against the created order. To think God's creation is malleable—that the sexes are interchangeable or that men and women can find personal fulfillment in other ways often leads to disaster, both personal and societal. Nothing ultimately functions correctly unless we use it in the way it was created to be used. To employ the human body and psyche in ways they were not created to be used will lead to the same kind of disaster as trying to use your automobile as a motorboat. You may feel exhilaration and freedom as you fly through the air after driving your car off the pier, but it will not float for long when it lands in the water.

God Designed Marriage to Be a Permanent Union

The notion of two becoming "one flesh" is pictured ultimately in the sexual union of husband and wife. Jesus Christ affirmed the permanence of marriage when He said, "What God has joined together, let not man separate" (Matthew 19:6). Permission to divorce was granted only "because of the hardness of...hearts" (Matthew 19:8). Divorce is an exception to what was ordained by God as a permanent union of husband and wife.

Elton Trueblood wrote these words more than fifty years ago. He could not have possibly imagined how prophetically relevant they would be today:

> Divorce, though sometimes justified, must always be looked upon as *failure* [italics in original]. A divorced couple must see that they have failed in the most important undertaking of their lives. Divorce may sometimes be the lesser of two evils, but in any case it is evil and we dare never look upon it with complacency. In short, if our society is to be strong and the lives of children protected, the marriage vow must be taken with complete seriousness. It must become a matter of conviction. It is interesting to note that there is some progress in the Bible in regard to divorce, but that the movement is not, as we might suppose, toward greater looseness; it is a movement toward greater strictness.[29]

God Designed Marriage to Provide Spiritual Unity Between Husband and Wife

Humans were created as physical and spiritual beings. Oneness is a matter not only of physical joining but of spiritual joining as well. The apostle Paul highlighted the spiritual joining in 1 Corinthians 6:15–17 when he warned against a Christian man joining himself to a harlot and becoming "one body with her." He then pointed out that human marriage between a male and a female carries the exalted honor of reflecting the nature of our union with Christ. He said that "he who is joined to the Lord is one spirit with Him" (v. 17). We are not joined to Jesus Christ physically, but we are joined spiritually. The highly spiritual nature of the human marriage union is often demonstrated in the Bible as a model or type of the union we have with God.

God Designed Marriage for the Purpose of Procreation

Shortly after Adam and Eve were created, they received their first commission: "God blessed them, saying, 'Be fruitful and multiply'" (Genesis 1:22). This command was repeated at the "second beginning" of humanity following the great flood: "God blessed Noah and his sons, and said to them: 'Be fruitful and multiply, and fill the earth'" (Genesis 9:1). "Procreation is part of God's creation mandate for the man and the woman... [It] ensures the continuation of the human race and enables it to fulfill God's mandate of cultivating the earth for God."[30]

The Pew report I cited earlier shows that this priority for marriage has been largely lost today. When the researchers asked married individuals, "Why get married?"...

- 93 percent said for love.
- 87 percent said for a lifelong commitment.

- 81 percent said for companionship.
- 59 percent said for having children.
- 31 percent said for financial stability.[31]

The Pew Research Center reported that this heavy emphasis on love was likely a first in human history. In the past, people in general have realized that love alone is not reason enough for marriage, and the biblical model supports this thesis. I don't want to be misunderstood here; I believe, as the apostle Paul did, that love is vital in marriage (Ephesians 5:25, 28; Colossians 3:19). But when you make love the sole reason for marriage, you ignore criteria even more basic and open a Pandora's box of problems. Christian scholar Dinesh D'Souza explains:

"But why should we prevent people who love each other from getting married?" Here is the problem. Marriage is defined as the legal union of two adults of the opposite sex who are unrelated to each other. This is the basic definition. Now let's assume we revise the definition to permit gay marriage. What if a group of Mormons, joined by a group of Muslims[,] presses for the legalization of polygamy? The argument proceeds along the same lines: "I want to have four wives, because we all love each other." And another man says, "Why shouldn't I be able to marry my sister?" And yet others make more exotic claims: "I love my dog and my dog loves me."

The point is that love is a desirable, but not sufficient, condition for marriage. Why, then, does society have these specific criteria? Why privilege this particular arrangement [of an unrelated man and woman] and grant it special legal status, including the social recognition and tax benefits that go with it? The reason is that marriage is the incubator of children. It is the only known mechanism for the healthy cultivation of the next generation.[32]

Another author said it this way: "It may seem a gratuitous paradox, but the truth is that marriage is more important than love. Marriage is more important than love because it is the normal situation out of which true and abiding love arises. The popular notion, much encouraged by light fiction and the motion picture, is that love is primary, marriage being a dull anticlimax. But this is vast error."[33]

God brought two perfect, sinless people together in the Garden of Eden, a man and a woman who knew the perfect love of God. They did not get married to find love but to walk together in the unity and purpose God created them to fulfill: the primary task of birthing and raising the next generation. And in the process, love happened.

God Designed Marriage as a Principal Building Block of Society

I've stressed this fact several times in this chapter; now I want to explore its origin. In the Garden of Eden, God instituted no other organization or structure for humanity besides marriage. He intended procreational marriage to be the solid link in the chain of human progress and society. Strong heterosexual marriages, and the resulting children and families, serve as an organizing force in a disorderly world. Not only do loyal marriages serve as a conduit for the channeling and containing of adult sexual and emotional energy, they also serve as a source of wisdom and instruction for succeeding generations of young people who rise to take their places in society. It is from strong, loyal marriages that young people learn what it takes to create oases of love and order and strength in a cultural desert of shifting moral sand, reshaped daily by the winds of convenience and preference.

When God's design for marriage is ignored, the well-being of an entire society is at risk. In December 2010, the annual *The State of Our Unions* report was released jointly by the National Marriage Project at the University of Virginia and the Center for Marriage and Families at the Institute for American Values. The subtitle of the report reads, "When Marriage Disappears: The New Middle America." The report states:

> Marriage is not merely a private arrangement between two persons. It is a core social institution, one that helps to ensure the economic, social and emotional welfare of countless children, women, and men in this nation...
>
> The disappearance of marriage in Middle America would endanger the American Dream, the emotional and social welfare of children, and the stability of the social fabric in thousands of communities across the country.[34]

Christians, especially, need to think again about the origins and importance of marriage. It is significant that while Adam was single, Satan did not approach him or tempt him to disobey God. He waited until after Adam's marriage to launch his attack. You would think it easier to attack one person instead of two, but by waiting he was able to attack not just an individual, but also God's foundational building block for harmony and stability—marriage. By attacking marriage, he was able to create division and disharmony between humans themselves as well as between humans and God. Satan still follows that strategy today. He knows that, as goes marriage, so goes stability in the societies of the world. The more disruption he can create in societies through attacking marriages, the better for his efforts at getting people's eyes off God and onto their own survival.

Andreas Köstenberger, coauthor of *God, Marriage, and Family: Rebuilding the Biblical Foundation*, warns,

> If God the creator in fact, as the Bible teaches, instituted marriage and the family, and if there is an evil being called Satan who wages war against God's creative purposes in this world, it should come as no surprise that the divine foundation of these institutions has come under massive attack in recent years. Ultimately, we human beings, whether we realize it or not, are involved in a cosmic spiritual conflict that pits God against Satan, with marriage and the family serving as a key arena in which spiritual and cultural battles are fought.[35]

Sometimes the battlefront of that spiritual conflict becomes starkly visible, as it did when President Obama set the U.S. government in opposition to traditional marriage. The battle against marriage is no longer a vague, spiritualized warfare. It has tangibly entered the arena where we must arm ourselves with God's truth and call on God to give us the courage and discernment to uphold and boldly defend what we know is right. At stake is the very future of our society.

God Designed Marriage to Be a Picture of His Relationship with Israel and Christ's Relationship with the Church

In Genesis 2:24–25 we read, "A man shall leave his father and mother and be joined to his wife, and they shall become one flesh. And they were both naked, the man and his wife, and were not ashamed." The Hebrew word for *one* is the same as is used in Deuteronomy 6:4–5 concerning God: "Hear, O Israel: The LORD our God, the LORD is one! You shall love the LORD your God with all your heart, with all your soul, and with all your strength."

The oneness to be found in marriage is the same kind of oneness found in the Trinity. God is three persons in one. Husband and wife are two persons who become one through marriage. The oneness that exists between a man and his wife cannot be experienced in the union of a woman with a woman or a man with a man. Male and female were created as complementary units in order to know intimacy with the opposite sex. This kind of complementary oneness is impossible between two people of the same sex.

Marriage is so sacred in the eyes of God that He chose it as the Old Testament picture of His relationship with the people of Israel. When Israel chose to worship other gods, this was considered adultery on her part (Jeremiah 3:6, 8).

In the New Testament, the marriage image continues as the picture of the relationship between Christ and the Church. The Church is the bride and Jesus Christ is the Groom (Ephesians 5:22–33).

The New Testament teaches that there is nothing more intimate than the relationship of Christ and His Church. To illustrate this oneness, the Holy Spirit chose the only relationship in human experience that could come close: the relationship between a man and his wife.

When I first began pastoring more than thirty years ago, I was called on to officiate weddings. I didn't know what to say, so I found a traditional wedding ceremony in a manual that had been compiled by Dr. Billy Melvin. In the years since, I've adapted the words and used them repeatedly. I call it my "Traditional Ceremony." As I later learned, it's based on the ceremony taken from the Book of Common Prayer, which dates back to 1549 and to the Reformation in England:

> Dear friends, we are gathered here in the sight of God and one another to join together this man and this woman in holy matrimony. Marriage is the first institution given for the welfare of the human race. In the Garden of Eden, before sin or death ever occurred, God saw that it was not good for the man to be alone. He made a helpmate suitable to him and established the rite of marriage, while heavenly hosts witnessed the wonderful scene.
>
> Originated in divine wisdom and goodness, designed to promote human happiness and holiness, this rite is the foundation of home life and social order and must remain till the end of time. It was sanctioned and honored by the presence and power of Jesus at the marriage in Cana of Galilee.
>
> It was commended by Paul to be honorable among all men and signifies unto us the mystical union that exists betwixt Christ and His Church. Therefore, it is not to be entered into unadvisedly or lightly, but reverently, discreetly, advisedly, and in the fear of God.

Better than anything else I've ever seen, the words of this ceremony summarize what the Bible says about the sanctity and holiness of marriage. It seems to me that the one sentence in the middle sums up this entire chapter: "Originated in divine wisdom and goodness, designed to promote human happiness and holiness, this rite is the foundation of home life and social order and must remain till the end of time." This is the set of scales that gives us a true and accurate reading of the moral and spiritual weight of marriage.

Is the future of traditional marriage in trouble in America? Is it in danger of becoming obsolete? I never thought I would see the day when the answer to those questions could be "Yes"—but that day has arrived. Our selfish natures, our increasingly godless culture, and our very government are hard at work against God's first ordained institution. Fortunately, to paraphrase Christ, "What God has ordained, no man or government can destroy" (see Matthew 19:6). But that requires the people of God to preserve, protect, and defend marriage from every form of attack. This means we must work on three fronts: our own marriages, the marriages of people we love, and the institution of marriage in society. Let us be vigilant and stick to our prayers.

We can't always control the choices of a secular society, but as children of God living biblically in a corrupt culture, we can guard our own marriages in both concept and practice. And in so doing, we can show the world what it's missing.

We began this chapter by telling the story of Prince William and Kate Middleton living together for eight months before formally marrying on April 29, 2011.

Despite their moral failure, they did get married in a traditional Christian ceremony watched by an estimated two billion people around the world. During the ceremony, the name of Jesus Christ was proclaimed many times, and Kate's brother, James, even read a passage from Romans chapter 12, urging the couple to resist the cultural pull toward worldliness. The presiding minister (the Archbishop of Canterbury) also prayed a prayer needed by all our marriages and all in our world today:

> *O Eternal God, Creator and Preserver of all mankind, giver of all spiritual grace, the author of everlasting life: send thy blessing*

upon these thy servants, this man and this woman, whom we bless in thy name; that, living faithfully together, they may surely perform and keep the vow and covenant betwixt them made, whereof this ring given and received is a token and pledge; and may ever remain in perfect love and peace together, and live according to thy laws; through Jesus Christ our Lord. Amen.[36]

The archbishop concluded his sermon with this prayer:

God the Father, God the Son, God the Holy Ghost, bless, preserve, and keep you; the Lord mercifully with his favour look upon you; and so fill you with all spiritual benediction and grace, that ye may so live together in this life, that in the world to come ye may have life everlasting. Amen.[37]

CHAPTER 5

When Morality Would Be in Free Fall

February 26, 2011, was a sad day in my hometown of San Diego. The San Diego State University Aztecs hoped to pay back the visiting Brigham Young University Cougars, who had defeated them on the basketball court earlier in the season. But it wasn't to be.

BYU beat our team soundly and suddenly started looking like a contender as a top seed in the upcoming "March Madness"—the NCAA basketball tournament.

A week after the San Diego State game, BYU officials suspended one of their star players from the team, effectively negating any chance the Cougars had for a trip to the Final Four. The player's offense was a violation of the university's honor code—a code signed by every student at the university. And it is a code with teeth. The school's no-tolerance policy for violations resulted in a star player's losing his spot on the squad—and the Cougars' losing a shot at a national title.

There was immediate pushback from the media and public at large, of course: How dare the university discipline a star player? But cooler, wiser heads began to speak out as if there just might be something to this "honor" thing. Pat Forde, an ESPN columnist, expressed his personal assessment of the school's decision:

> What makes this such a powerful testament is the fact that so many schools have cravenly abandoned their standards at such a time as this, embracing athletic expediency over institutional principle. It happens so often that we don't even raise an eyebrow at it anymore. Player arrests or other antisocial behaviors are minimized as youthful mistakes, with strenuous institutional effort put into counterspinning any negative publicity.[1]

And John Canzano at the *Oregonian* newspaper in Portland, Oregon, wrote, "At a moment like this, watching BYU wave off a [sophomore] who started 26 games, it's evident that their success is not accidental...Just maybe...the notion that good values and a willingness to think long term has some worth. Because the alternative has left the rest of college athletics feeling like a slimy and dark underworld."[2]

The idea of an honor code is not unique to BYU. All the American military academies have honor codes, as well as some of the most prestigious secular universities. But most of them are limited, dealing specifically with academic honesty when taking tests or completing academic assignments. But the Brigham Young University code is all-encompassing, which is why the athlete in question was called to account. In part, the BYU honor code requires students to . . .

- Be honest
- Live a chaste and virtuous life
- Obey the law and all campus policies
- Use clean language
- Respect others
- Abstain from alcoholic beverages, tobacco, tea, coffee, and substance abuse
- Participate regularly in church services
- Observe the Dress and Grooming Standards
- Encourage others in their commitment to comply with the Honor Code[3]

Since BYU is a religiously affiliated private university and most of the thirty-four thousand students are members of the Mormon religion, the code is more strict than that of a secular school. But even non-Mormon students attending BYU are expected to adhere to the honor code, with the exception of the requirement to regularly attend church services. Students—whether Mormon or not—know going in what is expected.

Having sat behind the president's desk of a college myself, I can tell you the heartache that comes from disciplining a student athlete needed by his school's team. But I can also tell you that nothing will serve a young person better than learning early in life that choices have consequences.

Madison Sarratt, former dean of Vanderbilt University, instituted an honor code system for all Vanderbilt students that remains firmly in place today. He is famous for having said to one of his classes something that serves as a credo for the university: "Today I am going to give you two examinations, one in trigonometry and one in honesty. I hope you will pass them both, but if you must fail one, let it be trigonometry, for there are many good [people] in this world today who cannot pass an examination in trigonometry, but there are no good [people] in the world who cannot pass an examination in honesty."[4]

In schools of the past and in a diminishing few today, we find a strong emphasis on exemplary moral behavior. This emphasis is crucial to an orderly society, not only in our educational institutions but also in our families, our communities, our nation, and even our churches. Anywhere we have a gathering of two or more people, morality becomes a factor in relationships, personal safety, property rights, and commerce.

C. S. Lewis tells us that morality is concerned primarily with three things: "Firstly, with fair play and harmony between individuals. Secondly, with what might be called tidying up or harmonizing the things inside each individual. Thirdly, with the general purpose of human life as a whole: what man was made for."[5]

In order for fallen humans to survive in an orderly society, a moral compass by which one navigates through life is absolutely essential.

Morality is more than just not cheating on a university trigonometry test; it is all-encompassing, providing a guide to every area of life. I never thought I would see the day when America's moral compass would lose its orientation. But it has happened. Our moral compass seems no longer to have a "true north." The needle spins crazily, looking for a direction on which to settle, a direction that can lead a nation on a path of integrity and morality.

For an example of this spinning compass needle, let's return briefly to college sports. In 2010, *Sports Illustrated* magazine and CBS News conducted a six-month investigation on crime and college football.[6] They found that 7 percent of the players on the preseason top twenty-five football teams (204 players) had been charged with or cited for a crime—nearly 40 percent of those involving serious offenses such as assault and battery, domestic violence, and robbery.[7] If even half that number committed actual crimes and were prosecuted, shouldn't we have heard about a wave of repercussions at universities across the land like we heard about the one athlete at BYU? Do acts such as assault and battery, domestic violence, and robbery not qualify as violations of some kind of code for university athletes?

I'm not picking on athletes here. I'm citing them as an example of a systemic problem in America. It's as if immorality is in the water we drink and the air we breathe. It no longer surprises us that coaches, when millions of dollars of endorsement and television and tournament receipts hang in the balance, sometimes choose to lighten or postpone a player's discipline when the player is caught in an immoral situation. But an episode of CBS's *60 Minutes* shows that such compromise is the name of the high-stakes game, not only in our schools. It also occurs openly among high officials in government.

When a network correspondent interviewed Pennsylvania governor Ed Rendell in a segment that aired in early 2011, the subject was gambling in his state. (There are now twice as many slot machines as ATMs in Pennsylvania.) Governor Rendell saw legalized gambling as a way to make up serious shortfalls in the state's budget.

When pressed by the *60 Minutes* correspondent about gambling addictions and the loss of badly needed family incomes to gambling, the governor responded by saying gambling "is a decent way to raise revenue where…the biggest downside is that some people lose their paychecks…If they were going to lose it anyway [in casinos in neighboring states] let's get the upside."[8] So it's a trade-off—all the well-documented and destructive downsides of gambling for the upside of money in the state budget. (That downside for Pennsylvanians and the upside for the state treasury amounted to $1 billion in 2010.) The governor took great offense at the correspondent's challenge concerning the morality of such a revenue-generating scheme and shouted in frustration toward the end of the interview, "You're idiots if you don't get that!"

This now passes for "decent" (to use the governor's word) in America? *Merriam-Webster* defines *decent* as "marked by moral integrity, kindness, and goodwill."[9] Is instituting a rigged system where the house (the state, in this case) wins and thousands of citizens lose an act of moral kindness and goodwill? Of course, we could give Pennsylvania credit for resisting the siren song of legalized gambling as long as it did. The only two states where all forms of gambling are still illegal are Utah and Hawaii. All other states allow some type of gambling: charitable, pari-mutuel, lotteries, commercial, Native American casinos, or racetracks.[10]

Another example of a wildly spinning moral compass occurred in 2009 when a Nevada state senator attempted to levy a tax on prostitution in his state. Gambling tax revenues were down in Nevada, so taxing the state's legalized prostitution, which had never been taxed, seemed like a well waiting for a bucket. Instead of introducing legislation to make the immoral act of prostitution illegal, this senator wanted to affirm its legality by taxing it to increase declining state tax receipts. (His motion was defeated.)[11]

While many Americans may participate in gambling, prostitution, abortion, pornography, and other legal behaviors that soil the American conscience, most seem to realize there's a disconnect between what is legal and what is truly moral. And, like children who lose respect for parents who are living inappropriate lives, we lose respect for those in authority who compromise absolute morality when passing laws for financial or political advantage. In the Gallup organization's 2010 poll on the perceived honesty and ethics of various professions, only 12 percent of the population gave state government officials a "very high/high" rating. Members of the U.S. Congress fared even worse: Only 9 percent of the population rated their honesty and ethical standards as "very high/high," with 57 percent saying their standards are "very low/low."[12]

Still not convinced that the needle on America's moral compass is wavering? What would you say if you knew that child sexual slavery was widespread? I'm not talking about what goes on in some steamy, seedy city in Southeast Asia, the world headquarters of the child sex trade. I'm talking about America. At least it's not legal like prostitution in Nevada, but it is practiced here nonetheless. In fact, a recent study discovered that more than five thousand children were identified as "domestic minor sexual slaves" in Las Vegas alone.[13] And Atlanta "has become a hub of child prostitution and other forms of commercial sexual exploitation of children."[14] Another hub is Dallas, site of 2011's NFL Super Bowl XLV. The preponderance of unattached males in attendance with plenty of money to spend makes the Super Bowl "one of the biggest human trafficking events in the United States," according to Texas state attorney Greg Abbott.[15]

Couple those facts with the viral spread of child pornography on the Internet—"the new silent child abuse"[16]—including bestiality with children,[17] and one wonders if America can sink any lower. While levels of morality are at all-time lows, jail and prison populations in America are at all-time highs. In 2009, just under a million American adults were in local jails, and the same number were on parole. One and a half million were in prison, and just over four million were on probation. That total—7.2 million American adults incarcerated or on probation—compares with 1.7 million in 1980.[18]

Given these realities, it should come as no surprise that in January 2011 Gallup reported that only 30 percent of Americans expressed satisfaction with the current moral and ethical climate in the United States, marking a new low.[19] What's more, an astounding 76 percent of Americans say the moral condition of America is getting worse.[20] Had I been polled in that survey, I would have voted with the majority in both cases.

The necessity of morality is more critical in America than in any other society on earth because we have more freedom. Because America is a democracy, "Americans have to be more self-governing, show more restraint, be more respectful of their neighbors." Thus read a statement issued in conjunction with a meeting of the Council on Civil Society held at the University of Chicago in 1998.[21] If morality is important in a democratic society, it is even more important in the spiritual society of Christ's Church. And there are signs that morality is breaking down there as well.

Shifting Moral Standards of Christians

The title of a study issued by the Barna Group says it all: "A New Generation of Adults Bends Moral and Sexual Rules to Their Liking." The report stated that attitudes of Christian believers born between 1965 and 1983 were "virtually identical" to the attitudes of nonbelievers regarding eight of the sixteen moral behaviors measured.[22] These included gambling, pornography, abortion, sex outside of marriage, same-sex marriage, and use of illegal drugs.[23]

In a summary statement, David Kinnaman, the director of the study, wrote, "This research paints a compelling picture that moral values are shifting very quickly and significantly *within* the Christian community as well as outside of it" (italics in original).[24] While the loss of a moral compass in society at large is troubling, it is even more troubling when followers of Jesus Christ—those who are called to be "salt and light" in the world (Matthew 5:13–16)—lose theirs. The very contrast between light and darkness suggests that those with the light are to illuminate the moral and spiritual way in the world. But if they lose their way, how will those in darkness be guided?

Obviously, this discussion begs the underlying question: Who defines what is moral? As America leans more and more toward humanism, the source and standards for morals and ethics are increasingly up for grabs. The moral standards America sets for its citizens by enacting them into law come from America's collective consciousness—or, specifically, from that of the lawmakers. All types of religious, spiritual, historical, and personal opinions are thrown into the mixer, and after debate, trade-offs, compromises, gauging voter opinion, and pressure from the executive branch, out comes a moral standard, for better or worse.

For Christians, the moral code is much more inclusive, more specifically defined, and has a more authoritative source. Comparing the Christian moral code to the American moral code is like comparing Brigham Young University's honor code, which covers all of life, with the honor codes of other universities, which typically address only matters of concern to the academic institution. The Christian moral code is all-inclusive, whereas the American moral code cares little about matters of private personal behavior. In America, for instance, there is no law against premarital sex, but in the kingdom of God there is such a law. Unlike the American moral code, which is based on the ever-changing will of the people, the Christian code of morals and ethics is found in the Bible and is based on the moral and ethical character of God.

It is clear, however, that the majority do not look to the Bible for their moral compass. As Doug Webster has written, "Contemporary ethics is shaped more by the ethos of a culture than the moral order revealed in God's Word."[25] Given the high number of citizens claiming to be Christian in our nation, that means even they are following the postmodern pattern of self-determined morality.

For today's Christians to "[bend] moral and sexual rules to their liking" (to quote the Barna study above) says a lot about how they view the Bible as a source of authority in their lives. When challenged, some Christians appeal to the lack of biblical clarity on activities such as gambling, drug use, and drinking alcohol. Granted, the Bible doesn't say anything specifically about the morality of these activities. But there are certainly indirect biblical approaches to these subjects (like the stewardship of one's money and personal health and drunkenness) that provide clear moral guidance. On other areas of life queried by the Barna study—sexual, marital, and gender issues—the Bible provides clear and direct moral guidance.

So it's difficult to see how Christians could claim lack of biblical clarity on moral issues as a basis for bending the rules. Rather, it always comes down to the issue of elevating one's personal desires over God's, of setting oneself up as a moral authority over the moral authority of God as revealed through His Word.

The Solid Moral Foundation for Christians

God's moral and ethical laws were given first to Moses in ten parts known as the Decalogue, or the Ten Commandments. Later, six hundred–plus laws were added to expand the implications of the ten fundamental laws, to remain in effect for the life of the nation of Israel. Then, Jesus Christ delivered a kingdom commentary on God's laws in the Sermon on the Mount to highlight their spiritual dimensions—the spirit of the law added to the letter. The civil and ceremonial laws given to Israel were not applied in the New Testament to the Church, but the requirements of the Ten Commandments are all repeated for application to the Church in the New Testament save one: the injunction to keep the Sabbath day holy (the fourth commandment).

The most concise summary of God's laws for those who claim to follow Him was given by Jesus in Matthew 22:37–40: " 'You shall love the LORD your God with all your heart, with all your soul, and with all your mind.' This is the first and great commandment. And the second is like it: 'You shall love your neighbor as yourself.' On these two commandments hang all the Law and the Prophets."

Love God (the first four of the Ten Commandments) and love

your neighbor (the remaining six)—the two simplest and most sub-
lime statements of morality ever uttered. No person who loves God
with heart, soul, and mind, and loves his neighbor as himself, will
ever be accused of bending or breaking God's moral laws.

For those Christians who think that living under grace in the
New Testament means morality is no longer the hyperissue it might
have been under the Old Testament law, the Bible offers several
clarifications:

First, through the prophet Jeremiah in the Old Testament, God
promised to take His laws off of stone tablets and put them in the
minds and write them on the hearts of His people (Jeremiah 31:33).
That promise was part of the provision of the new covenant that
was instituted through the shed blood of Christ: "This cup is the
new covenant in My blood, which is shed for you" (Luke 22:20). In
other words, by the indwelling Spirit of God, the laws of God—His
standards of morality—move from being an external to an internal
reality. God's law is no longer something to be read, examined, and
debated as an intellectual matter. It becomes part of the heart and the
mind of the one united to God by faith in Christ. As the great Bible
commentator Matthew Henry wrote, "When the law of God is written on our hearts, our duty will be our delight." The law changes from
being a burden that keeps us from pleasure to a guide that leads us to
a wholly new kind of pleasure—the pleasure of walking in God's best
plan for our lives. As Jesus said, "My yoke is easy and My burden is
light" (Matthew 11:30).

In addition, we will find that conforming to God's law in our
hearts allows us to experience in all activities of life the specific kind
of pleasure and satisfaction God meant for us to find in that particu-

lar activity. So the laws are entirely for our benefit; they are given not to prevent pleasure, but to increase it.

Second, the apostle Paul clarifies what grace doesn't mean: It doesn't mean that God's law has been nullified. Anticipating that he, by his preaching of grace, might be accused of antinomianism (negating the obligation to live a lawful life), Paul wrote, "Do we then make void the law through faith? Certainly not! On the contrary, we establish the law" (Romans 3:31). He says that we are not free to disregard God's moral laws just because we live under grace (Romans 6:1–2). And he confirms what Christ taught about love being the fulfillment of the law (Romans 13:8–10). As we noted above, we follow the law because we love God, knowing that His ways are always best for us and increase our joy.

So New Testament Christians are in no way exempt from the moral and ethical requirements of God's law. Indeed, we have an even higher motivation for fulfilling God's moral law: love. Grace means living a moral life not because we have to but because we want to.

Third, Paul puts an even sharper point on making moral choices by saying, "All things are lawful for me, but not all things are helpful; all things are lawful for me, but not all things edify. Let no one seek his own, but each one the other's well-being" (1 Corinthians 10:23–24). There may be an action or choice that breaks none of God's laws yet is still not "helpful" or "edifying." The Christian Gospel moves us to a higher plane in life. No longer do we look out only for our well-being but also for the well-being of others. If something is "lawful" on the basis of the letter of the law, yet it has the potential for hurting another person or tarnishing our testimony for Christ, then it becomes unlawful for us.

Fourth, when a Christian acts immorally, he or she negates the reason for the death of Christ on the cross. Christ died to satisfy the demands of the law: "The soul who sins shall die" (Ezekiel 18:4, 20). Christ died and was raised from the dead to pay the penalty of the law and break its power over us. The law was good, but because we were sinners, we could not obey it. Thus we failed to be what God created us to be and incurred the condemnation that comes from breaking the law and the enslavement that comes from being subject to it (Romans 6:1–14; 8:1). But by His death, Christ took the penalty we deserved.

Considering everything that is bound up in the cross and the empty grave, our choice to bend the moral requirements of the law of God is an outrageous affront to the One who suffered and died to free us from the power of sin. Why would anyone who claims to have accepted God's gift of forgiveness for breaking the law choose to insult the Christ who procured that gift through His own suffering?

But the most delicate take on the laws of God is the one provided by Jesus Himself in the Sermon on the Mount—the place in which He corrected human interpretations of the law with divine interpretations, where He revealed to His followers the difference between the letter and the spirit of the law.

Strength and Light by the Law

When one of my sons was a student at a college in the beautiful Blue Ridge Mountains of western North Carolina, we sometimes visited him during the winter—occasionally following a snow or ice storm. If a storm brought a particularly wet snow or covering of ice, the tall, thin pine trees would be bowed over from the weight or often toppled over due to their shallow root systems. But in the midst of the trees that succumbed to the storm, others—the hardwoods native to the area—would be standing erect and tall. Silently, like guardians of their heritage, they would bear the weight of the snow and ice without bending or breaking.

It was God's intent in the Old Testament for His people to be like those Appalachian hardwoods—the oaks, maples, ashes, and hickories of the human forest. The laws of God were intended to be the fiber in the human trunk that enabled Israel to stand strong in the family of nations, bowing neither to trouble, trial, nor temptation. Being shown the ways of righteousness, and then choosing those ways, would set Israel apart from all other peoples on earth: "It shall come to pass, if you diligently obey the voice of the LORD your God, to observe carefully all His commandments which I command you today, that the LORD your God will set you high above all nations of the earth" (Deuteronomy 28:1).

It was Israel's job to magnify the character of God—revealed through the law of God—in the earth. It was also Israel's calling to be a light to the Gentiles as she followed her coming Messiah:

Indeed He says,
"It is too small a thing that You should be My Servant
To raise up the tribes of Jacob,
And to restore the preserved ones of Israel;
I will also give You as a light to the Gentiles,
That You should be My salvation to the ends of the earth."
(Isaiah 49:6)

It was always God's intent for salvation to go to the ends of the earth. This is repeated as an injunction for the Church, God's new light, in Acts 1:8. Here it becomes clear that the phrase "to the end of the earth" is not merely a geographical reference but a spiritual one as well. The "end of the earth" is a dark place. To come from that place into a place of reconnecting with the Creator-God of the universe requires light. And that which set Israel apart as a light, in contrast with the darkness of the world, was the law of God. If Israel walked in God's law, she could lead others into the righteousness of God—the light that dwelt in her midst. But if she ignored the law of God, she would become as dark as the nations around her:

> If you do not carefully observe all the words of this law that are written in this book, that you may fear this glorious and awesome name, THE LORD YOUR GOD, then the LORD will bring upon you and your descendants extraordinary plagues—great and prolonged plagues—and serious and prolonged sicknesses. Moreover He will bring back on you all the diseases of Egypt, of which you were afraid, and they shall cling to you. Also every sickness and every plague, which is not written in this Book of the Law, will the LORD bring upon you until you are destroyed. You shall be left few in number, whereas you were as the stars of heaven in multitude, because you would not obey the voice of the LORD your God. And it shall be, that just as the LORD rejoiced over you to do you good and multiply you, so the LORD will rejoice over you to destroy you and bring you to nothing; and you shall be plucked from off the land which you go to possess.
>
> Then the LORD will scatter you among all peoples, from one end of the earth to the other, and there you shall serve other gods, which neither you nor your fathers have known—wood

and stone. And among those nations you shall find no rest, nor shall the sole of your foot have a resting place; but there the LORD will give you a trembling heart, failing eyes, and anguish of soul. Your life shall hang in doubt before you; you shall fear day and night, and have no assurance of life. In the morning you shall say, "Oh, that it were evening!" And at evening you shall say, "Oh, that it were morning!" because of the fear which terrifies your heart, and because of the sight which your eyes see. (Deuteronomy 28:58–67)

Israel's dual role of strength and light was dependent on one thing: adherence to the laws of God. Failure to keep God's law—meaning, failure to manifest the character of God in the earth—would result in the loss of both strength and light. Sadly, that is what happened to the nation more than once.

It is no surprise, then, to find Jesus, in the introduction to His teaching on the law in the Sermon on the Mount, picking up the themes of strength, uniqueness, and light: "You are the salt of the earth… You are the light of the world" (Matthew 5:13–14). For Jesus' followers to fulfill those roles requires a proper understanding of the spirit of the law—what God really meant when He said, "Thou shalt not…"

Let me be clear before proceeding: The Church is not Israel. Our relationship to the laws of God is both different from theirs and the same. It is the same in that following God's moral standards is the only way to be strength and light in the world. It is different in that we don't try to follow the law to attain righteousness in God's sight, as Israel did. Instead, through our faith in Christ we are credited with His righteousness because He kept the law perfectly in our place. We now receive the law of God written on our minds and in our hearts. As Paul wrote, we do not nullify the law as Christians; rather, we uphold it (Romans 3:31). We do not keep the law to become the people of God but to manifest our relationship with God and to be salt and light in the world.

What does it mean to be salt and light in the world? Salt is strong because it overcomes bacteria that would cause food to rot and decompose. It is unique in that it adds flavor to food and creates thirst in those who consume it. We are to do the same. As we keep God's law and manifest His character, we preserve the character of His creation; we prevent the deterioration and degeneration of human society and we add a unique flavor to it. We hope to create a thirst for God in those whose lives we touch.

The role of light is obvious—to bring truth into spiritually dark places. And what truth are we to bring? To "love the LORD your God with all your heart, with all your soul, and with all your mind," and to "love your neighbor as yourself" (Matthew 22:37, 39). Think how different the world would be if those two summary laws, on which "hang all the Law and the Prophets" (v. 40), were kept by all the human race! And think how much more powerful and effective the Church of Jesus Christ would be if Christians were not bending God's rules to satisfy themselves.

Christians who decide to adjust their moral stance to align more favorably with that of the world would do well to remember Jesus' words at the beginning of the Sermon on the Mount:

> Do not think that I came to destroy the Law or the Proph-
> ets. I did not come to destroy but to fulfill. For assuredly, I say
> to you, till heaven and earth pass away, one jot or one tittle

will by no means pass from the law till all is fulfilled. Whoever therefore breaks one of the least of these commandments, and teaches men so, shall be called least in the kingdom of heaven; but whoever does and teaches them, he shall be called great in the kingdom of heaven. For I say to you, that unless your righteousness exceeds the righteousness of the scribes and Pharisees, you will by no means enter the kingdom of heaven. (Matthew 5:17–20)

The Pharisees' moral standard was external. They carefully tithed in great detail, even down to giving a percentage of their herbs, while at the same time neglecting "the weightier matters of the law: justice and mercy and faith" (Matthew 23:23). They kept the letter of the law but ignored the spirit of it. They kept their hands clean but failed to cleanse their hearts (Matthew 23:27). They were guilty of the same thing for which their forefathers were condemned: honoring God with their lips while their hearts were far from Him (Isaiah 29:13).

The warning to today's church is this: Going through the motions of morality is not the morality God desires. Clean hands do not make a clean heart. But the opposite is true: Moral hearts will make moral hands. If we commit to keeping the spirit of the law, the letter of the law will, by default, be kept as well. And that is precisely the message Jesus delivered on that mountainside in Galilee.

The Spirit of God's Law

You have no doubt heard people say (perhaps you have thought it yourself), "Surely God doesn't expect me to risk my job by refusing my boss's orders to break my word with a client." "Surely God doesn't expect me to stay married to a husband I no longer love." "Surely God doesn't expect me to change my lucrative career just because I can't be with my family on weekends." "Surely God doesn't expect me to _____." Fill in the blank with any standard of morality or ethics that seems to rob you of your expectations. That kind of thinking permeates morality today, even among those who profess to follow Jesus:

- Men and women think to themselves, *I won't have an actual affair, but I'll allow myself to have an "emotional affair" with my coworker. God will understand.*
- Politicians say to one another (in essence), "You scratch my back, and I'll scratch yours." They aren't willing to stand by their convictions without a promise that it won't cost them.
- Spouses divorce one another without biblical cause: "God knows my needs and that they aren't being met in this marriage."
- People harbor grudges and wait for an opportune time to pay back a wrong suffered.
- Angry people justify harsh words toward others by the fact that they are not physically attacking the person. Words become an acceptable substitute for murder.
- Those who have had disagreements appear cordial on the outside but choose not to forgive in their hearts: "God expects me to be nice to this person even if I can't forgive [him or her]."

America is not a completely immoral, out-of-control society, but we have chosen to live with certain areas of immorality. We have allowed ourselves to go "this far" but no farther. And yet where we are today would have been absolutely unthinkable in the recent past, which means in the not-too-distant future we will likely be at a place we consider unthinkable today. If we don't draw a line in the sand and close the "morality gap"—the distance between what we know God expects and what we are willing to allow as acceptable behavior—the consequences will be impossible to imagine.

The religious environment of Jesus' day was very much like ours today. Religious leaders were willing to conform themselves to the outward demands of God's law while reserving a reduced realm of "internal immorality." Jesus addresses this morality gap in the Sermon on the Mount (Matthew 5:21–47) by addressing six errors people commonly make when applying biblical morality to their personal behavior. The overall effect is a major correction to the misconception that the appearance of the kingdom of God removed the requirements of God's law upon its citizens.

To bookend this exposition, Jesus made two statements that apply to each of the six points. He began by saying that He did not come to destroy the law but to fulfill it (Matthew 5:17). And He concluded by saying, "Therefore you shall be perfect, just as your Father in heaven is perfect" (v. 48). Perfect? Yes, perfect—a standard that puts us between a rock and a hard place: God expects moral and ethical perfection, but such perfection is impossible by fallen man on his own. The tension between God's absolute standard and man's inability to meet it sets up the unfolding resolution found in the Gospels of the New Testament: What is impossible for man is possible for God; God has sent His Son to keep the law for us that we might inherit His righteousness.

In his commentary on Matthew's Gospel, Professor Michael Wilkins compares this six-part section of Matthew to the Bill of

Rights in the U.S. Constitution.[26] The Bill of Rights was added to the Constitution to ensure that the new nation's government continued into the future in accordance with the framers' intent. Just so, Jesus' purpose in Matthew 5:21–47 is to ensure that God's intent for the law is maintained and clarified. Jesus "reassures his listeners and chastens his opponents, who perhaps believe that Jesus' announcement of the arrival of the kingdom of heaven will abolish the Law and the Prophets."[27]

To illustrate His point—which was to close the morality gap between God's intent for the law and the way the law was practiced— Jesus chose six examples. They are easy to identify by the sixfold repetition of the phrases "You have heard that it was said...But I say to you..." (Matthew 5:21–22, 27–28, 31–32, 33–34, 38–39, 43–44). In each case Jesus points out the letter of the law as it had been repeated for centuries, and then points out how far this traditional interpretation has missed the mark. In doing so, He illustrates what He meant in His introduction—that He came not to destroy the law but to fulfill it. He came to illustrate in His own life and teaching what being perfect should actually look like.

The benefit to studying Jesus' words on the true meaning of morality and ethics is that they expose the rationalizing and justifying human beings are capable of—including Christians. It is (sinful) human nature to want to take the path of least resistance, to do just enough to get by, to appear moral without having to do the hard work of self-discipline and self-denial and sacrifice that results in our being truly moral and ethical people.

As we explore these six moral and ethical topics, keep in mind that they were important issues in the civil and religious culture of Jesus' day. While He could have touched on additional topics related to our day, the point is still made: God expects more of us than we expect of ourselves. What passes for morality in America gets a failing grade in the kingdom of God.

Illustration 1: What You've Heard Said About Murder (Matthew 5:21–26)

The Old Testament law was clear: "You shall not murder" (Exodus 20:13). Is this confusing? Does this need clarification? In the physical sense, no. If you don't murder a person, you have not broken the law. If you do murder a person, you have. Seems clear enough. But Jesus was going for something deeper.

Murder is the taking of a human life. But Jesus is suggesting there is more than one way to do this. Attacking a person with a knife or a gun is one way, but attacking someone with anger or hateful words is another. The latter methods of attack may not take a person's physical life, but they can certainly kill a person emotionally or spiritually. And another thing to consider: Anger is often a prelude to physical violence or murder. If you are angry enough to rage at someone with hateful words, you might be near the tipping point.

So don't feel morally superior just because you've kept the letter of the law and never physically murdered anyone. Jesus said your angry or hateful words have violated the spirit of the law. In the kingdom of God, taking a person's emotional or spiritual life is as bad as taking his or her physical life. As the Puritan theologian Thomas Watson put it, "Malice is mental murder."

Illustration 2: What You've Heard Said About Adultery (Matthew 5:27–30)

As with murder, the prohibition against adultery was clear in the law: "You shall not commit adultery" (Exodus 20:14). Obviously, this referred to a married person engaging in sexual acts with someone besides his or her spouse. But as with the illustration of murder, Jesus takes the issue beyond the physical to the spiritual. For a man to look at another woman lustfully constitutes the same betrayal as to engage in a sexual act with her. Why? Because it reveals the same lack of respect for that person, the same disrespect for one's spouse, and the same discontent with one's place in life. The consummation of a sex act is just the outward manifestation of a sin that has already occurred in the heart.

When a former U.S. president declared, "I did not have sexual relations with that woman," he was telling the truth in terms of sexual intercourse.[28] But he was splitting the same moral hairs that Jesus condemns in this illustration. We are not truly moral because the body is pure, but only if the heart and the mind are pure as well (1 Samuel 16:7; Psalms 19:14; 24:4).

Illustration 3: What You've Heard Said About Divorce (Matthew 5:31–32)

Divorce was not specifically addressed in the Ten Commandments but was addressed in Deuteronomy 24:1–4 as an adjunct to the prohibition against adultery. Moses prescribed a "certificate of divorce" when a man divorced his wife as a legal form of protection for her against further exploitation by the divorcing husband. Not addressing those technicalities, Jesus gets to the heart of the moral matter here (and in Matthew 19:4–9) by saying that any man who divorces his wife "for any reason except sexual immorality causes her to commit adultery" (Matthew 5:32). "Don't talk to me about certificates and procedures," Jesus is saying. "God never intended for there to be divorces—He allows it at all only because of the hardness of your hearts" (see Matthew 19:8).

Of Jesus' six first-century illustrations of shallow ethics and morality, this one applies most to the twenty-first-century church. Christian
husbands and wives in deplorable numbers have broken their marriage covenant with the spouses of their youth (Malachi 2:14) without
biblical grounds. This is not a call for condemnation or guilt on these
people, on neither Jesus' part nor mine. But it is a stark reminder of
how easy it is to drift from God's standards when His standards
conflict with our convenience or comfort.

Illustration 4: What You've Heard About Oaths (Matthew 5:33–37)

When most people read the third of the Ten Commandments—"You
shall not take the name of the LORD your God in vain" (Exodus
20:7)—they think it refers to not using God's name as part of a curse
word. It certainly could include that, but it really addresses using
God's name in an oath or promise—swearing on God's name that
you will do the thing you promised (for example, expressions like "By
God..." and "May God strike me dead if I don't..."). If you swore
"by God" and then didn't keep your oath, you would have used God's
name in vain. You would have used the trust people have in God to
get them to trust you. This means you would risk making them feel
negatively toward God if you failed to follow through. The only reason oaths were necessary at all was because people weren't true to
their word.

Jesus said oaths are not necessary for people with integrity: "Let
your 'Yes' be 'Yes,' and your 'No,' 'No'" (Matthew 5:37). We betray
the same mistrust in people today when we say, "Do you promise...?"
Truly ethical people don't have to swear or promise. They say what
they mean and mean what they say.

Illustration 5: What You've Heard About Retaliation and Payback (Matthew 5:38–42)

The Latin legal phrase *lex talionis*—law of retaliation—is based on the Old Testament teaching in Deuteronomy 19:21: "eye for eye, tooth for tooth, hand for hand, foot for foot." The point of the law was to limit retribution. Punishment for a crime was not to go beyond the amount of the victim's loss.

But Jesus turns the law around and says, in effect, "You don't have to pay anyone back for evil done to you." Instead of being careful to limit the judgment against an evil person, do whatever you can to avoid conflict altogether. If someone sues you, it is better to give him what he wants than to get embroiled in a court battle. In fact, "If anyone wants to sue you and take away your tunic, let him have your cloak also" (Matthew 5:40; see also 1 Corinthians 6:1–11). Kingdom ethics and morality do not focus on revenge and retaliation. They focus instead on peace, as Jesus makes clear in His commendation for peacemakers early in the Sermon on the Mount (Matthew 5:9). In God's economy, evil is not overcome with more evil but with good (Romans 12:21).

Illustration 6: What You've Heard About Enemies (Matthew 5:43–47)

"You shall love your neighbor as yourself" (Leviticus 19:18) is a central part of the Old Testament law. In Matthew 22:39, Jesus cited this as the second-most-important commandment. But here in His Sermon on the Mount, Jesus points out how this Old Testament law had been reworded to suit the mores of the day: "You have heard that it was said, 'You shall love your neighbor and hate your enemy'" (Matthew 5:43). The problem is, the words *hate your enemy* do not occur in Leviticus 19:18 or anywhere else in the Old Testament. The idea that God approved of hating one's enemy was a theologically misinformed flip side of the "love your neighbor" coin. It seemed logical and suited fallen human temperaments—so it became unofficial law.

But Jesus turns man's morality on its head and essentially says, "In the kingdom of God we are to love our enemies as well as our neighbors." This was a radical idea in Jesus' day, given Israel's history of enemies—Egyptians, Moabites, and other "-ites," Assyrians, Babylonians, Greeks, and, in the days of Jesus, Romans. Many Jews—especially many of the religious leaders to whom Jesus' words were directed—even considered all Gentiles their enemies. Jews would often greet Gentile tax collectors publicly for the sake of appearance (5:47), all the while considering them enemies in their hearts. When it comes to love, a truly moral and ethical person has no enemies.

As we can see by Jesus' six-point exposition, the spirit of God's law requires total transparency in the life of the Christian. The world around us may either ignore God's moral standards or comply with them for the sake of expediency or appearance, but the Christian may do neither. We are to obey the spirit of all God's laws in order to represent Him faithfully in this world. Or, as Jesus put it, "You shall be perfect, just as your Father in heaven is perfect" (Matthew 5:48).

Just a few decades ago, I never imagined that we would live in a time like today. It's a day in which many obvious violations of God's absolute moral code are not only committed openly and without shame, but even enshrined into law. And lawmakers are being urged to enact laws legitimizing even further violations. But as I've said before, we should not be surprised or disheartened. Historically, Christians have more often than not lived in a world that ignored or was hostile to the moral law.

It is, therefore, incumbent on us as Christians to be salt and light—to live in such a way that we not only respect and observe absolute morality but also live above the minimum physical standards, as Jesus enjoined us to do in the six points above. God has honored us with the crucial responsibility and glorious opportunity to live lives that demonstrate His nature to a wayward and searching world.

We can be eternally thankful that the One who is perfect has enabled us to perform this function by living within us and moving us toward the goal of being as perfect as our Father in heaven.

CHAPTER 6

When the Bible Would Be Marginalized

Something has happened in America that once seemed unthinkable to me. When I was a boy growing up and even a young man in school, biblical principles had a strong influence in society.

I don't mean everyone was religious, or even that religion was dominant in everyone's thinking. Yet there was a pervasive respect for the
Bible, and biblical principles were evident in the general shape of
the culture and the mores of the people. It never occurred to me that
the Bible could be marginalized and even vilified publicly as it is today.

When we look at American history, we find that this change is even
more dramatic than what I've seen in my lifetime. This is nowhere
more evident than in public education. To show you what I mean,
look at the following sampling of an early child's poem:

A: In Adam's Fall we sinned all.
B: Heaven to find, the Bible mind.
C: Christ crucify'd for sinners dy'd.
D: The Deluge drown'd the Earth around.
E: Elijah hid by Ravens fed...

In 1690, most children in New England learned their alphabet
from this poem. It is from an elementary textbook for public schools
titled *The New-England Primer*, which was first published between
1687 and 1690 in Boston. It was based on *The Protestant Tutor*, which
the same printer, Benjamin Harris, published in England before he
sought religious freedom in America.

Did you pray the following prayer as a child or teach it to your
children?

Now I lay me down to sleep,
I pray the Lord my soul to keep,
If I should die before I wake,
I pray the Lord my soul to take.

It may surprise you to learn that this nighttime prayer was first published in *The New-England Primer*, along with numerous other instructional and spiritual guides for children—all with a thoroughly Puritan, biblical foundation.

One writer explains the significance of the *New-England Primer* with these words:

> This is the single most influential Christian textbook in history. Most scholars agree that most, if not all, of the [American] Founding Fathers were taught to read and write using this volume which is unsurpassed to this day for its excellence of practical training and Christian worldview. First published in 1690, the goal of the *Primer* was to combine the study of the Bible with the alphabet, vocabulary, and the reading of prose and poetry.[1]

Though *The New-England Primer* was used extensively even into the eighteenth and nineteenth centuries, it was gradually replaced by another series of books known as McGuffey Readers. These readers were several volumes of books teaching basic alphabet and reading skills for young ages. William McGuffey was born in 1800 and grew up in Ohio in a committed Christian family. Even as a teenager his twin passions consumed him: education and preaching the Gospel. After receiving his own excellent education, he was hired to write four reading instructional books for elementary students. These were published by 1837. His brother added two more volumes in the 1840s. Millions of American children in public schools learned to read using McGuffey's Readers, and the fact that William McGuffey's biblical Christianity permeated the books was not a problem. For instance, Lesson XVIII in *McGuffey's Eclectic Primer* (1836) reads,

THE SETTING SUN

Look at the sun! See, it sinks in the West. Who made the sun?
It was God, my child. He made the sun, the moon, and the stars.
God made each tree and herb, the tall oak, and the low bush.
God bids the trees to put forth their leaves, and at His word
    they fade and fall.
He bids the wind to blow, and He bids it to cease...
God sees and knows all things. He sees me when I rise from my
    bed.
He sees me when I go out to work or play, and when I lie down
    to sleep.
If God sees me, and knows all that I do, He must hear what I say.
Oh, let me speak no bad words, nor do any bad act;
for then God does not like bad words or bad acts.[2]

While not as overtly biblical and theological as *The New-England Primer*, the original editions of the McGuffey Readers presented learning from a biblical foundation and reinforced biblical principles of morality and life in its lessons. But when William McGuffey died in 1873, his beloved readers underwent a radical overhaul. America was changing into a pluralistic society—a melting pot of religions and worldviews. The six volumes of the readers, plus the primers and spelling books, were made totally secular:

The revised Readers were compiled to meet the needs of national unity and the dream of an American melting pot for the world's oppressed masses. The Calvinist values of salvation, righteousness, and piety, so prominent in the early Readers, were excluded from the later versions. The content of the books was secularized and replaced by middle-class civil religion, morality and values. McGuffey's name was featured on these revised editions, yet he neither contributed to them nor approved their content.[3]

And he would likely never have approved the changes had he been around to prevent them. For instance, Lesson XVIII (cited above) in the "Revised Edition" (1881, 1896) of the *Eclectic Primer* bears no resemblance to McGuffey's original. All references to God, His sovereignty over nature, and man's accountability to Him are gone. Lesson XVIII is now about Sue and her pet bird.[4]

Do you detect a trend in American education here? In the eighteenth century *The New-England Primer* was *explicitly* biblical. In the nineteenth century the original McGuffey Readers were *implicitly* biblical. In the late nineteenth and early twentieth centuries, the revised McGuffey Readers were *wholly secular*. And then came a great sea change: modern, twentieth-century education under the influence of John Dewey, the father of progressive American education.

John Dewey (1859–1952) was a psychologist and philosopher who was most responsible for how American children are educated today. He changed the priority in education from acquiring knowledge to experiencing knowledge: "In the 1920s/1930s, John Dewey became famous for pointing out that the authoritarian, strict, pre-ordained knowledge approach of modern traditional education was too concerned with delivering knowledge, and not enough with understanding students' actual experiences."[5]

Dewey was not against students' acquiring knowledge; he was against teaching it to them instead of helping them discover it through experience. Thus he changed American education from the didactic transfer of knowledge to the modern view that experience is what drives the acquisition of knowledge.

This distrust of "delivering knowledge" led Dewey to abandon the system of education that delivered knowledge based on a biblical worldview. In making this move he turned his back on a proven system of education and instigated an experiment that put the well-being of our nation in jeopardy. God said through the prophet Hosea, "My people are destroyed for lack of knowledge. Because you have rejected knowledge, I also will reject you from being priest for Me; because you have forgotten the law of your God, I also will forget your children" (Hosea 4:6).

Israel was destroyed not for "delivering knowledge" but for abandoning knowledge. The people perished because they elevated experience over knowledge. Jesus Christ rebuked the leaders of Israel in His day because they had "taken away the key of knowledge" (Luke 11:52), which is a right understanding of God's Word.

The correct relationship between knowledge and experience is set forth clearly in Deuteronomy:

> Hear, O Israel: The LORD our God, the LORD is one! You shall love the LORD your God with all your heart, with all your soul, and with all your strength. And these words which I command you today shall be in your heart. You shall teach them diligently to your children, and shall talk of them when you sit in your house, when you walk by the way, when you lie down, and when you rise up. You shall bind them as a sign on your hand, and they shall be as frontlets between your eyes. You shall write them on the doorposts of your house and on your gates. (6:4–9)

The truth was too vital to leave to chance discovery. The focus was on *teaching* the truth as set forth in the Ten Commandments: There is only one God, and He is to receive the wholehearted affections of His people. Fathers were to communicate that truth, instilling the objective law of God into their children throughout all the experiences of life. But the purpose of experience was not to *discover* truth; it was to learn how life must be *conformed to* truth.

On July 21, 1620, when a portion of the Puritan congregation in Leyden, Holland, was on the dock ready to depart for the New World aboard the *Mayflower*, pastor John Robinson delivered a farewell sermon. He was not going with this initial group of his congregation, yet he felt responsible for sending them off with an admonition to keep their priorities straight in America. He told them,

> Brethren, we are now quickly to part from one another, and only the God of heaven knows whether I will see your face again. I charge you before God and His blessed angels that you follow me no further than you have seen me follow the Lord Jesus Christ. I am verily persuaded that the Lord yet has more truth to break forth from His holy Word.[6]

The wisdom and light these intrepid Pilgrims would need in the New World would "break forth" not from their experience and discovery, but from two objective benchmarks: the Lord Jesus Christ and the teachings of Scripture.

Sadly, over more than three centuries those objective standards slowly disappeared from American public education. From *The New-England Primer* to John Dewey, knowledge went from being Bible-based to being experience-based. With armed security guards now patrolling public schools and American teenagers lagging far behind their international peers in math and science, we can't help but draw negative conclusions about this change in our educational priorities. Instead of having the Bible quoted in school textbooks, today the Bible can hardly be opened in public schools.

The Marginalization of the Bible

I know America is no longer a Christian nation (that is, a nation governed largely by biblical principles), and it is not the kingdom of God on earth. I agree with our Founding Fathers that no religion should be legally sanctioned by our government. Yet, as the quotes above from Deuteronomy and Jesus Himself show, a nation's well-being depends on objective knowledge of God's truth. America's Founding Fathers knew this. Although they insisted on religious neutrality (not religious expulsion), most of them were either Christians themselves or, like Benjamin Franklin and Thomas Jefferson, readily acknowledged the high value of the Bible's teachings in the life of society. But in our journey from Plymouth to pluralism, the Bible has been downgraded from taught to tolerated in the public square. And from taught to virtually banned from public schools. From being a rule of faith and practice, the Bible has become a relic of history—a negative cultural icon used to illustrate the narrow-mindedness of our nation's founders.

As much as I hate to say it, the public square and public schools are not the only venues in which the Bible's status has been downgraded and its message diluted. It's also happening in the last place we should expect it: in the Christian Church itself. The church, which should stand firm and exercise a positive effect on society, has instead allowed itself to be affected by our culture's growing marginalization of the Bible. And that brings us to the heart of this chapter. My primary concern is not the place of the Bible in public education. The brief historical survey I've given you is merely a prelude to a lamentable fact about the American church: *As goes the culture, (too often) so goes the church.*

Maybe we shouldn't be too surprised that America is drifting away from God's truth. History shows that nations tend to do that. But I never thought I'd see the day when the Bible would lose its pride of place in the Christian Church in America. Yet we see mounting evidence that the church is shifting in the same direction as public education—from *propositional* knowledge to *experiential* knowledge.

In short, not only has the Bible been marginalized in American culture; it is becoming marginalized in the church.

The Meaning of Marginalization

Marginalization is a big word that we don't hear very often. *The American Heritage Dictionary* defines *marginalize* as "to relegate or confine to a lower or outer limit or edge, as of social standing."[7] Within the same general range of meaning are words like *banish, deport, exile, expel, blacklist, boycott,* and *shut out.*

But there is a significant difference: Those words represent overt exclusionary actions that are instigated in a point of time. It's easy to know when you've been banished, deported, or blacklisted. Such actions do not merely push you aside or render you irrelevant; they exclude you absolutely. For instance, Leo Tolstoy's nonfiction book *The Kingdom of God Is Within You,* the culmination of thirty years of reflections on Christianity, was banned in Russia—utterly excluded, not marginalized. A second example of this type of exclusion is the burning of non-Nazi books in Germany in 1933.

Another difference between marginalization and overtly exclusionary actions is that the latter is often done—at least in the Church—with the hope of achieving repentance and restoration (1 Corinthians 5:1–5; 2 Corinthians 2:5–11).

Marginalization is different on both counts: It happens slowly, and the goal is a reduction in influence, not restoration. Marginalization usually happens when those in power stop giving credence to a person or an idea. In the workplace, a particular employee might be excluded from significant policy meetings or social gatherings. The goal is not to get rid of the employee but to *move him or her to the margin or edge of the community.* It's what happens in junior high school when a clique of "cool kids" shuns a fellow student in order to minimize his participation in their activities.

In a similar way, the Bible has been marginalized in modern culture. It has been pushed to the edge in public education, in the town square, and out of the decision-making processes of our official institutions. It has been relegated to a place of irrelevancy to the perceived needs of modern people. It is treated either as a relic of history, an icon of the unenlightened past, or as the sole property of religious people who want to live in their own little world. Those who honor the Bible are tolerated as long as their biblical principles do not spill over into public activity.

Here is what I find really worrisome about this sad state of affairs: If 75 to 85 percent of Americans identify themselves as Christians, how is it possible that the Bible is so marginalized in the life of the nation? Professing Christians represent a strong majority of the nation's population, yet the Book they depend on as the sole source of information about their faith is being marginalized to a status of irrelevancy.

One of the conclusions I can reach from this paradox is that Christians are being drawn into the values of an increasingly secular culture, which is imposing its negative influence on their values and diluting their allegiance to the Book on which their faith is based.

Modern, Marginal Christians

"If God spare my life, ere many years pass, I will cause a boy that driveth the plow shall know more of the Scripture than thou dost."[8] Those words were spoken around 1521 by Englishman William Tyndale to a local clergyman. Most English clergymen in Tyndale's day were woefully ignorant of the contents of the Bible, and with good reason: Bibles in English were not allowed in sixteenth-century England. They were published in Latin, a language read only by the educated and priests, because only priests were deemed capable of rightly interpreting Scripture. (In 1519 Catholic officials put to death a woman and six men for having taught their children English versions of the Lord's Prayer, the Ten Commandments, and the Apostles' Creed!)[9] But because Tyndale believed that every English-speaking person deserved to have access to the Bible in English, he labored to produce the first complete New Testament (and part of the Old Testament) in English translated directly from the original Hebrew and Greek texts.

Finding no support for his efforts in England, the Oxford- and Cambridge-trained scholar, fluent in no fewer than eight languages, left for Germany in 1524, never to see England again. Finding supporters there, he completed the New Testament in English in 1525 and printed six thousand copies, of which only two have survived.

Church officials in England did everything they could to eradicate (as opposed to marginalize) Tyndale's translation—preaching against it and buying copies and burning them. The money from the purchase of the copies was often smuggled back to Tyndale to support his continued work.

After completing the translation of the Pentateuch (Genesis–Deuteronomy) in 1530, he was apprehended in Brussels, imprisoned for a year and a half, then strangled and burned at the stake in 1536. Reportedly, his last words were, "Lord, open the king of England's eyes!" As historian Tony Lane explains, Tyndale's work and death were not in vain: "By 1539 every parish church in England was required to make a copy of the English Bible available to all its parishioners. All the available translations were substantially based upon Tyndale's. Thus while Tyndale had not been personally vindicated, his cause had triumphed, as had his translation."[10]

Just as William Tyndale gave his life for the sake of the Bible in the sixteenth century, many are risking their lives for the Bible in oppressed nations today. Andrew van der Bijl (called "Brother Andrew" and "God's smuggler") risked his life smuggling the Bible into Communist countries during the Cold War. The ministry he leads today gets the Bible and Christian literature into the hands of the persecuted church.[11]

The contrast between these Christians and today's Christians in the West is striking. On one hand we have people laying down their lives to expand the Bible's influence, and on the other we have modern churches being willing to allow the Bible's influence to recede toward the vanishing point, even in their own lives. The explanation for this contrast is the luring influence of the culture; again, as goes the culture (too often), so goes the church. When the secular culture marginalizes the Bible and Christians don't counter by elevating its place in their own spheres of influence, then Christians unwittingly participate in its marginalization. While the church should be influencing the culture, we are allowing the culture to seduce and diminish the church. Marginalization can occur so subtly that even committed Christians may not realize it is happening or that they are contributing to the problem.

How can Christians prevent this slippage into irrelevance? One way is to recognize the potential dangers and be vigilant against them. To that end I have identified five ways, discussed below, in which followers of Christ are contributing to the marginalization of the Word of God.

Forming an Improper Allegiance to Authorities

Christians have a healthy respect for authority, and for good, biblical reasons. Christians are to submit to one another: wives to husbands, children to parents, slaves to masters, younger people to older people, and so on (Ephesians 5:21–22; 6:1, 5; 1 Peter 2:18–21; 5:5). We are also told to submit to governing authorities (Romans 13:1–7; 1 Peter 2:13–17). It is possible, however, for well-meaning Christians who want to be good citizens to take the principle of submission to government further than they should.

Until recent years, most citizens were familiar with the Bible-friendly history of America's founding. The original Pilgrim founders came to the New World in search of religious freedom. The framers of the Constitution not only robustly embraced this freedom, they also endorsed biblical values and even wove them into America's system of laws. For the first two hundred–plus years of our history, these principles were diligently followed, making it easy to be a Christian in America. But things have changed. The Bible is no longer quoted or referenced in the halls of government or education as it was in the beginning. This makes it easy for Christians committed to submitting to leaders to be lulled into thinking that official indifference toward the Bible sets an example to follow.

So if civil authorities decide to marginalize the Word of God, each Christian must give himself or herself a wake-up call, saying: "Even though my leaders and my culture want to marginalize God's Word, I am responsible as a steward of God to uphold His Word in every dimension of my life...in private, in public, at home, and at church. As a Christian I am never free to move God's Word to the edge of my life, regardless of what those around me or in authority over me may do." When facing a similar dilemma, Peter and the other apostles said, "We ought to obey God rather than men" (Acts 5:29).

We can be lulled into complacency by adopting uncritically the principle of submission to government on the assumption that the Christian history of our nation makes it safe to let our leaders do our thinking for us. But we cannot do this in our post-Christian nation where God's Word is being marginalized. Nothing could be more dangerous for Christians and churches than to wander thoughtlessly down this path of increasing biblical indifference—a path that could well lead to a place where the Bible is not merely marginalized, but banned outrightly.

Failing to Count the Cost of Loyalty

We pray that no citizen in our country will ever have to pay the price for adherence to the Bible that William Tyndale did. But it could happen. Many Christians in repressive nations are risking their lives today for the privilege of having even a page or some small portion of the Scriptures.

In our nation, and even in our Christian churches, we see a growing unwillingness to hear and honor the Word of God. This means that while adherence to the Bible may not mean risking our lives, there may be other prices to pay.

We find an example in the Old Testament when King Ahab of Israel and King Jehoshaphat of Judah made an alliance to go to war. Jehoshaphat insisted that they inquire of the Lord before advancing, so Ahab brought together four hundred of his prophets who gave the king a unanimous green light. But Jehoshaphat was suspicious of such blanket approval. He asked Ahab if there was not "a prophet of the Lord" available (1 Kings 22:7). "There is still one man," Ahab replied, "Micaiah the son of Imlah, by whom we may inquire of the Lord; but I hate him, because he does not prophesy good concerning me, but evil" (v. 8). Ahab didn't like the prophet Micaiah because he would not conform to the king's expectations. Micaiah's rule of practice was, "As the Lord lives, whatever the Lord says to me, that I will speak" (v. 14).

But to satisfy Jehoshaphat, Micaiah was called. He prophesied that the military venture would be a disaster and revealed that a lying spirit had spoken through the four hundred prophets of Ahab. One of Ahab's officers slapped Micaiah in the face, and Ahab decreed that the prophet be thrown in prison and given nothing but bread and water until Ahab returned from battle. But Micaiah would not relent. He said to Ahab: "If you ever return in peace, the Lord has not spoken by me" (v. 28). Ahab refused to listen to Micaiah's word from God and was killed in the battle.

Those who are loyal to the Word of God, in the face of a majority who are not, will likely pay a price. They may be mocked and ridiculed and, like Micaiah, even suffer physically. A Christian who attends a city council meeting and expresses a strong biblical conviction may be laughed at. A Christian teenager who takes his Bible to school for an after-school Bible study may be ridiculed by his peers. A Christian legislator who presents a bill and defends it from a biblical perspective may be accused of violating church-state separation. Any one of these Christians may be labeled as a religious fanatic.

Most Christians who face this kind of mild persecution lose nothing but their standing in the minds of those who have gone far down the secular road. For some Christians, however, that pressure is too strong, the price too high. What others think of them holds too high a place in their values. But as a Christian it is your responsibility not to be conformed to the world around you (Romans 12:2), but to remain loyal to the Word of God regardless of the cost.

Fearing Intellectual Rejection

Many Christians today are ashamed to be identified as a follower of Jesus or a believer in the Bible because they have bought into the common error of thinking that belief requires blind faith, while disbelief springs from rigorous intellectual analysis. These Christians fly their faith under the radar to avoid losing intellectual credibility in the eyes of others.

This fear has been exacerbated by the books and arguments of the New Atheists, whom I mentioned in chapter 1. They write eloquently, speak persuasively, and argue convincingly, giving them an intimidating presence in the cultural conversation about God. As a CNN article put it in 2006, "What the New Atheists share is a belief that religion should not simply be tolerated but should be countered, criticized and exposed by rational argument whenever its influence arises."[12] (This moves them beyond subtle marginalizing to outright blacklisting.)

Perhaps the best-known of the New Atheists is British scholar Richard Dawkins. See if his assessment of belief in God makes you feel a little defensive of your faith: "We cannot, of course, disprove God, just as we can't disprove Thor, fairies, leprechauns and the Flying Spaghetti Monster...But, like those other fantasies that we can't disprove, we can say that God is very, very improbable."[13] So, if you believe in God—and by extension, in the divinity of Jesus and the Bible—your faith is as intellectually indefensible as belief in "Thor, fairies, leprechauns and the Flying Spaghetti Monster." Not every Christian is willing or able to counter such a caricature, even though the apostle Peter said we should "always be ready to give a defense to everyone who asks you a reason for the hope that is in you, with meekness and fear" (1 Peter 3:15).

Many Christians do not realize that we need not be ashamed of the intellectual defensibility of our faith. The Bible and its claims are solidly backed by extremely strong evidences. Many intellectual giants have been believers, such as Augustine, Aquinas, Milton, C. S. Lewis, and Solzhenitsyn.

At least on equal intellectual footing with the New Atheists was the Swiss theologian Karl Barth. His *Epistle to the Romans* was a turning point in reversing the tide of liberalism and skepticism concerning the Bible that swept over Europe in the late nineteenth and early twentieth centuries. His thirteen-volume *Church Dogmatics* is one of the most important theological works in church history. Though Karl Barth was not always as orthodox as one would like, the application of his intellectual gifts to the defense of the triune God of the Bible was a welcome event in an otherwise unorthodox period of European church history.

In spite of his towering intellect, Barth understood that faith is not dependent on one's intellectual prowess. Beneath all the evidences and arguments for the truth of God and His Word is a simplicity of truth that both intellectuals and the most uneducated Christian can hold with confidence. To illustrate, it is said of Karl Barth that while speaking at Princeton University on a 1962 lecture tour, he was asked to summarize the millions of words contained in his *Church Dogmatics*. Thinking for a moment, he replied: "Jesus loves me, this I know, for the Bible tells me so."[14]

This juxtaposition of intellect with the simplicity of faith should inspire every Christian to take heart. Clearly, it is not necessary to be as brilliant as the New Atheists or the greatest of theologians to say with conviction, "The Bible tells me so." Although belief in God and His special revelation in Scripture are intellectually defensible, they do not require our defense in order to be trustworthy. Nor does every question have to be answered in order to replace shame with confidence. The apostle Paul carefully explained why no one should be intimidated by those who use intellectual prowess to marginalize God and His Word (1 Corinthians 1:18–2:16).

When you are in a situation where you are tempted to back away from asserting your belief in the Bible because you feel this kind of shame, you should ask yourself, *Whose opinion counts, anyway: my peers' or God's?*

Jesus, the Living Word of God, has strong words for any who find themselves ashamed of the Word of God: "Whoever is ashamed of

Me and My words, of him the Son of Man will be ashamed when He comes in His own glory, and in His Father's, and of the holy angels" (Luke 9:26).

Falling into the Tolerance Trap

If America has a new religion, surely it must be the religion of tolerance. Its primary dogma is taken from noncommittal postmodernism, which says that all religions deserve equal respect. No problem there. But postmodernism goes on to say that all religions are equally valid and true since life and history have no central "meta-story"—no central script by which all other stories are measured. Jesus, on the other hand, insisted, "I am the way, the truth, and the life. No one comes to the Father except through Me" (John 14:6). The narrowness of Jesus' exclusive claim can be embarrassing to Christians who have grown up in the pluralistic soup of the last several decades. It puts Christianity out of step with today's culture.

The paradox of tolerance in modern society is that Christians lose in two ways: Because of the supposed narrowness of our views, we are labeled the most intolerant of all religions. At the same time, we are the least tolerated of all religions. Because of that double-barreled assault, many Christians have grown afraid to utter the words "The Bible says…" or "God says…" or "Jesus says…" We have become hesitant about quoting the Bible for fear of offending those who have bought into pluralistic tolerance. I recognize that many Christians have earned the accusation of being offensive by their actions, attitudes, or use of the Bible as a hammer rather than a source of love, life, and comfort. But if we are not guilty of a lack of love, then neither should we be fearful of being an offense. Indeed, regardless of how lovingly the Bible is communicated, it contains within its message an inherent risk of offense. The apostle Peter said as much when he quoted from Isaiah and the Psalms in 1 Peter 2:6–8:

> Look! I'm setting a stone in Zion, a cornerstone in the place of honor. Whoever trusts in this stone as a foundation will never have cause to regret it. To you who trust him, he's a Stone to be proud of, but to those who refuse to trust him, the stone the workmen threw out is now the chief foundation stone. For the untrusting it's...a stone to trip over, a boulder blocking the way. (The Message)

Do you see Peter's point? The "stone in Zion" is Jesus (and by extension in our day, the message of the Bible *about* Jesus). To some people the stone becomes the foundation of their lives, but for others He is "a stone to trip over, a boulder blocking the way."

How can the same stone be both a blessing and an offense? The answer has to do not with the stone but with our response to the stone. If a Christian woman is afraid to share with her Muslim neighbor what the Bible says about Jesus for fear of offending a new friend; if a preacher is afraid to quote what the Bible says about heaven and hell for fear of offending some wealthy donors; or if a Christian politician is afraid to identify himself with the truth of Scripture for fear of losing votes—those people have agreed with our culture that the Bible is offensive and should be moved to the outer perimeters, where it won't impede progress or upset the status quo.

But it's important to realize that the Bible is offensive only to those who choose to be offended because it requires of them something they don't want to give—a change of direction, abandoning a pet sin, giving up certain habits, or revamping their lifestyle. Thus they dismiss the Bible as mythical or an outrageous intrusion on their freedom. As the apostle Paul wrote, "The message of the cross is foolishness to those who are perishing, but to us who are being saved it is the power of God" (1 Corinthians 1:18). Being afraid of how others might respond to the Bible is one way in which Christians participate in its marginalization.

Feeling the Pressure to Compete

Finally—and here I speak mainly to pastors—churches sometimes marginalize the Bible because of the ongoing pressure for attendance and dollars. When it comes to attracting people, more and more, churches find themselves competing with America's entertainment culture.

As the senior pastor of a large church responsible for bringing glory to God on Sunday mornings, I fully recognize the thinness of the line that threads through the concepts of entertainment, education, edification, and excellence. I am aware that neither God nor my fellow pastors have appointed me to create a checklist to keep churches from stepping from one side of that line to the other. Yet I again caution us all to remember: As the world goes, (too often) so goes the church.

Pastors today are often judged more on their ability to make a congregation laugh and enjoy the assembly than on the biblical content of their preaching. There is nothing wrong with laughter and joy in the church on Sunday morning. With so much crude and unedifying humor in the world today, laughing to the glory of God provides a wholesome and refreshing alternative.

My concern is that wholesale adoption in our assemblies of the methods of the entertainment culture with its emphasis on continual excitement, sound-bite doses of information, and the latest in high-tech gimmickry can leave little time for teaching and preaching the Word of God. In Acts 2:42, the very first item on the list that characterized the assembly of the first church in Jerusalem was continuing "steadfastly in the apostles' doctrine." This shows that more than anything else, the content of the Bible is what the Spirit of God uses to renew the mind of one who is transferred from darkness to light through faith in Christ (Romans 12:2; Colossians 1:13–14). It is truth, Jesus said, that sets people free from the patterns of sin and releases them into the liberty of life by the grace of God (John 8:32). And that truth is contained in the Bible.

Pastors, it is up to us to make the Word of God a priority in the life of the church—from children's Sunday school to adult classes and home groups. We cannot improve on what appears to have been the pattern in the early Church: the careful reading and explaining of the apostles' letters as they circulated through the new churches. We call it expository preaching today, but it is nothing more than taking followers of Jesus through the same "apostles' doctrine" that the early Church learned—verse by verse, Sunday after Sunday, week after week, watching believers grow up "till we all come to the unity of the faith and of the knowledge of the Son of God" (Ephesians 4:13).

The alternative is to see Christians remain as "children, tossed to and fro and carried about with every wind of doctrine, by the trickery of men, in the cunning craftiness of deceitful plotting" (Ephesians 4:14). As this verse warns, when the absolutes of the Bible are neglected, Christians lose the anchor that holds them steady and gives them security in a world groping blindly for meaning and purpose. The only way to counteract such chaos is to restore the Bible to its rightful place in our churches so our members will restore it to the center of their lives and reflect its principles in our culture.

I am not opposed to striving for excellence, interest, and appeal in our churches. If whatever mix of education, edification, entertainment, and excellence we craft into them results in Christian maturity through the faithful teaching of the "apostles' doctrine," then I believe God is pleased. But if our attempts to draw people with the techniques of the entertainment culture push the Bible to the edges of our worship services and our churches' educational ministries, we are contributing to its marginalization in our culture.

Churches ultimately play a pivotal role in whether the Bible is pushed to the margins or elevated to the center of a culture. What adults see prioritized in their church will influence the priorities they pass on to the next generation.

Numbers Tell a Shocking Story

The idea that the Bible is being marginalized in our culture and churches is not merely a private opinion. Simple observation proves that the Bible is no longer influencing or shaping the policies of government, education, business, sports, and entertainment as it did in the past. There are exceptions, of course. I am grateful that the oldest and most respected American business magazine, *Forbes*, prints on the last page of each issue a favorite Bible verse sent in by a reader. And there are countless individual teachers, coaches, company owners— even some politicians—who make faithfulness to the Bible a hallmark of their vocational and personal lives. But overall, one sees little of the Bible's influence in our nation's public arena or institutions.

Even more telling is the research undertaken by polling organizations such as the Barna Group, Gallup, Pew Research, and others. This research is both illuminating and discouraging in what it reveals about the place the Bible holds in the lives of Christians. And we have to assume that the role of the Bible in individual Christians' lives reflects, to some degree, its role in the lives of the churches they attend.

This first set of numbers, compiled in December 2010, focuses not specifically on the Bible but on the influence of religion in America. Since "religion" includes Christianity, which holds the Bible to be a central source of its authority, this poll gives us our first indirect evidence of the Bible's increasing marginalization. The following results were compiled when Gallup asked a cross section of Americans, "At the present time, do you think religion as a whole is increasing its influence on American life or losing its influence?":[15]

	1957	2010	
Increasing its influence	69%	25%	(a decrease of 44%)
Losing its influence	14%	70%	(an increase of 56%)
No change in influence	10%	2%	(a decrease of 8%)

The Barna Group released a set of data in October 2009 that opened the window of insight further still; 43 percent of those surveyed believed the Bible, the Quran, and the Book of Mormon "offer the same spiritual truths."[16] And while 90 percent of those over the age of 64 viewed the Bible as a sacred book, only 67 percent of those between the ages of 18 and 25 did so.[17]

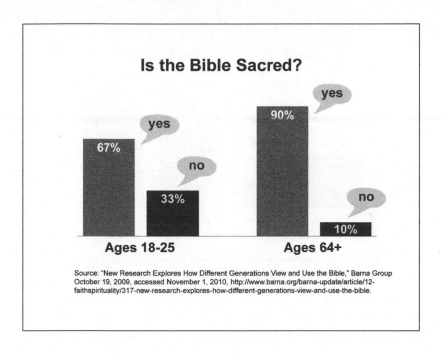

Is the Bible Sacred?

Ages 18-25: yes 67%, no 33%

Ages 64+: yes 90%, no 10%

Source: "New Research Explores How Different Generations View and Use the Bible," Barna Group October 19, 2009, accessed November 1, 2010, http://www.barna.org/barna-update/article/12-faithspirituality/317-new-research-explores-how-different-generations-view-and-use-the-bible.

A disturbing trend in the Barna research regards age. The statistics could just be telling us that as people mature, their respect for the Bible grows. This may be true for many, but I want to provide you with additional results from the Barna research so you will understand why we should be concerned for our young people.

It appears that the younger generation is simply a reflection of the culture in which they live, a culture that is losing confidence in the Bible. For instance, to this statement—"The Bible is totally accurate in all of the principles it teaches"—the responses in agreement are illustrated in the graph on the next page. [18]

In light of the fact that the younger generation appears to doubt

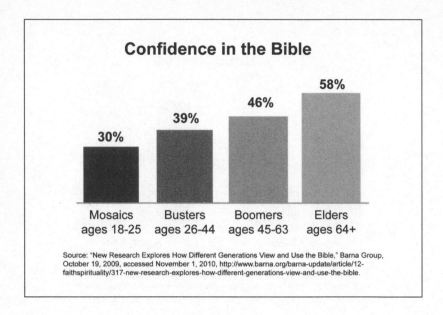

Confidence in the Bible

Mosaics ages 18-25: 30%
Busters ages 26-44: 39%
Boomers ages 45-63: 46%
Elders ages 64+: 58%

Source: "New Research Explores How Different Generations View and Use the Bible," Barna Group, October 19, 2009, accessed November 1, 2010, http://www.barna.org/barna-update/article/12-faithspirituality/317-new-research-explores-how-different-generations-view-and-use-the-bible.

the trustworthiness of the Bible, you may be wondering how their view of the Bible can be described. David Kinnaman, who directed the Barna study, helps answer that question by explaining that the "central theme of young people's approach to the Bible is skepticism. They question the Bible's history as well as its relevance to their lives."[19]

It's not surprising that these decreasing confidence levels correlate closely with the amount of time each of these age-groups spends with the Bible personally. In response to this statement—"Spent time completely alone where you prayed and read the Bible for at least 15 minutes"—the responses in agreement are shown in the graph on the following page.[20]

A radical trend toward marginalizing the Bible becomes starkly evident when we remember *The New-England Primer* and the

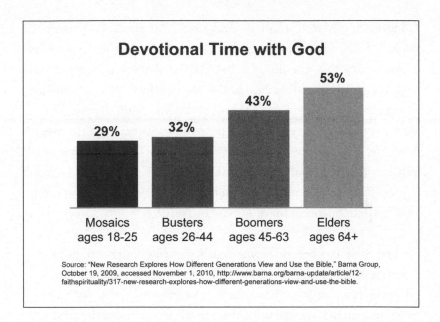

Devotional Time with God

Mosaics
ages 18-25
29%

Busters
ages 26-44
32%

Boomers
ages 45-63
43%

Elders
ages 64+
53%

Source: "New Research Explores How Different Generations View and Use the Bible," Barna Group, October 19, 2009, accessed November 1, 2010, http://www.barna.org/barna-update/article/12-faithspirituality/317-new-research-explores-how-different-generations-view-and-use-the-bible.

McGuffey Readers I cited earlier—schoolbooks used by millions of American children and approved by their parents. When the Bible was pervasive in culture, there was no skepticism about its truth or its relevance. But a slow, subtle, steady shift in how our nation views the Bible has pushed it out of the center of culture to the inconsequential edges. It has been marginalized beyond anything I could ever have imagined in my youth. And though it pains me to say it, responsibility for that marginalization must be laid largely at the feet of Christians, whose views are represented in the cultural surveys cited above.

Here's more evidence of marginalization: In 1982, the ninety-seventh United States Congress, by joint resolution, authorized President Ronald Reagan to proclaim 1983 the "Year of the Bible." That resolution passed and became Public Law 97-280.

Fast-forward to May 2009, when a group of sixteen members of

Congress introduced a bill to designate 2010 another "Year of the Bible." OneNewsNow of American Family News Network conducted a poll asking this question: "What are the chances Congress would approve a bill designating 2010 as the 'Year of the Bible'?" Of the 7,681 respondents, 86 percent said the probability was "slim to none."[21] They were correct—Congress did not pass the measure. In only twenty-seven years American leaders moved from official affirmation of the Bible to refusing to affirm it. And most Americans probably didn't notice. That's how marginalization happens: slowly, subtly, but surely.

Christian historian Mark A. Noll has written,

> The Bible has been a permanent fixture in American culture since the beginning of the European settlement of North America... Scripture has always been extraordinarily potent in American life... Until some time in the late nineteenth century or early in the twentieth, the Bible existed as the most coherent, the most widely respected, and the most powerful of those means by which American[s] ordered their daily existence and made sense of the universe in which they lived.[22]

When the Pew Research Center reported on the shallow amount of Bible knowledge possessed by most Americans, Nicholas Kristof, a columnist for the *New York Times*, posted a response that concluded by saying, "The most crucial element is perhaps not what is in our scriptures, but what is in our hearts."[23] As vital as Scripture is, it remains ineffective as long as it is merely ink on paper closed up in a leather binding. It gains power in our lives when it is planted in our hearts and produces the fruit of God's work in a world that sorely needs it.

Ruby Scott was a missionary with Wycliffe Bible translators who worked in the dense tropical jungles of Chiapas, in southern Mexico. Her goal was to translate the Bible into the Tila language for the Tili Chol Indian tribe. During the course of her work, she also shared the Gospel verbally with the villagers, and a church was planted. As time went by, the entire region became eager for the Bible, and Ruby was constantly bombarded with the question: "How much longer before we have the Book?"

When the project was nearly completed, Ruby took her language helper, a young man named Aureliano, to Mexico City to work on the final drafts. One day as they labored over the final product, Aureliano reached over and tenderly touched the foot-high pile of printouts on the desk. "Ruby," he said with a sense of wonder, "I'm the first Tila man to have *all* of this book in my hand. I feel like a king on the throne as I sit here day after day and read God's Word."[24]

Ruby later wrote, "That night I lay awake remembering the soft look in Aureliano's eyes and the awe and reverence in his voice as he read God's Word—God's Holy Word. What had happened in my heart? Had I become so used to reading that beautiful message that I no longer felt the wonder of it? Had I allowed some of the awe and marvel of the Book to slip away? How long had it been since I felt like royalty because I could read the most important Book in the world? Tears filled my eyes. 'Oh God,' I prayed, 'make my heart tender toward you—tender toward your Word, the Living Everlasting Word.' "[25]

The answer to today's alarming marginalization of the Bible is for every Christian to take Ruby Scott's prayer to heart. Pray that God will restore our wonder in the astounding fact that the Creator of heaven and earth loved us so dearly that He gave us His loving and guiding Word, which gives us knowledge of His amazing sacrifice and draws us toward Him and His redeeming love. Be assured that He will hear such a prayer. And if enough Christians restore the Bible and the One it tells us of to the center of our lives, our nation and its culture may yet be transformed.

CHAPTER 7

When the Church Would Be Irrelevant

"And now, by the authority invested in me by the World Wide Web, I pronounce you husband and wife."

Those were the words spoken by the female minister at a wedding attended by the son of a friend of mine. While the wedding service was apparently traditional enough, the minister's words of pronouncement set tongues a-wagging during the reception: "Who is that minister?" "How do you get authority to marry from the World Wide Web?" It turns out her credentials were credible—in a modern sense. Her ministerial license had apparently been acquired from an Internet diploma mill. Laughable, yet legal in the eyes of the law.

For decades now, Christian weddings have been conducted outside the four walls of a church. And, strictly speaking, there's nothing wrong with that. It is God who sanctifies marriages, not religious buildings. But such trends are another sign of the increasingly optional status of the Church in American society. Whereas a community's churches used to be considered a source of life and light, increasingly their light has grown dimmer when it comes to their connection with life's most serious moments. Many people view churches as having little to say that is more relevant than what can be found on television talk shows or in Internet advice columns. And so they stay away.

Some people do still try to find their way into the church but find the welcome mat missing. So they look elsewhere for answers. One such person was a young painter whose portrayal of the institutional church in two of his paintings is a sad commentary on how the church can make herself irrelevant.

At best, we would have to say that the thirty-seven years of Vincent Willem van Gogh's life (1853–1890) were tormented ones. The Dutch painter, recognized as a master only after his self-inflicted death, was known mostly for failure and rejection during his lifetime. In all matters of the heart—romance, painting, and faith—his efforts went unrewarded. From a human perspective, it is not difficult to understand his despair. Just a few days before ending his life he painted *At Eternity's Gate* (1890), a bleak picture of a man sitting in a wooden chair with his head buried in his hands. While the work is not known as a self-portrait, when we consider it in light of his suicide shortly afterward, it was almost certainly a portrayal of van Gogh's despairing mind-set.

Scholars and historians have speculated about the root of van Gogh's apparent mental illness, but with no definitive conclusions. One wonders if his ultimate rejection of himself was an expression of the rejection he suffered at the hands of many others during his life, not the least of which was the established church in his day.

Before making a serious commitment to art, van Gogh aspired to be a Christian minister or missionary. His father was a Dutch Reformed minister and his grandfather a trained theologian, so he grew up with a sensitivity to God and to people and their need for Him. At one point he apprenticed himself to a Methodist minister for a period, then he studied in Amsterdam to take exams for entrance into theological studies. He failed those exams and subsequently failed another three-month course of study at a Dutch school where he studied to become a missionary. In 1879 he became a temporary missionary in a coal-mining village in Belgium and sought to identify with the difficult lives of those to whom he ministered—living in a hovel and sleeping on a bed of straw. His ministry and lifestyle appalled the local officials, who discharged him for "undermining the dignity" of the clergy. He was forced to abandon his missionary work and what he felt was his first, true calling: to be a Christian minister of the Gospel.

In the last year of his life, van Gogh produced two of his best-known paintings: *The Church at Auvers* and *Starry Night*, both of which contain a village church in their center. In these paintings, van Gogh's Postimpressionist style is striking. *Starry Night* is a nocturnal scene in which the deep blues of the sky and the darkened homes in the valley are punctuated by yellow lights—stars and the moon in the sky and warm glows from the windows of the houses that surround the church. But noticeably, there is no light emanating from the church. It sits in silent shadows, its windows black and empty in stark contrast to the lights coming from the nearby homes.

If *Starry Night* did not make a strong enough statement about the Church, the message of *The Church at Auvers* is undeniable. In fact, author Leonard Sweet has called the painting "the most haunting in the history of religious art."[1] The easiest way for you to see the power of both paintings is to view them on the Internet, but I'll do my best to describe *The Church at Auvers* for you.

This church was familiar to van Gogh from his travels, and he painted it in detail. It dominates the entire center of the canvas. The foreground in front of the church consists of a patch of grass and wildflowers and a roadway approaching the church. These features are sunny and bright, while the sky in the background is a deep, dark blue transitioning upward into black, much like the colors of the sky of *Starry Night* but less active and more foreboding. The church is a lumpish, inelegant structure squatting beneath that sky, its windows the same cold blue and its walls dull and bland, seemingly in the shadow of some ominous thing above that imposes its ominous presence on the brightness of the world.

Two additional features add to the story of this church. First, it has no doors—at least none that are visible. And second, the road leading to the church splits into a "Y" right in front of the church, with the two branches bypassing the church on either side, presumably reconnecting on the other side. A woman walking toward the church on the left-hand branch tells us that the daily travels of the townspeople on the road take them *by* the church, not *to* the church.

Because the church has no doors, people on the outside can't get in and people on the inside can't get out. In other words, there is no traffic from the town into and out of the church. Whatever the church has inside that might be of benefit, the people outside have no access to it. And whatever the people outside might need from the church, those inside can't reach them to give it.

Sitting as it does in the middle of the road, the church appears as a giant obstacle in the way of daily commerce—something to be bypassed as one pursues life's appointments and priorities. The church sits in the way of life—a dark obstructing presence, a lifeless relic that people bypass to avoid its cold, inhibiting shadow.

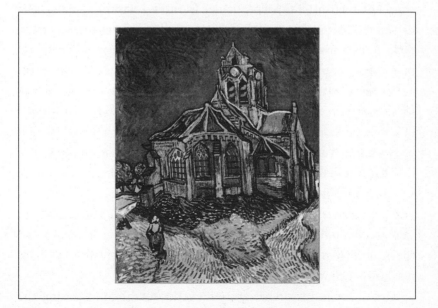

These are my interpretations, not van Gogh's, but they are also held by many others. The artist himself left no written records of what he wanted the two paintings to say about the church in his day. But given his failure to qualify to serve God through the church because of its formidable entrance standards, it is not difficult to imagine him viewing the church as a dark place, devoid of light, impossible to enter, and an obstacle in his life's path. If I have interpreted van Gogh correctly, and if van Gogh's perceptions of the church in his day were even partially valid, his paintings are a sad commentary on the relevance of the institution as he knew it.

As I thought on these paintings, I wondered, *If van Gogh could paint the American church in 2011, how would he portray it?* If he rendered faithfully the physical realities of today's churches, we might see a surface contrast that differs from these nineteenth-century churches in terms of three particular features—darkness, doors, and driveways. Many of today's churches are full of light emanating from racks of overhead stage lights of all colors, rotating siren lights, and pulsating strobe lights. The doors would be numerous and wide open as the seeker-style of ministry makes the church building as well as its service as accommodating as possible to the world. And instead of a lone peasant woman walking around the church, people would be swarming from the parking lot and pouring into the building.

That would be the surface appearance of the church if van Gogh simply painted what he saw with his physical eyes. But does the surface appearance reflect the true reality of the Church? If van Gogh were to manipulate the sky, the foreground, the light, the shape, and the position of the church in order to reflect its inner reality, I wonder just how much we would like that painting.

I'm all for full churches and energetic worship and getting the message out. *But sometimes I wonder if the Church's best efforts to make herself relevant are causing her to become more irrelevant than ever.* I wonder if a true painting of the church of today might look a little more like van Gogh's *The Church at Auvers* than we'd like to admit.

I agree with these thoughts from my friend Chuck Swindoll:

We live in a time with a lot of technology and media. We can create things virtually that look real. We have high-tech gadgets that were not available to previous generations. And we learned that we could attract a lot of people to church if we used those things. I began to see that happening about twenty years ago. It troubled me then, and it's enormously troubling to me now because the result is an entertainment mentality that leads to biblical ignorance...

Some time ago a group of church leaders decided that they didn't want to be hated. They focused just on attracting more and more people. But if we're here to offer something the world can't provide, why would I want to copy the world?[2]

Martyn Lloyd-Jones said, "When the Church is absolutely different from the world, she invariably attracts it. It is then that the world is made to listen to her message, though it may hate it at first."[3]

I wonder and worry about the same things Charles Swindoll and Martyn Lloyd-Jones have noted. And not just about *your* church, but about my church as well. It's a constant struggle to define relevance by the Bible instead of by the world's standards. I never thought I'd see the day when the Church of Jesus Christ was perceived as irrelevant. But that day has arrived, and I think the Church has to assume some of the blame. If the Church is being ignored because we preach the message of "Jesus Christ and Him crucified" (1 Corinthians 2:2), or because the Gospel has become "a stumbling stone and rock of offense" (Romans 9:33) to the world, that's one thing. But if we are deemed irrelevant because we're an anemic version of the world's entertainment options or because we aren't playing the world's game nearly as well as the world does, then that's another thing. That's a tragedy.

If we're going to be attacked or ignored by the world, it might as well be for turning the world upside down as the early Church did (Acts 17:6).

What Is the Church?

Often people confuse "Church" with "church"—the former being the universal body of believers in Christ; the latter being a building constructed for the purpose of a local part of the Church meeting together for worship, instruction, service, and fellowship.[4] That confusion developed easily in America where churches have proliferated. Many New England towns and villages are characterized today by the houses of worship built hundreds of years ago as the nation was settled.

One of the clearest places in America to distinguish between "Church" and "church" is Palmyra, New York (population 7,762 at the 2000 Census). Founded in 1782, this small town is a place where, at least in the nineteenth century, the Church and churches were anything but irrelevant. As one of only a handful of towns in the world that have four churches built on the four corners of the intersection of two major streets or roads, in Palmyra you'll find the following churches at one intersection: Presbyterian (built in 1832), Methodist

(1867), Baptist (1870), and Episcopal (1873). All four are beautiful, traditional brick churches with tall steeples piercing the New York sky.[5]

Every Sunday, Christians in Palmyra fill four different churches to worship God, probably in much the same way as they have for more than a century in that historic setting. What happens when these Christians worship in these buildings is that the *Church* is filling the *churches*.

In the New Testament, the Greek word for church is *ekklesia*, which literally means "called-out ones" (*ek*, "out of," plus *kaleo*, "to call"). *Ekklesia* referred to any assembly of people who were called together for a particular purpose, and the New Testament writers applied this term to those called together by God. It occurs 114 times in the Greek New Testament, and it always refers to people, not buildings.

In his best-selling book *Being the Body*, Charles Colson provided a powerful illustration of the true meaning of the Church:

> One of our favorite pictures of the church comes from the late Richard Halverson, friend and mentor. Dick was chaplain of the U.S. Senate, but before that he was pastor of Washington D.C.'s large Fourth Presbyterian Church. He had been leading that church for years when suddenly, one night, he saw his church clearly for the first time.
>
> He was flying into Washington one day at dusk. At that time the approach path to Washington's Reagan National Airport happened to pass directly over Fourth Presbyterian Church. Dick pressed his face against the window to catch a glimpse of the building from the air. But everything on the ground was shrouded in the shadows falling over the city as the sun set. Dick could not find his church.

He leaned back in his seat, gazing at the Washington sky-line, always an inspiring sight. As his eyes followed the Potomac River, he could see the skyscrapers of Rosslyn, just across Key Bridge from Georgetown. Then, in the distance to the left, the White House, the lights of the Labor Department, the distant glow of the Capitol dome.

As he stared out the window, he began mentally ticking off the names of members of his congregation who worked in those office buildings and government bureaus. Disciples he had equipped to live their faith. And suddenly it hit him.

"Of course!" he exclaimed to the startled passenger in the next seat. "There it is! Fourth Presbyterian Church!"

The church wasn't marked by a sanctuary or a steeple. The church was spread throughout Washington, in the homes and neighborhoods and offices below him, thousands of points of light illuminating the darkness.[6]

The great English Bible translator William Tyndale wisely sought to avoid the confusion between "Church" and "church" by translating *ekklesia* as "congregation" instead of "church" so that the reference to people was always preserved. Alas, church politics got in the way. England's King James I, titular head of the Church of England, would not hear of his translators' (who were working on the Authorized, or King James Version) copying the Puritan Separatist Tyndale's work, so he made his translators render *ekklesia* as "church" instead of "con-gregation." By the early 1600s, when his translation was prepared, there were many churches (church buildings) in Europe, which set the stage for four hundred years of confusion as to what "church" means: people or buildings? As I have said, in the New Testament it always refers to people.

I have spent the time to define the word *church* for this reason: When we talk about the relevancy of the Church of Jesus Christ, we are talking about people—the followers of Jesus. Buildings and institutions don't set agendas or make decisions: People do. Jesus didn't send a church building into the world to make disciples in every nation, He sent people (Matthew 28:19–20). So when Christians ask whether or not the Church is having an impact on the world, there is one place to look: in the mirror.

Indeed, an argument can be made that churches have contributed to the institutionalizing of what was intended to be a dynamic, ever-expanding and ever-maturing human organism. When Emperor Constantine made Christianity the official religion of the Roman Empire in the fourth century, he did what Roman emperors had always done: They had provided money for the building of temples to Roman deities; he (and other emperors to follow) funded the building of churches. Prior to that, the Church had met in homes (Romans 16:5; 1 Corinthians 16:19), in public places (Acts 2:46), and in other noninstitutional settings (Acts 1:13). But as the official Roman Church began building churches throughout Europe, the die was cast: The Church became institutionalized and tied to its property.

Lest I sound "anti–church building," let me assure you, I'm not. I believe buildings play a key role in the success of the Church over time. All the benefits that accrue to a nuclear family from having a physical structure to call home accrue to church families as well. The "Church gathered" is the flip side of the "Church scattered." Both are important, and church buildings allow the Church to gather for worship and for instruction and fellowship, while discipleship and accountability are best accomplished in the "scattered" mode of small groups and Christian influence in commerce and the workplace.

The point I am making is this: We must maintain a clear understanding of the difference between Church and church—and the priority of the former over the latter. Church buildings can necessitate huge investments of resources for construction and maintenance, and they are only temporary. Keeping the focus on people is the biblical priority and will result in the Church's remaining relevant.

Is the Church Irrelevant?

Some people think so. Recently there has been a flurry of disturbing books and reports questioning the condition and relevance of the American church. The titles speak for themselves: *Quitting Church*; *Life After Church*; *So You Don't Want to Go to Church Anymore*; *They Like Jesus but Not the Church*; and *The American Church in Crisis*. Certainly, the irrelevance of the Church has become a very relevant topic of discussion among Christians and non-Christians alike.

In 2010, the Barna Group compiled a survey of opinions about Christians from a cross section of Americans—and the results were not encouraging.[7] On the positive side, respondents noted that Christians in America help the needy, engage in evangelism, protect American values, strengthen marriages, and discourage abortions. But the highest percentage of respondents to cite a positive attribute of Christians (helping the needy) was only 19 percent—less than one-fifth of Americans surveyed. According to 11 percent, Christians had made no positive contributions to America at all, and another 25 percent could not name a single positive contribution made in recent years.

It's true that these last two numbers combined represent a minority of Americans, but the fact that so many Americans view those who represent the Church as irrelevant is troubling.

On the negative side, the largest number of respondents (20 percent) cited violence or hatred in the name of Christ as the reason for their low opinion of Christianity. Other positions or activities that drew sharp criticism were opposition to gay marriage, the Church's involvement in politics, and recent sexual abuses involving Catholic priests. Obviously, some of these complaints, like opposition to gay marriage, come with the biblical territory the Church must stake out and defend. A certain percentage of the population is going to think badly of Christians for narrow moral views even if those views are right. In other cases, the criticism is deserved. Sexual predation of children, moral failures among *any* clergy, hate-filled rhetoric—these acts are unacceptable, and we deserve whatever judgment accrues from such failures.

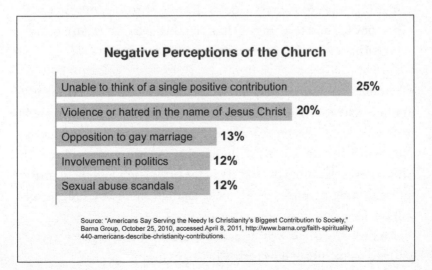

Negative Perceptions of the Church

Unable to think of a single positive contribution	25%
Violence or hatred in the name of Jesus Christ	20%
Opposition to gay marriage	13%
Involvement in politics	12%
Sexual abuse scandals	12%

Source: "Americans Say Serving the Needy Is Christianity's Biggest Contribution to Society," Barna Group, October 25, 2010, accessed April 8, 2011, http://www.barna.org/faith-spirituality/440-americans-describe-christianity-contributions.

194 I Never Thought I'd See the Day!

Overall in the Barna research, the list of complaints about Christians was longer than the list of commendations. And that shouldn't be. When I read from history how Christians were described in the early years of the Church, it makes me long for that kind of relevancy today. For example, an early Christian leader named Justin Martyr (ca. AD 150) wrote to the Roman emperor Antonius Pius, challenging him not to believe false reports about Christians and inviting him to come and inspect their activities for himself:

> To avoid anyone thinking that this is an unreasonable and reckless declaration, we demand that the charges against the Christians be investigated. If these are substantiated, we should be justly punished. But if no one can convict us of anything, true reason forbids you to wrong blameless men because of evil rumors. If you did so, you would be harming yourselves in governing affairs by emotions rather than by intelligence... It is our task, therefore, to provide to all an opportunity of inspecting our life and teachings... It is your business, when you hear us, to be good judges, as reason demands.[8]

Would the Church today invite the public and the government to examine everything about its activities without fear of what might be found? Justin Martyr makes it clear that the early Church had no such fear. The three extensive quotes that follow show why the early Church was relevant to the society of the time, and I find them inspiring as shining examples of what the Church should be today—and still can be.

An early Christian writing called *The Epistle to Diognetes* (ca. AD 130) gives a picture of how early Christians lived:

They dwell in their own countries, but simply as sojourners. As citizens, they share in all things with others and yet endure all things as if foreigners. Every foreign land is to them as their native country, and every land of their birth as a land of strangers. They marry, as do all others; they beget children; but they do not destroy their offspring. They have a common table, but not a common bed. They are in the flesh, but they do not live after the flesh. They pass their days on earth, but they are citizens of heaven. They obey the prescribed laws, and at the same time surpass the laws by their lives. They love all men and are persecuted by all. They are unknown and condemned; they are put to death and restored to life. They are poor yet make many rich; they are in lack of all things and yet abound in all; they are dishonored and yet in their very dishonor are glorified. They are evil spoken of and yet are justified; they are reviled and bless; they are insulted and repay the insult with honor; they do good yet are punished as evildoers. When punished, they rejoice as if quickened into life; they are assailed by the Jews as foreigners and are persecuted by the Greeks; yet those who hate them are unable to assign any reason for their hatred. To sum it all up in one word—what the soul is to the body, that are Christians in the world.[9]

And from the *Apology for the Christians* (ca. AD 197) of Tertullian, an early Church father, we have this description of how money was used in the early Church:

There is no buying and selling of any sort in the things of God. Though we have our treasure-chest, it is not made up of purchase-money, as of a religion that has its price. On the monthly day, if he likes, each puts in a small donation; but only if it be his pleasure, and only if he be able: for there is no compulsion; all is voluntary. These gifts are...not spent on feasts, and drinking-bouts, and eating-houses, but to support and bury poor people, to supply the wants of boys and girls destitute of means and parents, and of old persons confined now to the house; such, too, as have suffered shipwreck; and if there happen to be any in the mines or banished to the islands or shut up in the prisons, for nothing but their fidelity to the cause of God's Church, they become the nurslings of their confession. But it is mainly the deeds of a love so noble that lead many to put a brand upon us. See, they say, how they love one another, for they themselves are animated by mutual hatred. See, they say about us, how they are ready even to die for one another, for they themselves would sooner kill.[10]

Rodney Stark, a modern scholar who has written extensively about early and modern Christianity, says this about the relevance of the Church in its early years:

Christianity revitalized life in Greco-Roman cities by providing new norms and new kinds of social relationships able to cope with many urgent problems. To cities filled with the homeless and impoverished, Christianity offered charity as well as hope. To cities filled with newcomers and strangers, Christianity offered an immediate basis for attachment. To cities filled with orphans and widows, Christianity provided a new and expanded sense of family. To cities torn by violent ethnic strife, Christianity offered a new basis for social solidarity...And to cities faced with epidemics, fire, and earthquakes, Christianity offered effective nursing services... For what they brought was not simply an urban movement, but a new culture capable of making life in Greco-Roman cities more tolerable.[11]

At the very least, we can say that the Church *has been* relevant. And there is evidence that it is still relevant today.

The Value of the Church

Since 1997, Professor Ram A. Cnaan has been studying what local churches are "worth." His unique approach, which is from a nonreligious, social-science perspective, surprised me: He assessed the value of *all* a local church contributes to its community—goods and services of all kinds. This year (2011) he will release his newest research on twelve historic Philadelphia churches. Preliminary figures indicate that one of those churches, Philadelphia's First Baptist Church, conservatively contributed $6,090,032 to the local economy annually—nearly ten times its annual budget. Cnaan determined the economic impact of First Baptist Church by placing a monetary value on the presence and services of the church. Among the contributions listed were the stimulus of the church budget to the local economy, the value of education provided by the church's educational ministries, and the savings to the community because of the church's counseling efforts to prevent suicide, addiction, crime, and divorce. Reading this study made me realize an entirely new dimension of the universal Church's relevance and value.[12]

But here's the more important dimension of relevance—one that can't be measured with a calculator: the spiritual impact in people's lives. Philadelphia resident Dennis Wright, struggling with AIDS since the mid-1980s, was searching for something more spiritual than what he had found at various nonchurch support groups. So he plugged into the Hospitality Center at Philadelphia's Saint Luke and the Epiphany Church. When asked about the value, in dollars, he had received from the group at the church he said, "A dollar value? I don't know what I would put for that. I owe my life to the church."[13]

There it is: "*I owe my life to the church.*" Try telling Dennis Wright that the Church is irrelevant in the modern world. Or try telling it to yourself or to someone you know or love. What price can be placed on being reconciled to God? On having sins forgiven? On seeing your children find a place where they are loved and accepted? On having a small group to meet with regularly? On prayer and counsel? On having a pastor meet you at the hospital in the middle of the night when there is a family emergency? Dennis Wright's confession—"I owe my life to the Church"—could be repeated countless times in this modern era. The impact of the Gospel of Jesus Christ in human terms cannot be measured. In eternal terms, it cannot even be imagined.[14]

No, the Church doesn't always get it right. Unsavory and regrettable things have happened to people "in church" or in the name of Christ throughout history. But that doesn't negate the good that has been done and will continue to be done. It doesn't make the Church irrelevant.

The Value of Heritage

It breaks my heart, referring back to the Barna survey, that 11 percent of respondents said Christianity had made no positive contributions to the United States and that 25 percent could not cite a single positive contribution made by Christians in America in recent years. The saddest fact is that those respondents don't realize that they, by living in America, are reaping the benefits of the biblically based foundations on which the nation was built. It seems that more and more, people do not understand that the founders of our nation used biblical values as their model to design a government that would preserve our most precious freedoms. For example, consider how the following dimensions of America's government directly reflect biblical values:

- Constitutional (covenantal) government—a mutual agreement between governor and governed. (Reflects the covenant between God and Israel.)
- Representative government—governors chosen from among the people. (Reflects the way New Testament Church leaders are selected.)
- Equality of all—all citizens have equal standing before the law in a republic. (Reflects the biblical idea that all stand equally before God.)
- Rule by law—laws of man must reflect the revealed laws of God rather than the whims of a monarch. (Reflects the biblical idea that the Creator-God of Scripture is the Lawgiver and Judge of all.)
- Liberty—all have the right to freedom. (Reflects the liberty and freedom from condemnation found in Christ Jesus.)
- Recognition of the depravity of man—man is not capable of governing himself; laws are needed to keep depravity in check. (Reflects the biblical notion that "all have sinned" [Romans 3:23])
- Separation of powers—executive, judicial, legislative branches. (Reflects the tripartite rule of God as outlined in Isaiah 33:22: "The LORD is our Judge, the LORD is our Lawgiver, the LORD is our King; He will save us.")

Unfortunately, several generations of Americans have grown up completely unaware of the nation's true and full history and the role Christianity has played in creating and preserving the "land of the free and the home of the brave." That is not to say that all the framers were evangelical Christians—they weren't. But even those who were not Christians recognized the moral, spiritual, and ethical value of the Bible's teachings and built those values into the warp and woof of the nation they were creating. It's another example of the Church's relevance to modern American life.

James Russell Lowell (1819–1891) was a Harvard-trained lawyer who established his place in American history as a social critic, magazine editor, publisher, and language professor. He often used his rigorous and lengthy poems as his tool of choice. After teaching at Harvard for twenty years, he was appointed as U.S. ambassador to Spain and then to England. Lowell was once at a banquet where detractors were attacking Christianity, and especially its missionary endeavors. He rose to speak and said the following:

> I challenge any skeptic to find a ten square mile spot on this planet where they can live their lives in peace and safety and decency, where womanhood is honored, where infancy and old age are revered, where they can educate their children—where the Gospel of Jesus Christ has not gone first to prepare the way. If they find such a place, then I would encourage them to emigrate thither and there proclaim their unbelief.[15]

Lowell spoke those words in the late nineteenth century after witnessing what is now referred to as the great age of missionary expansion. Christian missionaries from the West began crisscrossing the globe in increasing numbers, taking the Christian Gospel to primitive and undeveloped cultures. As the Gospel was embraced, primitive cultures were transformed in the way Lowell described.

Unfortunately, biblical Christianity is no longer being preached from every pulpit in the land. As a result, America is losing her spiritual way, and it is due, in no small part, to the fact that the church has lost *her* way. I believe with all my heart: As goes the church, so goes the nation. If the spiritual light of the nation has grown dim, and righteousness has not been preserved, it's because two things are missing: spiritual salt and light (Matthew 5:13–16).

What Makes the Church Relevant?

The value of the Church can be measured by three vital dimensions, which combine to make it relevant to society—indeed not only relevant, but absolutely crucial to society's continuation. To understand the Church's value to the world, let's examine these three dimensions one by one.

The Church's Purpose: The Glory of God

For half a century, the faithful parishioners of the old First Church of Christ in Unionville, Connecticut, had missed their steeple. The rugged stone spire, first built in 1885, had loomed above the town's center with quiet dignity. But the tower suffered deterioration and was torn down. Church members wanted to replace the steeple, but the project was too expensive.

Then Verizon Wireless came to the rescue. When the phone company needed to build a cell phone tower in Unionville, locals were worried about disfiguring the village landscape. So the phone company spent more than $500,000 to rebuild the church's steeple, not out of stone, but out of steel and fiberglass so radio waves could bounce from antennas hidden inside the structure. Some of the church members hesitated, but in the end most agreed with the project, especially as the new steeple was expertly designed to match the rest of the building. As one member said, "We thought it would be nice to have a steeple again."[16]

No one really knows who first topped a church building with a steeple, but the practice dates back about fourteen hundred years to when churches had clock towers and bell turrets, which were often the tallest structures in town. These towers and turrets provided commanding views for watchmen, and they are still seen in many European towns. They are the ancestors of today's steeples.

"Just as we associate shapes with items such as stop signs, the Coca-Cola bottle, the Nike swoosh, or the Red Cross, so too the shape of a steeple represents the church," said one steeple-maker, Douglas Caudle of Piedmont Fiberglass in North Carolina.[17]

Another steeple manufacturer, Jerry Bennett, whose company manufactured the world's tallest steeple, a 229-foot structure atop First Baptist Church of Huntsville, Alabama, put it this way: "A steeple points one to the heavens…Through city streets, across the valleys and lakes, through the countryside far and wide, the steeple declares Christ."[18]

I love steeples for that reason. They point toward the heavens and direct the eye upward to our risen Savior. Preachers come and go. Songs become popular and fade into forgetfulness. Trends and methods change with the years. Personalities dominate the pulpit then are buried in the church cemetery. Even church architecture changes in fad and fashion. But throughout all these changes, church steeples have remained a constant tradition. Their styles and materials may change, but I am thankful that those aspiring spires still point toward the heavens, because they are fitting symbols for one central purpose of the Church that is not faddish and does not change: to direct people's lives upward toward the glory of God.

According to author Brett McCracken, "True relevance is seeking the true faith that transcends all boxes and labels...Things that are permanent are not faddish or fickle or trendy. They are solid. The word *relevant*, however, seems to imply temporality. I think we need to fess up to the truth that nothing temporal is really all that relevant at all, in the long run. True relevance *lasts*."[19]

As the fads and trends around us come and go, one person endures: Jesus Christ. He "is the same yesterday, today, and forever" (Hebrews 13:8). He is exalted in the heavens, and the earth is His footstool. Someone said that Jesus Christ is the meeting place of eternity and time, the blending of deity and humanity, the junction of heaven and earth.

In his work titled *Explore the Book*, Dr. J. Sidlow Baxter notes:

> Our Lord's message was Himself. He did not come merely to preach a Gospel. He Himself is that Gospel. He did not come merely to give bread; He said, "I am the bread." He did not come merely to shed light; He said, "I am the light." He did not come merely to show the door; He said, "I am the door." He did not come merely to name a shepherd; He said, "I am the shepherd." He did not come merely to point the way; He said, "I am the way, the truth, and the life."[20]

The purpose of the Church is all about glorifying our wonderful Savior, Jesus Christ. As our eyes look upward toward the heavens, we gladly turn away from our own earthly idols and cast our crowns at His feet, knowing that He will not share His glory with any other object of worship (Isaiah 42:8). "You are worthy, O Lord, to receive glory and honor and power; for You created all things, and by Your will they exist and were created" (Revelation 4:11).

The Church's Priority: The Great Commission

There is nothing more relevant to each and every soul in the universe than the good news of Jesus Christ. Michael Horton writes,

> The Good News concerning Christ is not a stepping-stone to something greater and more relevant. Whether we realize it or not, there is nothing in the universe more relevant to us as guilty image-bearers of God than the news that he has found a way to be "just and the justifier of the one who has faith in Jesus" (Rom. 3:26).[21]

> It is only in the gospel where we see God's merciful love and pure justice embrace at the cross. Precisely where our message and mission seem most odd, counterintuitive, and even offensive are they the most interesting and relevant. The story we have to tell to the world is not told in different ways in other religions. The gospel is the strangest thing we will ever hear—or tell. And if it isn't true for all of us, then it isn't true for any of us.[22]

A relevant Church must be carried along by the fresh winds of the Great Commission. At the end of Matthew's Gospel, Jesus tells us to go into all the world, winning, baptizing, teaching, and making disciples in all nations (Matthew 28:18–20). At the beginning of Acts, He says to His followers, "You shall receive power when the Holy Spirit has come upon you; and you shall be witnesses to Me...to the end of the earth" (1:8).

The Lord Jesus promised to build His Church, and the gates of hell cannot prevent it (Matthew 16:18). Even if the Church is reduced to a tiny, persecuted, ridiculed minority in the Western world, she can confidently pursue the priority her Savior has given her. Whether we're respected in society or neglected and abused, we have a mission—to take the good news of Christ to the ends of the earth and to bring the Gospel within earshot of anyone willing to listen. We aren't here to be successful, influential, wealthy, famous, or praised by a degraded society. We're here to pave the way for the Lord's return by sowing the Gospel, both person-to-person and nation-to-nation.

The Church's Program: The Great Commandment

Our ministry of compassion is one aspect of our faith that critics cannot deny. The world respects our historic concern for the poor, the innocent, the downtrodden, the sick, the underprivileged, the orphans, the widows, and the needy. The pundits may rail against our stand on immorality, but they respect our help for the homeless. The Bible says, "Live such good lives among the pagans that, though they accuse you of doing wrong, they may see your *good deeds* and glorify God" (1 Peter 2:12 NIV, emphasis mine here and in the following verses).

Jesus said, "Let your light so shine before men, that they may see your *good works* and glorify your Father in heaven" (Matthew 5:16). Paul said that we have been "created in Christ Jesus for *good works*, which God prepared" for us to do (Ephesians 2:10).

We're to be like Dorcas, who "was full of *good works* and chari-table deeds which she did" (Acts 9:36). We're commanded to be rich in *good works*, prepared for every *good work*, equipped for every *good work*, zealous for *good works*, and in all things showing ourselves to be a pattern of *good works* (1 Timothy 6:18; 2 Timothy 2:21; 3:17; Titus 2:14; 2:7).

The good deed you or I do for someone authenticates our testi-mony, shares the compassion of our Lord, and paves the way for our message. In his book titled *The Great Commandment Principle*, David Ferguson recounts one occasion when the churches' love for one another led to a transformed life:

It was a balmy November evening in Titusville, Florida, and the Friday night service was nearing conclusion. I was speaking to about a thousand pastors and lay leaders gathered for one of our regional ministry training conferences. My text was Romans 12:15: "Rejoice with those who rejoice; mourn with those who mourn." During our time of worship we experienced the first part of that verse, rejoicing together in God's goodness and grace. Then I emphasized the testimony of love that results when we share our hurts and discouragements *with* one another and receive God's comfort *from* one another as the Bible instructs.

At the close of my message I encouraged everyone to turn to someone nearby—spouse, family member, or friend—and share a memory of personal pain. It could be as small or great a pain as they cared to disclose, something recent or from the past. As each individual spoke, his or her partner was to listen and express godly comfort.

As people shared their hurts and comforted one another, many exchanged spontaneous, tender embraces, and a few tears began to flow. I slipped away from the platform and circled behind the crowd near the main doors, rejoicing as I contemplated the Father's joy.

While I stood there watching, the door opened behind me, and a man walked in. He was about thirty years old, nice looking, and casually dressed. I found out later that Ray, who was not a believer, lived in the neighborhood and was out for an evening walk. Curious about why the church parking lot was full on a Friday night, he had stepped inside to take a look.

He walked over near me and surveyed the sea of people. Obviously perplexed at the sight, he asked, "What are they doing?"

"They're comforting one another," I explained.

Ray continued to watch the people share their hurts and tenderly embrace—married couples, single adults, and entire families. Tears formed in his eyes, and there was a longing in his voice. "That's what *I* need."

Sensing a divine appointment, I said, "Are there stressful or painful things going on in your life right now?"

Ray nodded. He explained that his job at the nearby Kennedy Space Center was in jeopardy due to cutbacks. Furthermore, he had just gone through the pain of placing his mother in a nursing home. At about the same time, his fiancée had broken up with him. This young man was in a world of hurt!

Others gathered around Ray and shared God's love with him by comforting him. The unexpected outpouring of love from total strangers lifted a great burden from Ray, and before the evening was over, he committed his life to Jesus Christ.[23]

When the Church manifests the life of the Lord Jesus Christ, then the Church will be just as relevant in our day as He was in His. Mission, mercy, meeting needs, maintenance, manifesting the power and love of God—all these and more are facets of the Church's mandate to make disciples through faithfully teaching all that Jesus commanded His first disciples (Matthew 28:19–20).

In a powerful commentary on the Church, Steven J. Lawson offers an analysis and prescription for today's Church that serves as a fitting conclusion to this chapter:

As the church advances into the twenty-first century, the stress to produce booming ministries has never been greater. Influenced by corporate mergers, towering skyscrapers, and expanding economies, bigger is perceived as better, and nowhere is this "Wall Street" mentality more evident than in the church. Sad to say, pressure to produce bottomline results has led many ministries to sacrifice the centrality of biblical preaching on the altar of man-centered pragmatism.

A new way of "doing" church is emerging. In this radical paradigm shift, exposition [of the Bible] is being replaced with entertainment, preaching with performances, doctrine with drama, and theology with theatrics. The pulpit, once the focal point of the church, is now being overshadowed by a variety of church-growth techniques, everything from trendy worship styles to glitzy presentations to vaudeville-like pageantries. In seeking to capture the upper hand in church growth, a new wave of pastors is reinventing the church and repackaging the gospel into a product to be sold to "consumers."

Whatever reportedly works in one church is being franchised out to various "markets" abroad. As when gold was discovered in the foothills of California, so ministers are beating a path to the doorsteps of exploding churches and super-hyped conferences where the latest "strike" has been reported. Unfortunately the newly panned gold often turns out to be "fool's gold." Not all that glitters is actually gold.

Admittedly pastors can learn from growing churches and successful ministries. Yet God's work must be done God's way if it is to know God's blessing. He provides the power and He alone receives the glory only as His divinely prescribed plan for ministry is followed. When man-centered schemes are followed, often imitating the world's schemes, the flesh provides the energy and man receives the glory... In a strange twist, the preaching of the cross is now foolishness, not only to the world but also to the contemporary church.[24]

May God grant His Church the discipline to stay focused and the desire to manifest the eternal relevance of Jesus Christ to a needy world.

CHAPTER 8

When a Muslim State Could Intimidate the World

In the Name of God, the Compassionate, the Merciful: All praise be to Allah, the Lord of the Universe, and peace and blessing be upon our Master and Prophet, Mohammad, and his pure Household, and his noble Companions and on all divine messengers. Oh, God, hasten the arrival of Imam Al-Mahdi and grant him good health and victory and make us his followers and those who attest to his rightfulness.[1]

If you are thinking that prayer was uttered in a religious service in an Islamic mosque somewhere in the Middle East, or even in one of New York City's more than one hundred mosques, you would be mistaken. The prayer was offered in New York City before the Sixty-fifth Session of the United Nations General Assembly on September 23, 2010—by Mahmoud Ahmadinejad, president of the Islamic Republic of Iran.

Imagine what would happen if an American president who embraces the Christian faith prayed the following before giving a speech at the United Nations:

> *Dear God, I pray You will hasten the coming of our Lord Jesus Christ; that You will grant Him victory over all His enemies; that You will establish His kingdom in power and righteousness; that You will cause every knee in the nations represented here today to bow before Him and confess that Jesus Christ is Lord over all. Amen.*

Even before the president had taken a sip of water and begun his speech, delegates in the General Assembly would be tweeting and texting their outrage around the world. The very idea of bringing God into a political body! What audacity this man has to pray that his particular God would establish a kingdom on earth! And to suggest that all other nations would become subject to *his* God and *his* political system! Outrageous!

Yet that is exactly what Mahmoud Ahmadinejad did at the United Nations, and I daresay you heard nothing about it. Concealed in his brief words—"hasten the arrival of Imam Al-Mahdi and grant him good health and victory"—is a prayer that the conqueror, whom Islamic peoples believe will come, will arrive soon and complete his conquest of all non-Islamic nations. It's an entire system of religious-political belief that controls the government of Ahmadinejad's nation, the Islamic Republic of Iran.

A generation ago it would have been unthinkable that the leader of a nation could with impunity pray such a prayer in such a place. Yet this prayer—and the absence of any public negative response to it—demonstrates the growing impact of this political leader from a country where church and state are one and the same.

Iran is a theocracy. The word *theocracy* is a combination of two Greek words, one meaning "God," and the other meaning "strength." A theocracy is a government where religious beliefs dictate political decisions—where God is the head of state. It is that theocratic system of beliefs that Ahmadinejad is using to destabilize the Middle East and intimidate the world community.

I never thought I'd see the day when an ancient, repressive nation could intimidate the modern world using threats based in theology. Yes, in my lifetime the world has seen other bullies with international aspirations: Germany's Adolf Hitler and the former Soviet Union's Nikita Khrushchev come to mind. But these leaders were different. Their aspirations were based primarily on military might and the desire for power.

Adolf Hitler was not the leader of a theocratic state, but Mahmoud Ahmadinejad is. And that difference is highly significant. I can think of nothing more volatile than a theocratic leader with nuclear capabilities in one hand and a divine mission from "God" in the other.

We have seen countless examples of this deadly combination of weaponry and religious fundamentalism on the part of Islamic believers who were willing to kill and be killed in the name of "God." Using a jetliner to bring down skyscrapers, strapping explosives to one's chest in a public marketplace, or sending a nuclear-tipped missile across the border of another country—it's all the same: chaos and killing in order to bring about the (so-called) will of God.

Life-or-death commitment to one's religious principles is to be commended. Jesus Christ told His followers to take up their cross if they intended to follow Him. He was telling them to be ready to die. The difference is that Jesus' message and ministry were based on love (John 13:34–35). Their deaths would be inflicted by those who reacted negatively to their message of love, whereas Islamic fundamentalists are encouraged to die in the process of killing others who do not believe as they do.

While Jesus will institute a theocracy on earth one day—a kingdom over which He will rule as King—that kingdom will be based on righteousness and justice and blessing and generosity, not on coercion, intimidation, and fear (Revelation 20:1–6).

Parsing the President's Prayer

To get the full picture of how Iran is threatening the world, let's unpack President Ahmadinejad's prayer at the United Nations.

He prayed for "the arrival of Imam Al-Mahdi," also called Muhammad Al-Mahdi. Just as Christians await the second coming of their Lord, Jesus Christ, so many Muslims await the appearance of "Imam Al-Mahdi." According to Shia Islam (the official religion of Iran), the Mahdi will be the twelfth imam (Muslim religious leader) in direct succession from the prophet Mohammad, the founder of Islam.

Shia means "followers of Ali." The adherents of Shia Islam believe their religion is the only way to the one god Allah, and these Shiites make up about 90 percent of Iran's population. They believe that the Mahdi was born in AD 869 and that he never died. Allah has hidden him since that time, intending to reveal him as the "savior of mankind" someday in the future.

Iran's leaders believe their country will become the welcoming nation for the Mahdi when he appears. In a speech delivered in December 2009, Ahmadinejad said that one of Iran's primary tasks as a nation is to prepare for their role in "the administration of the world."[2] Shia Muslims believe that "global Islamic rule" will be accomplished under the Mahdi. He is expected to come in the third millennium, which they claim "belongs to Islam and the rule of Muslims over the world."[3] Former Iranian president Ali Akbar Hashemi-Rafsanjani's principal foreign policy adviser wrote: "We have a huge position in the Islamic world. No country other than Iran can lead the Islamic world; this is a historical position."[4]

Shia Muslims like Ahmadinejad are not afraid of chaos. Indeed, they welcome it since it is during a period of chaos that the Mahdi, the savior, will appear. Ahmadinejad believes the United States knows this and is attempting to block Iran's rise to a leadership position in the Middle East, preventing her from being the nation to which the Mahdi reveals himself. He believes the U.S. is doing whatever it can "to prevent the coming of the Hidden Imam [the Mahdi] because they know that the Iranian nation is the one that will prepare the grounds for his coming and will be the supporters of his rule."[5] According to Ahmadinejad, the U.S. knows that "a divine hand will come soon to root out the tyranny in the world...They know that Iran is paving the way for [the Mahdi's] coming and will serve him."[6]

Ahmadinejad is known for his outlandish policy positions. Not only has he publicly denied that the Jewish Holocaust ever happened,[7] in his 2010 speech to the United Nations General Assembly, he stated that "the majority of American people as well as other nations and politicians agree" that the September 11, 2001, attack on America was not a terrorist attack but was "orchestrated" by the government of the United States.[8] He has also publicly declared that Israel will one day be "wiped out from the map."[9] This 2005 statement has become even more relevant in light of the possibility of Israel's taking military steps to thwart Iran's nuclear aspirations. In May 2010, Ahmadinejad's chief of staff, Esfandiar Rahim Mashaei, said that such an attack on Iran would result in Israel's destruction in less than ten days.[10]

Let's catch our breath and summarize:

- Shia Muslims are awaiting the return of the Mahdi, the twelfth imam, who will assume a leadership position over Islam.
- Iran believes that it is the preeminent Muslim nation and thus the host nation to which the Mahdi will return.
- Iran believes the United States is "the Great Satan," and that she is an ungodly, secularizing force, working behind the scenes to sabotage Iran's rise to prominence on the world stage.
- Iran believes that Israel has stolen the land of Palestine from its rightful Arab Muslim owners and should be "wiped out from the map."
- Iran is not afraid of conflict and chaos since such a setting is necessary in order for the Mahdi to return.
- Iran is on an accelerated path to acquire nuclear capability.
- Iran's political policies have one goal: to carry out Allah's will. It is this marriage of politics and theology that makes Iran the most destabilizing nation on earth today. Iranian leaders

believe their huge oil reserves are Allah's gift for the purpose of funding their Islamic agenda. Iran is not a toothless tiger.

Looking Behind the Curtain in Tehran

In the movie version of L. Frank Baum's *The Wonderful Wizard of Oz*, Dorothy and Toto, along with their three friends, travel to the Emerald City to see the Wizard of Oz. When they arrive they make a startling discovery: The fearsome face that is supposed to be the wizard is actually being projected and controlled by a man behind a giant curtain. The wizard is nothing more than a mouthpiece for the man behind the curtain.

If we look behind the curtain of the Iranian capital of Tehran, we will discover that the saber-rattling president of Iran is only a mouthpiece for the religious leaders of this Muslim nation. They remain "behind the curtain" pulling the strings. Remember: Iran is a theocracy—a marriage of church and state. President Mahmoud Ahmadinejad is the "state," and fundamentalist Shia Muslim clerics are the "church."

What Ahmadinejad says to the world is not of his own formulation. He is simply the public face for the fundamentalist Muslim clerics who are interpreting the will of Allah for the nation of Iran. What is new, however, is Ahmadinejad's willingness to express Iran's "militarist and messianic Islamism" on a public stage.[11] Iran is getting bolder about revealing publicly what has been happening behind the curtain for many years.

To fully grasp what is happening in Iran today, we must understand certain key events from its past. A nation that is thousands of years old like the Persian state of Iran has a detailed and complex history. So I'm going to greatly simplify the story and pick it up in the modern era beginning in 1979 when the last shah of Iran was deposed.

The shah had ruled as the leader of Iran since 1941. But because of his increasing alliance with the United States and Britain and his economic and cultural reforms, the Iranian religious leaders became increasingly opposed to his rule. Islamic clerics, especially those loyal to Ayatollah Khomeini, a cleric exiled under the shah's rule, led uprisings against the shah. He was deposed in January 1979 and fled the country with his family.

Into this vacuum of leadership moved the exiled Muslim religious leader Ayatollah Khomeini, and in April Iran became the Islamic Republic of Iran. A theocratic constitution was approved by December, and Khomeini seized power, becoming the supreme leader of Iran. Thousands who had been loyal to the shah were executed, and Iran became a nation led by a religious leader who governed by fundamentalist Islamic principles.

Here is what's important about this swift and dramatic transformation of Iran: When Khomeini seized power, he declared himself the supreme leader by invoking a historic and controversial teaching in Muslim tradition: the "Guardianship of the Religious Jurist." Khomeini declared himself to be this religious jurist—an heir to the prophet Mohammad and the imams who preceded him. As the religious jurist, he wielded "absolute authority and sovereignty over the affairs of the entire Muslim nation."[12]

Over time, Khomeini strengthened his hold on all things Iranian by adding to the new constitution provisions reflecting his assumed authority—like Principle 57: "The legislative, executive, and judicial branches in the Islamic Republic of Iran are under the supervision of the [religious jurist]"[13]—that is, Khomeini. The supreme leader is also the supreme commander of the armed forces. He declares war and peace and appoints or impeaches the president of Iran. As the highest religious and political authority in Iran, the supreme leader conjoins church and state. *The supreme leader, not the president, is the true head of Iran.*

Khomeini's goal following his restructuring of the constitution was to spread radical or fundamental Islam throughout the world. It is still the goal of the Islamic Republic of Iran to establish a caliphate uniting Muslims worldwide.

The Ayatollah Khomeini died in 1989 and was succeeded by Ayatollah Ali Khamenei (note the slight difference in the spelling of their last names), who remains supreme leader in Iran today. Khamenei assumed the role of religious jurist and continued Khomeini's radical policies toward worldwide Muslim unification and world domination. In 1989 he was quoted as telling a group of Hezbollah leaders from Lebanon:

Iran's Islamic revolution cannot be confined within borders, nations, or ethnic groups... It is in our revolution's interest, and an essential principle, that when we speak of Islamic objectives, we address all the Muslims of the world, and when we speak of the Arrogant West, we address all the oppressors of the world.[14]

That's what is going on behind the curtain in Tehran. In front of the curtain and acting as the face of Iran is Mahmoud Ahmadinejad, who was elected president of Iran in 2005 on a religious hard-line platform. But not all Iranians are happy with the militant, fundamentalist regime that controls Iran. There were massive protests in the streets of Tehran following the 2009 elections in which Ahmadinejad was reelected under suspicious circumstances. Those protests were brutally put down and drew criticism from many nations. France, Germany, the United Kingdom, and the United States declined to send Ahmadinejad the expected letters of congratulations upon his reelection.

Core Beliefs That Drive Modern Iran

Several core beliefs, both religious and political, provide the motivating fuel that defines the actions and purposes of modern Iran. Let's consider those briefly:

- Iran is a Muslim theocratic state in which policy is informed by religion.
- Iran is angry at the West for several reasons: for interfering in the affairs of the Middle East by blocking Iraq's invasion of Kuwait in 1990–1991; for invading Iraq and deposing Saddam Hussein in 2003 and occupying the country ever since; for invading Afghanistan following 9/11; for being Israel's chief ally; for lumping Iran in with other Muslim nations instead of recognizing her cultural "superiority"; and for spreading a decadent, secular worldview.
- Iran is angry with Israel for moving into Palestine and establishing a homeland in 1948 at the expense of the Arab Palestinians who were living there.

Iran's religious fundamentalism and her strident reaction to what she sees as offenses against her and Islam have made a large part of the world extremely nervous. Nations are apprehensive, not because she is the eighteenth-largest country in terms of landmass or because she has the third-largest proven oil reserves or the fourth-largest army. Iran represents a ticking time bomb because of her messianic arrogance and her determination to acquire nuclear capability.

As Israel's prime minister Benjamin Netanyahu has observed, "You don't want a messianic apocalyptic cult controlling atomic bombs... When the wide-eyed believer gets hold of the reins of power and the weapons of mass death, then the world should start worrying, and that's what is happening in Iran."[15]

Curiously, while Iran's nuclear capability scares all nations, it particularly scares the rest of the Middle Eastern nations. In the West, we tend to lump all Middle Easterners together as "Muslims" or "Arabs." This is our mistake, not theirs. It's due to our lack of knowledge of the basic religious and cultural history of the Middle East.

Iranians are not Arabs—they are Persians. The Persians and the Arabs do not even speak the same language. Persians speak Farsi and Arabs speak Arabic. What unites the Middle Eastern nations, however, is their Islamic religious heritage. But their ethnic, racial, and cultural differences are a tension point in the region.

The fact that Iran views itself as the "true" keeper of the Muslim faith—the nation to which the Mahdi will return; the nation where the religious jurist resides; the nation that insists on implementing the true, radical, militant Shia branch of Islam—makes her a bully in the eyes of the other Muslim nations. And they know that Iran is actively trying to spread her influence in the region.

Analysts believe that if Iran acquires nuclear weapons, the other nations in the region will be forced to follow suit. Given Iran's superior view of her role in the world, her neighbors cannot afford the risk that Iran would use her nuclear advantage to intimidate the other Muslim nations.

Some think the more moderate Muslim nations would welcome a military strike by Israel or the West on Iran's nuclear production facilities in order to throw water on Iran's burning desire to rule the Middle East.[16] The thought of a nuclear-arms race in the Middle East is a frightening prospect. According to Netanyahu, "The Middle East is incendiary enough, but with a nuclear-arms race, it will become a tinderbox."[17]

Persia and Israel: An Ancient Relationship

Make no mistake about it: At the top of Iran's agenda is the elimination, not necessarily of Jews per se, but of the formal State of Israel. Iran would like to see Jews go back to the nations where they lived prior to regathering in their homeland of Israel in 1948. But as we will see in a moment, Persians and Jews have not always had such an antagonistic relationship.

Let's do a quick point-by-point review of the historic high points of this relationship before exploring where it went wrong and what this means for the future:

- Late sixth-century/early seventh-century BC: The two southern tribes of Benjamin and Judah are taken from Jerusalem into captivity in Babylon.
- 539 BC: The Babylonian Empire is taken over by the Persians, and they inherit the captive Jews from Jerusalem.
- 538 BC: The Persian king Cyrus issues a decree that the Jews should rebuild their temple in Jerusalem (Ezra 1:2–3). He also

returns to them the priestly hardware taken from the temple by the Babylonian king Nebuchadnezzar.

- A succession of Persian kings—Darius I, Xerxes I, Artaxerxes I, Darius II—continue supporting the return of the Jews to Jerusalem as well as providing resources for rebuilding the temple, the wall, and the city. The rebuilding efforts are led by biblical heroes Zerubbabel, Ezra, and Nehemiah.

In summary, for more than 130 years there was a respectful and successful relationship between the Jews and the Persians.[18] But we know from the Bible how close that relationship came to ending abruptly and in blood! A plot formulated by a Persian official to exterminate all the Jewish people in Persia was uncovered and derailed only by the providence of God. That plot bears a sinister similarity to the diabolical hatred of the modern-day Persians (Iran's government) for Israel.

The story of God's intervention is recorded in the biblical account of Esther. This is where we find precedent for a future intervention that will also save the Jewish people from a genocidal attack. The story of Esther takes place during the reign of the Persian king Xerxes I (486–465 BC), also called Ahasuerus in some English translations.

The Persian Empire under Ahasuerus was huge: 127 provinces ranging from modern-day Iran in the north to India in the east to Ethiopia in the west (Esther 1:1).

The book of Esther opens with the first of ten parties mentioned in the account. At the end of one particular seven-day feast (Esther 1:5), Ahasuerus called for his wife, Queen Vashti, to appear wearing her crown before his gathering of dignitaries (Esther 1:9–11).

Vashti, who was in the process of hosting her own party, refused

(Esther 1:12). When Ahasuerus inquired of his advisers what should be done to Vashti for disobeying his command, this was their answer:

> Queen Vashti has not only wronged the king, but also all the princes, and all the people who are in all the provinces of King Ahasuerus. For the queen's behavior will become known to all women, so that they will despise their husbands in their eyes, when they report, "King Ahasuerus commanded Queen Vashti to be brought in before him, but she did not come." (Esther 1:16–17)

The king agreed with his advisers and banished Vashti from his presence forever. Following additional counsel from his advisers, he immediately began searching for a new queen to replace Vashti.

A sort of beauty pageant was held for the purpose of previewing the most beautiful young women in Persia, from which the king would make his selection. Among these women was a Jewess named Esther, an orphan who had been raised by her older cousin Mordecai. Mordecai cautioned Esther not to reveal her Jewish heritage as she was being considered by Ahasuerus. Incidentally, it is in connection with Mordecai that the term "Jew" is first applied to the people of God (Esther 2:5).

The king selected Esther to become the new queen of Persia. Shortly afterward Mordecai, who appears to have received a minor court appointment, discovered an assassination plot being hatched by two of the king's officials. Mordecai informed Queen Esther, who in turn informed the king, crediting Mordecai with the discovery of the plot. An investigation revealed the truth of Mordecai's accusation, and the two conspirators were executed. The whole event—names, dates, and places—was recorded in the king's record books and promptly forgotten. But the event will emerge again to become an important piece of the providential Persian puzzle we are piecing together.

Meanwhile, King Ahasuerus promoted a man named Haman to a prestigious position in his court. With the promotion came the obligation for Persians to bow down to Haman whenever he entered their presence. As a faithful Jew, Mordecai refused to bow before anyone except the God of Israel—the God of his forefathers Abraham, Isaac, and Jacob. When Haman observed Mordecai standing while the rest of his minions groveled before him, he was enraged.

In his anger, Haman decided on a preemptive strike: Not only would he have Mordecai put to death; he would avenge this insult to his honor by exterminating all the Jews in all 127 Persian provinces.

We can't help but wonder, is it really possible that this man would put thousands of Jews to death just because one Jew failed to acknowledge his royal stature? There must have been something else going on in his mind. And indeed there was—Haman was determined to use this occasion to settle an old score on behalf of his ancestors.

Haman was not a native Persian but an Agagite (Esther 3:1). The term "Agagite" leads us back almost a thousand years before Haman to Agag, the king of the Amalekites at the time of the Jews' exodus from Egypt. The Amalekites, descendants of Esau, were the first nation to attack Israel as they journeyed from Egypt to the Promised Land.

God pronounced His curse on the Amalekites, which would result in their total annihilation as a people (Exodus 17:8–16). In fact, Moses told the generation of Israelites who were entering the Promised Land that, once they got settled, they should "blot out the remembrance of Amalek from under heaven" (Deuteronomy 25:19).

Why were the Amalekites antagonistic toward the Hebrew refugees from Egypt? See if this diagram helps explain:

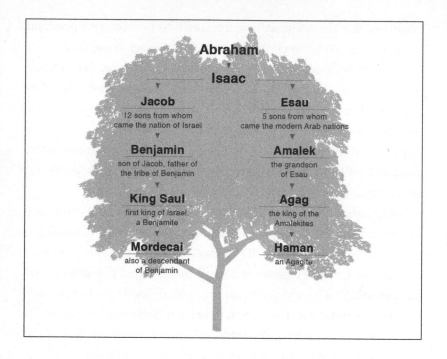

Abraham
▼
Isaac
▼
Jacob   Esau
12 sons from whom   5 sons from whom
came the nation of Israel   came the modern Arab nations
▼   ▼
Benjamin   Amalek
son of Jacob, father of   the grandson
the tribe of Benjamin   of Esau
▼   ▼
King Saul   Agag
first king of Israel,   the king of the
a Benjamite   Amalekites
▼   ▼
Mordecai   Haman
also a descendant   an Agagite
of Benjamin

Two facts in this chart have direct bearing on Haman's plan to exterminate Mordecai and all the Jews in Persia. First, Mordecai was a descendant of Jacob, and Haman was a descendant of Esau. If you recall your Old Testament history, it was because Jacob tricked his brother, Esau, that their father, Isaac, ended up giving the blessing of the firstborn to Jacob instead of Esau, to whom it rightfully belonged (Genesis 27).

The present-day antagonism of the Arab states toward the State of Israel is a continuing reflection of the murderous anger Esau initially felt toward Jacob for his deception. Ultimately Esau and Jacob reconciled, but their descendants have rarely lived peacefully together since.

Haman had a second reason for hating Mordecai and his people. Mordecai was a descendant of Kish, a Benjamite (Esther 2:5). Kish was the father of Saul, the first king of Israel. So both Saul and Mordecai descended from Kish.

As Israel's first king, Saul was commissioned by God to destroy the Amalekites for their attacks on the Jews as they journeyed from Egypt to the Promised Land.

King Saul did not fully obey this command. Instead of killing the Amalekite soldiers, all their livestock, *and* Agag the king, Saul spared the king's life and kept the best of the livestock (1 Samuel 15). That act of disobedience cost Saul the throne, and he was later killed by an Amalekite (2 Samuel 1:1–10).

The Amalekites were ultimately reduced to nothing by King David, but the years of hostility between Israel and the Amalekites would not have been forgotten by Haman in Persia centuries after Agag. So Haman (from the lines of both Esau and Agag) bore a double grudge against the Jews. When he discovered he had been snubbed by Mordecai, a Jew, he immediately saw it as an opportunity to destroy the Jews in one fell swoop, just as the Jews had destroyed his ancestors. It was too rich an opportunity to pass up. The big moment had come: It was payback time against Mordecai and the rest of the descendants of Jacob living in Persia.

Haman approached the king about ridding Persia of the Jews and presented a trumped-up list of charges about how they were multiplying, were disloyal to the king, and had no value to the Persians (Esther 3:8). Haman even offered to fund the massacre with a personal contribution of 10,000 talents of silver to the king's treasury. At today's silver prices, that's equal to about $348 million.

Ahasuerus, in an appalling display of misplaced trust or executive irresponsibility, told Haman to keep his money and do to the Jews "as seems good to you" (Esther 3:11). So Haman prepared an edict to the officials of the provinces, giving the genocidal instructions "to destroy, to kill, and to annihilate all the Jews, both young and old, little children and women, in one day...and to plunder their possessions" (v. 13).

Mordecai learned of Haman's plan, and he went into mourning for his people. When her cousin's condition was reported to Esther, she sent one of the king's advisers to see about him. Mordecai relayed to the adviser what Haman had done and begged him to ask Esther to intervene on behalf of their people, the Jews. Remember: The king did not know that his wife, Queen Esther, was a Jewess.

Royal protocol prevented supplicants from entering the king's presence unannounced, and violators were subject to the death sentence at the king's discretion. This rule extended even to the king's wives and family. So Esther told Mordecai to have the people fast for three days, and if she had not been invited into the king's presence, she would go before him uninvited. At the end of three days Ahasuerus had not requested to see Esther, so she mustered up her courage and approached the king.

Pleased to see his beautiful queen, the king granted her an audience and asked to hear her request. Esther chose not to reveal what was in her heart, but invited the king and Haman to a banquet she had prepared that very day. At the banquet, the king once again invited Esther to make her request. She answered by promising to reveal her request if the king and Haman would attend another banquet the following day.

Haman strutted out from the banquet swaggering with pride at having been included in an intimate banquet with the king and the queen of the empire. But at the palace gate he passed by Mordecai, who again did not bow to him, and immediately Haman's pride was eaten up by rage. He hurried home and had a gallows built, on which he intended to hang Mordecai immediately, ahead of the scheduled massacre.

That night, as the gallows were being built, King Ahasuerus could not sleep. So he whiled away the night by reviewing the recent records of his kingdom. He stumbled across the record of Mordecai's having saved him from the assassination plot on an earlier date and asked what had been done to repay this man for his loyalty. His advisers replied that nothing had been done.

King Ahasuerus asked if anyone was in the outer court, and he was told that Haman was there, waiting to see him. Haman had come to discuss the impending hanging of Mordecai! The king invited him to enter and immediately asked him what should be done to honor a loyal subject of the king. Haman assumed the king was planning to honor him, so he described the lavish gifts and public accolades that such a man deserved. The king agreed and told Haman to go at once, fetch Mordecai, and do for him all that Haman had described, for he was the man the king intended to honor!

Haman was stunned at this turn of events. He was mortified. He was utterly undone. But he had no choice but to obey the king. So he placed a royal robe on Mordecai, seated him on one of the king's horses, and paraded him through the streets, praising him and publicly proclaiming: "This is what is done for the man the king delights to honor!" (Esther 6:9 NIV).

That night, when the king and Haman joined Esther at her banquet, she revealed to the king that she was a Jewess and told him of Haman's plot to kill her kinsmen throughout the entire land of Persia. King Ahasuerus had Haman hanged on the very gallows he had prepared for Mordecai. For her loyalty, the king turned over to Esther Haman's vast wealth. Mordecai was made administrator of the estate and subsequently prime minister of Persia. A royal decree was issued counteracting the order to kill the Jews throughout the provinces of Persia. The king "commanded by letter that this wicked plot which Haman had devised against the Jews should return on his own head" (Esther 9:25).

God intervened. The plan of an evil official in the Persian Empire to exterminate the Jewish people in Persia was thwarted. And the king of Persia, through the influence of his Jewish queen, became the protector of the Jews.

Because of God's faithfulness to save His people, an annual two-day festival was proclaimed. The Feast of Purim is a time of celebrating, feasting, giving gifts to one another, and giving to the poor (Esther 9:21–22). Later, Esther added the features of "fasting and lamenting" to the celebration (Esther 9:31). The Feast of Purim is not mentioned again in the Bible, but it is celebrated by the Jewish people to this day.

The story of Esther in Persia is more than a story of drama and intrigue. It provides an ironic backdrop to the modern-day story of Iran's relationship to Israel. Prior to Esther's time, a series of Persian kings enabled the rebuilding of the Jewish homeland. In Esther's day, the Persian king became the protector of God's people. Contrast that with our day, when the Iranian president has become the world's most vocal and radical enemy of Israel and proposes the destruction of the Jewish state.

I believe the difference between then and now is best explained by one reality: the change of religions that occurred between the time of ancient Persia and the rise of modern Iran. It is commonly assumed that the religion of ancient Persia is the same as that of modern Iran. Nothing could be further from the truth. Esther's story occurred in the fifth century BC, when Zoroastrianism was the religion of Persia. Zoroastrianism is essentially a monotheistic religion with a belief in an uncreated creator, Ahura Mazda. A major difference between this Persian religion and Judaism was the Persians' dualistic belief in a destructive and evil energy that opposes good. Zoroastrianism remained the Persian religion until Islam conquered the Arabian Peninsula by AD 632 and the nation of Persia by AD 644.

More than a thousand years separate Esther's story from the rise of Islam in Persia. This shows us that Haman's evil motives toward Mordecai and the Jews had nothing to do with radical militant Islamic beliefs. (We have already learned what was fueling Haman's hatred.) The story of Esther reveals no hint of religious intolerance in Persia toward the Jews. Apparently the monotheistic Persians were content to allow the monotheistic Jews to live and worship alongside them.

Not so with Islam. Muslims do not think of Islam as being invented by Mohammad as we know it was. Rather, they believe that Mohammad was given the content of the Koran to call polytheistic worshippers back to true monotheism, which, in their eyes, is only the monotheism of Islam. In other words, Islam views itself as the one, true, monotheistic faith.

When Mohammad's teachings began to be spread by the sword across Arabia, the people were forced to worship the "one true God," which meant worshipping Allah according to the tenets of the Koran. And when Islam reached Persia in the seventh century AD, it wasn't enough that the monotheistic Zoroastrians in Persia worshipped one god; they had to worship Allah. The transition was gradual, but by the late tenth century AD, it was complete. Persia had become a Muslim nation.

In summary, we can draw these three conclusions that bear on today's international spread of Islam:

1. The more radical the branch of Islam, the less tolerant are its adherents toward other monotheistic faiths.
2. Islam is persistent. Muslims conquered Persia in AD 644, and by the tenth century Persia was Islamic. It took 350 years, but the conversion happened.
3. Shia Muslims, such as those who rule Iran, are not content with modern Muslims who possess a pluralistic attitude toward other religions. Their goal is the implementation of fundamentalist sharia law in all countries and cultures.

When you combine intolerance, persistence, and fundamentalism with the leverage of nuclear capability, you have a recipe for international disaster. It is a shame that modern Iran's attitude toward the Jews is not the same as that of ancient Persia; that Mahmoud Ahmadinejad has forgotten the benevolence of his forefather King Ahasuerus.

Europe and America

From what I've explained above, you can see that Iran, with its radical Islamic leadership and the potential of a nuclear arsenal, poses a threat not just to Israel but to other countries as well. Today they have begun to express particular hatred toward the European nations and the United States. Experts on Islam give three reasons for this growing anger against the West:

1. Loss of world domination
2. Loss of authority in Muslim lands
3. Loss of sanctity of the Muslim home

Many Muslims believe these losses result from Islamic peoples' adopting Western ideas and ways. While such Western ways are attractive to the masses within Muslim lands, Islamic leaders view them as subversive and an insult to Allah. Such influence by infidels—all nonfollowers of Islam—over faithful Muslims is "truly evil and unacceptable."[19]

But what about the outwardly moderate and peace-pursuing Muslims in Europe and America? Do they have the same ultimate theocratic goals as their violent Shia brothers? Or are they simply using more patient and peaceful means to someday see churches replaced with mosques and national flags of Western nations replaced with the Islamic crescent? Only God knows.

I am willing to take the word of people like General Georges Sada, a Persian Christian who rose to become the chief of the Iraqi air force under Saddam Hussein. He says, "Please understand that there are many Muslims who don't accept [the militant view] of Fatah and Jihad any longer."[20] But he also says,

I can assure you that the [militants] who are intent on destroying America won't be stopped by appeasement. They are not interested in political solutions. They don't want welfare—their animosity is not caused by hunger or poverty or anything of the sort. They understand only one thing: total and complete conquest of the West and the destruction of anyone who does not bow to them and their dangerous and out-of-date ideology of hate and revenge.[21]

While there is much we in the West may not understand about Islam, we can be sure of two things: First, that Iran is intent on creating instability in the Middle East in order to hasten the return of the twelfth imam of Islam. Second, we can also be sure that in God's future plan for Iran, there is a day coming when her theocratic hopes will be dashed. I believe the Bible clearly presents an end-time scenario that finds Iran, under the leadership of Russia, making one final attempt to destroy the Jewish people and the nation of Israel.[22]

The Battle of Gog and Magog—Ezekiel 38–39

At the beginning of the seven years of tribulation on the earth, a battle will be fought in which Russia assembles a mass of nations to attack Israel. On that list of nations you will find Persia (today known as Iran).

This battle, which is prophetically outlined in Ezekiel 38 and 39, is the most detailed prophecy concerning war in the entire Bible. I believe this invasion of Israel will occur either before or shortly after the beginning of the seven years of tribulation when Israel will sign a covenant with the Antichrist, the new leader of the European Union. Because of this agreement, Israel will be at peace with her Islamic neighbors. The people of Israel will be lulled into believing the European powers will protect them from any outside aggressor or invader, especially from Russia.

According to Ezekiel 38 and 39, Russia will lead these nations against Israel from the north for the purpose of taking a spoil and a prey from Israel. When it appears that all is lost and there is no hope for the Jewish nation, God will intervene with convulsions of the earth, confusion of the troops, contagions of diseases, and calamities from the sky.

All the armies of Israel's enemies will perish on the mountains of Israel and in the open fields. Ezekiel says the carnage will be so great that it will take Israel seven months to bury the dead (Ezekiel 39:12).

If, as I have said, these events occur at the beginning of the Tribulation period, and the Tribulation period begins immediately after the Rapture, and the Rapture, according to the Bible, could occur at any time, that means we might be on the threshold of this battle even as we speak.

God's Work in Iran Today

The utter annihilation described in that battle marks the future of Iran. But what about Iran in the present? In his *New York Times* bestselling book *Inside the Revolution*, Joel Rosenberg writes of the spiritual awakening currently taking place in the Middle East:

> You rarely even hear about it in churches in the West, in the East, or even in the Middle East. But the big, untold story is that more Muslims are coming to faith in Jesus Christ today than at any other time in history... Millions are finding that only Jesus Christ heals the ache in their hearts and the deep wounds in their souls.[23]

The stories coming out of modern-day Persia are strikingly similar to the story of Esther. What Satan has sought for his evil purposes has been turned back on his own head. Just as Haman sought to destroy the Jews and Mordecai, so Islam has attempted to drive Christianity from within Iran's borders. What is happening in Iran today almost equals the irony of the hanging of Haman on the gallows he built for Mordecai. Rosenberg records for us the words of a Christian leader in Iran:

It's ironic that when the Ayatollah Khomeini took power in Iran with his style of Islamic Shiite extremism that the true face of Islam was finally exposed not just to the Christian populace, but to the Muslims themselves... Before 1979, the demand for Bibles in Iran was never that great. Today, Iranians can't get enough of the Bible or biblical teaching. It is counterintuitive, I know, but it's as if God used that man, the Ayatollah... to expose Islam for what it is and for Muslims to say to themselves, "That's not what we want; we want something else. We want something better."[24]

An Iranian who directs one of the largest ministries of evangelism and discipleship to Shia Muslims in his country told Joel Rosenberg that he believes there are as many as seven million believers in Iran. That's about one out of every ten people.[25]

While many are coming to Christ through the showing of films like *The Passion of the Christ* or *The Jesus Film*, there are dozens more stories of people who are being brought to Christ through dreams:

One Iranian Muslim woman had a dream in which God told her, "Whatever the two women you are going to meet with tomorrow tell you, listen to them." Startled, she went through the next day curious who she would meet. She had no plans to meet anyone, but sure enough, at one point two Iranian Christian women came up to her and explained the message of salvation to her. She obeyed the Lord's directive from the dream, listened carefully, and then bowed her head and prayed to receive Christ as her Savior.[26]

I wrote about these dream claims in an earlier book and confessed that I did not know what to make of them. I am still not sure where to fit these stories into the framework of my theology, but I believe they are true and that God is doing an unusual work among the Muslim people.[27]

In his book *What Good Is God?* Philip Yancey tells about meeting believers with a Muslim background during his visit to the Middle East. Many of their conversion stories involved dreams:

One middle-aged woman told of reading the Koran and finding the prophet Jesus mysteriously attractive, even more so than Mohammed. The more she read about Jesus, the more she wanted to know him. She would hear strange words at night in her sleep: Messiah, child of God, lamb, sheep...Then she heard the words, "The truth will set you free," unaware that they came from the Christian Bible. One night she experienced a vision of Jesus beckoning her to follow. After several more such visions over the course of fourteen years, she declared herself openly as one of Jesus' followers. She spoke darkly of persecution from her family, but choked up before she could elaborate.[28]

These stories seem unorthodox to Western Christians, but before you discount their genuineness, be sure to read each story all the way to the end. Muslims who become Christians suffer rejection from their families and friends. They are often physically abused and sometimes even killed. Persecution and martyrdom are pretty effective authentications.

In this chapter we have seen why the day has come when an ancient nation, which once had no quarrel with God's people, has reared its angry head as a potential threat to the modern world. We have also seen how enemies of God can take such a nation from a coexistent stance to radical belligerence against God's people. We have also seen that no matter how high such a nation rises in power and influence, God will maintain His sovereignty as promised and save His own by bringing all His enemies to ruin on the shoals of their own pride and arrogance.

Perhaps one of the most important things we have explored is the fact that God, the persistent "hound of heaven," loves each of us as His dear creation and pursues us as individuals even inside the borders of nations hostile to Him. Iran as a nation may have risen against Him, but within that nation are people who can hear His voice when He calls and respond to Him with love and dedication.

That is why in our personal judgments we must remember who the enemy is. A given nation may have defied God, but within that nation are Christians and potential Christians who are not enemies but brothers and sisters. In our judgments we must never become "judgmental" in the sense that we make unwarranted assumptions about the power of God's Word or the length of His reach.

I remember the shock I felt several years ago when I saw a bumper sticker that asked, "Have you prayed for Saddam Hussein today?" I am sure you know what my answer was. But obviously the question has stayed with me because it requires an answer. As Christians, we are commanded to "love your enemies, bless those who curse you, do good to those who hate you, and pray for those who spitefully use you and persecute you, that you may be sons of your Father in heaven" (Matthew 5:44–45).

CHAPTER 9

When America Would Turn Her Back on Israel

If the topics I have addressed in the previous eight chapters of this book are serious, and I'm convinced they are, the topic of this chapter is *deadly* serious. Those chapters addressed a gradual decline in the quality of life in America; this chapter addresses the question of America's survival at all.

That is a dramatic statement, but not an overstatement. I believe America's future depends in large part on one simple factor: our relationship to the tiny nation of Israel.[1] And given the political trends in recent years, I believe America is putting her future at risk. We supported Israel in the mid-twentieth century when she was re-formed politically in her homeland. I never thought I'd see the day when we would abandon or diminish that support. But that day has come, and if we do not return to our previous supportive policies toward Israel, our future as a nation is in peril.

You may be wondering whether my thinking is upside down. America is the world's greatest superpower; Israel is a tiny sliver of land accommodating only a few million citizens. One would think that America is the key to Israel's survival, not the other way around. Given our history of vast military and economic aid packages to Israel over the years, it would seem that America could use the threat of withdrawn aid to leverage her influence over Israel and get that tiny nation to do whatever we want. Surely a larger benefactor nation holds in its hand the survival of a smaller dependent nation. Instead, I am saying the opposite is true: Israel is the key to America's survival. Here's why.

It is clear that America's leaders—at least in recent administrations—have not been looking at Israel with spiritual or biblical eyes. Had they done so, one small verse would have guided all their policy decisions regarding Israel: Genesis 12:3. That verse records God's promise to Abraham and his descendants:

I will bless those who bless you,
And I will curse him who curses you;
And in you all the families of the earth shall be blessed.

You would think that no national leader who reads that verse would do anything to hinder the blessing and prosperity of the Jewish people and thereby ensure judgment upon his nation. God has a perfect track record for keeping His promises—a fact irrefutably demonstrated by several thousand years of history. Yet in spite of God's well-demonstrated trustworthiness, American leaders in recent years have rationalized and justified their way into denying Israel the free expression of her sovereignty as a nation. America has tolerated and coddled, and even financially supported, some of Israel's neighbors who have openly declared that their goal is to drive the Jewish people from their homeland and scatter them back into their pre-1948 "homes" around the world—if not to exterminate them altogether.

No nation should take lightly the promise of God in Genesis 12:3— if for no other reason than self-preservation. And that includes America. Even if American leaders don't fully understand or agree with the Judeo-Christian teachings of the Bible, matching up Genesis 12:3 with the thousands of years of Israel's history should be convincing: Bless Israel and you'll be blessed; curse Israel and you'll be cursed.

God's Providence in the Story of Israel

What is so special about Israel? Why is it that this one little nation should occupy a place of such importance in the world as to be a key to the survival of other nations? To answer those questions we must look briefly at the beginnings of the nation of Israel.

While Israel is often called "God's chosen people," it is more accurate to speak of a "chosen person"—Abraham—from whose loins would come a people that would belong to God in a special way.

Rather than *choosing* an existing nation, God chose a progenitor and *created* a nation through him and his wife, Sarah. That nation became God's chosen people. The phrase "chosen people" does not occur in the Bible (NKJV), but there are abundant references in Scripture to the idea: "Blessed is the nation whose God is the LORD, the people He has chosen as His own inheritance" (Psalm 33:12).

The best summary of how and why Israel became the chosen people of God is in Deuteronomy 7:6–8:

> You are a holy people to the LORD your God; the LORD your God has chosen you to be a people for Himself, a special treasure above all the peoples on the face of the earth. The LORD did not set His love on you nor choose you because you were more in number than any other people, for you were the least of all peoples; but because the LORD loves you, and because He would keep the oath which He swore to your fathers.

Clearly, there was nothing inherent in Israel herself that caused God to embrace her as His people. Indeed, Moses spoke the words in Deuteronomy to a new generation of Israelites whose parents had been poverty-stricken slaves in Egypt for four hundred years—not exactly the kind of résumé that would make a people appealing to a God who wanted to show off His best work. Instead, Israel became the people of God for two reasons: (1) because of a promise He made to Abraham centuries before; and (2) because of God's faithful love in keeping His promises.

Here is the complete promise God made to Abraham (Genesis 12:1–3, italics added):

The LORD had said to Abram:
"Get out of your country,
From your family
And from your father's house,
To a land that I will show you.
I will make you a great nation;
I will bless you
And make your name great;
And you shall be a blessing.
I will bless those who bless you,
And I will curse him who curses you;
And in you all the families of the earth shall be blessed."

As you can see by the lines in italics, this passage contains the words of warning we are considering in this chapter.

The question arises, Why such a warning? What is so crucially important about Israel that God protects her by promising to bless her benefactors and curse her enemies? The answer is found in the words that bookend the warning: "And you [Abraham and your descendants] shall be a blessing...And in you [Abraham and your descendants] all the families of the earth shall be blessed." There it is. Through His chosen people, God intended (and intends) to bless the rest of the human family. He chose a Mesopotamian man named Abram and promised that he and his descendants would be a channel of that blessing. The entire population of Planet Earth—every man, woman, and child—was destined to be blessed through the nation of Israel. Therefore, people who recognize God's purposes for Israel and do whatever they can to preserve, protect, and defend Israel will likewise be preserved, protected, and defended. God, to whom Israel belongs, will see to it.

Conversely, people who stand in the way of Israel's prosperity—and thus to humanity's blessings—will find themselves standing in the direct path of God's purposes for Israel on earth. And history gives us the tragic story of what happens to anyone, individually or nationally, who puts himself in that unenviable position.

It is no more complicated than that. God created a people for Himself in order to bless the human family. And He will bless those who bless His people—Israel, or the Jews. Those who stand in the way of Israel, not to mention persecute Israel, will find themselves experiencing the judgment of God.

God's Promise of a Land for Israel

As we just read in Genesis 12:1–3, part of God's promise to Abraham was a land in which he and his descendants would dwell. That land was known as Canaan when Abraham first arrived there. But it became known as the Promised Land when Israel moved into it following her exodus from Egypt. Not only did God promise to Abraham the land "from the river of Egypt to the great river, the River Euphrates" (Genesis 15:18; see also Genesis 13:15, 17; 15:7; 24:7), He also promised it to Abraham's son Isaac (Genesis 26:2–5), Isaac's son Jacob (Genesis 28:13; 35:12), and Jacob's twelve sons and their descendants (Exodus 33:1–3).

We know from biblical history that Israel moved into this land and prospered exceedingly. She became a rich and powerful nation to be reckoned with under the successive reigns of her great kings David and Solomon. But then an ungodly spirit of pride and comfort set in, along with sensual temptations from the religions surrounding her, and the nation fell away from godly principles to the point that God stepped in and imposed disciplinary action. He allowed the Jewish people to be conquered and dispersed throughout the nations of the world.

Israel began moving back to the land following World War I, under the British Mandate of Palestine, and then in earnest following World War II. Tension developed between the returning Jews and the Arabs then living in the land, who did not then take, and have not since taken, kindly to Israel's "coming home." This tension came to a head when Israel's statehood was announced in 1948.

It is easy to slip into a sympathetic mode toward these occupying Arabs. But the bottom line is this: The land belongs to God (Psalm 24:1), and God gave it to His chosen people, Israel, as an "inheritance...forever" (Joshua 14:9).

To get a proper perspective on the reality of the situation, consider this illustration: You are sitting in your reserved seat at a theater production. Just before the curtain rises, you get an important call on your cell phone. So you leave your coat in your seat and go to the lobby to return the call in private. You return to discover a stranger sitting in your seat on top of your coat. The squatter refuses to leave and finally does so only after an embarrassing scene in which ushers force him to abandon a seat for which he cannot prove "ownership." You, however, have your reserved-seat ticket stub, so access to the seat is restored to you.

In that illustration, the theatergoer is Israel; the seat is Israel's homeland; the ticket is the Bible where legal assignment to the land is recorded; the temporary vacancy of the seat represents Israel's temporary absence from the land (from AD 70 to 1948; Romans 11:11–32);

the squatter represents various groups who availed themselves of the opportunity to take the land in Israel's absence; the coat represents the historical artifacts throughout the land that attest to Israel's previous habitation; and the usher, at least in 1948, is the League of Nations, followed by its successor, the United Nations, who said, "This is Israel's seat." In truth, Israel didn't get all her land back in 1948. But she got enough, including part of Jerusalem, to establish a formal presence there. She gained access to all of Jerusalem in 1967.

The Jews were not restored to their homeland because they earned the right or turned back to God. They are by no means perfect. They have so far failed as a people to corporately embrace the Messiah who came to suffer and die for them—though one day they will (Zechariah 12:10; Romans 11:26). But her lack of perfection is no reason to deny her permanent place in the plans of God. Israel remains to this day the apple of God's eye (Deuteronomy 32:10). And woe to any nation—including the world's remaining superpower—that tries to deny that fact for the sake of politics, preference, or popularity.

No race or nation has lived as long, contributed as much, and *survived as much persecution* as the Jews. No other race or nation has ever had the phrase "chosen people of God" attached to them as the Bible attaches it to the Jews. Would anyone be so bold as to say there is no connection between the Jews' uniqueness and endurance and their "chosenness"? I certainly would not. In fact, I would say the opposite: The uniqueness and the greatness of the Jewish people are a direct result of their being the chosen people of God, the apple of God's eye. It is their very existence that supports their claim to a supernatural beginning and continuance.

Thomas Newton, bishop of Bristol, England, from 1761 to 1782 and an expert in biblical prophecy, summarizes well the warning that accompanies Israel's uniqueness:

> The preservation of the Jews is really one of the most signal and illustrious acts of Divine Providence...And what but a super-natural power could have preserved them in such a manner as none other nation upon earth hath been preserved? Nor is the providence of God less remarkable in the destruction of their enemies, than in their preservation...We see that the great empires, which in their turns subdued and oppressed the people of God, are all come to ruin...And if such hath been the fatal end of the enemies and oppressors of the Jews, let it serve as a warning to all those, who at any time or upon any occasion, are for raising a clamor and persecution against them.[2]

The warning is clear: Support Israel and be blessed, or oppress her and be cursed. For America today the question is: Will we support Israel's return to her homeland and continue to aid her progress in fulfilling God's purpose to be a channel of blessing to the world?

There was a time when America answered yes to that question, and I believe America's blessing and greatness are due in part to that answer. America has been blessed because we have blessed the Jewish people in many ways since her founding in 1948. Today, however, I fear America has lost sight of her responsibility to bless the people of God. And I fear we may suffer for that loss just as many other nations have suffered in the past.

I fear that the former bishop of Bristol's warning would fall on deaf ears in Washington today. America is not persecuting Israel, but we are certainly "raising a clamor" against her desire to exist as a peaceful, productive, and sovereign nation. From his eighteenth-century vantage point on history, the bishop could survey the abundant debris that remained of nations who dared to raise a hand against the nation God handpicked as His own. And from our vantage point in history, we have even more evidence than the bishop had. How much stronger would his warning be today had he lived to see the bombed-out ruins of Germany after that nation eliminated one-third of the world's Jewish population? Yet, in spite of America's access to such overwhelming evidence, we are failing to learn from history's illustrations of the truth of Genesis 12:3: Bless Israel and be blessed; curse Israel and be cursed. And paraphrasing the Spanish philosopher Santayana, "Those who fail to learn from history's mistakes are doomed to repeat them."[3]

God's Punishment of the Enemies of Israel

The prophet Zechariah declared that God sent him to the nations that "plunder" Israel, "for he who touches [Israel] touches the apple of His eye" (Zechariah 2:8). Later, he mentions by name some who would fall under God's judgment: Hadrach, Damascus, Hamath, Tyre, Sidon, Ashkelon, Gaza, Ekron, Ashdod—a roll call of peoples that had lifted a hand against God's chosen nation (Zechariah 9:1–7). Then Zechariah says, speaking for God, "I will set up camp in my home country and defend it against invaders. Nobody is going to hurt my people ever again. I'm keeping my eye on them" (v. 8, The Message).

Just as Zechariah called the roll of ancient, local nations that cursed Israel and were in turn cursed by God, we can, from our historical vantage point, add even more ancient and modern names to the list: Egypt, the "-ite" nations surrounding the Promised Land—Amorites, Kenites, Kenezzites, Girgashites, and others. Later nations include Assyria, Babylon, Greece under Alexander the Great, the Roman Empire, Spain following the Spanish Inquisition, many modern Arab nations, and post-Holocaust Germany. Not all these nations were totally destroyed, but all suffered various degrees of judgment—and some still do today!

One nation, Great Britain, deserves an extended look because of its unique connection to Israel in modern history, as well as its connection to America's history and cultural values.

Great Britain was the last great world empire leading into the twentieth century. At its height, Great Britain controlled more land and people around the globe than any other nation in history. The British Balfour Declaration, approved in 1917, "[favoured] the establishment in Palestine of a national home for the Jewish people"[4] and pledged Britain's efforts to that end. Following World War I, the League of Nations gave Great Britain administrative oversight of much of the Middle East, including Palestine, in what was called the British Mandate of Palestine. Britain's rule lasted until 1948 when the British Mandate of Palestine ended and the United Nations partitioned Palestine into two states—Jewish and Arab. The Jews accepted the U.N. partition plan, but the Arabs did not. The U.N. declared Israel a state on May 14, 1948, one day before the British mandate ended. Civil war erupted between Jews and Arabs over land and rights, followed by major wars in 1967 and 1973. In these wars Israel gained control of even more land, further deepening Arab resentments.

Between the 1917 Balfour Declaration and the 1948 ending of the British Mandate of Palestine, Great Britain slowly but steadily withdrew her support for the regathering of the nation of Israel. At times she supported Israel while simultaneously supplying arms and support to Arabs. An award-winning 1960 movie, *Exodus*, based on Leon Uris's historical novel by the same name, pictured Britain's quandary following World War II and her desire to be free of her entanglement with the Jews. Jews all over Europe were in refugee status following World War II and were sent to detention camps in places like the island of Cyprus under British administration. These Jews wanted to get to Palestine, but the British wouldn't let them—setting up the plot of the movie. The film depicted the efforts of a Palestinian Jew to get a freighter of six hundred Jews from Cyprus to Palestine and the growing Jewish-Arab conflict they faced on arrival.

A piece of dialogue from the film captures the British predicament—dialogue between an American nurse on Cyprus and the British general in charge of the Jewish detention center:

NURSE: I saw the people on that ship. They're not dangerous. They're just poor, miserable people. Why can't you let them go?

GENERAL: You must understand that we British have shown, throughout our history, an extraordinary talent for troublesome commitments. Palestine is a British Mandate imposed upon us by the League of Nations, which makes us responsible for keeping peace in the area. The Arabs simply won't keep the peace if we allow further Jewish immigration.

NURSE: I don't know much about the Mandate. But I do know the Jews were promised a homeland in Palestine.

GENERAL: During the First World War, Britain needed and accepted Jewish support from all over the world. In return, the Balfour Declaration of 1917 made such a promise [of a home-

land]. That promise was reconfirmed during World War II...
Thousands of Palestinians [Jews] fought with us.

NURSE: How can you promise something and then not deliver it?

GENERAL: England was fighting for her life in 1917. Nations are
very like people in such circumstances. They make promises
they're not immediately able to fulfill. During that same crisis,
we made the Arabs certain assurances. Hence, they have their
claims, too. The Arabs are fanatics on the subject of Jewish
immigration. Just now, we need their goodwill.

NURSE: How is it going to end?

GENERAL: I don't know. The whole question now is before the
United Nations. I hope they solve it. The sooner I stop oper-
ating detention camps the happier I'll be. That goes for every
British officer and soldier I know.[5]

In short, Great Britain promised a Jewish homeland to the Jews
(the 1917 Balfour Declaration) and almost immediately reneged.
Through their role as administrator of Palestine, they stopped Jewish immigration that could have saved millions of lives. America's
President Roosevelt expressed to Secretary of State Cordell Hull his
consternation at Britain's backing away from the Balfour Declaration,
saying, "I was at Versailles and I know that the British made no secret
of the fact they promised Palestine to the Jews. Why are they reneging
on their promise?"[6] To gain Arab support, Great Britain made promises covering most of the Arab Middle East. Great Britain's actions, in
spite of what they had promised in 1917, severely limited Israel's ability to establish a homeland.

When the United Nations partition of Palestine came up for a vote in 1947, Great Britain abstained—she refused to take a side or a stand for Israel. Great Britain assumed that an Arab-Jewish civil war would immediately result in the Arabs' overpowering the Jews, and that would be the end of the matter. But they did not take into account God's promises to restore Israel to her homeland. Nor did they take into account God's promise in Genesis 12:3 regarding those who either bless or curse Israel. It is no surprise that one can begin charting the decline of the British Empire during the same years that they were reneging on their promise of a Jewish homeland for Israel.

The decline of modern Great Britain has not gone unnoticed. A 2009 *Newsweek* article observed,

> Suddenly, the sun that once never set on the British Empire is casting long shadows over what's left of Britain's imperial ambitions, and the country is having to rethink its role in the world—perhaps as Little Britain, certainly as a lesser Britain...As William Hague, [Prime Minister] Cameron's deputy and shadow foreign secretary, said in a recent speech: "It will become more difficult over time for Britain to exert on world affairs the influence which we are used to."[7]

God's Preservation of America Because of Israel

From America's founding, the Jews have been a welcome part of the nation. Ever since the first twenty-three Jewish immigrants landed in New Amsterdam (later New York City) in 1654, America has, for the most part, been a place of safety and prosperity for the Jewish people. It is estimated that 250 Jews were living in the American colonies in the early 1700s.[8]

It's a little-known fact that a Jewish businessman played a significant role in keeping alive General George Washington's struggling Revolutionary army. Haym Solomon was a Polish Jew who immigrated to America in 1775 and became financially successful as a broker of overseas trade deals. The British arrested him more than once for his American sympathies, but he continued to use his financial skills to raise money for the Revolution. On one occasion, Washington needed to march his army to engage the British in what proved to be the final and decisive battle of the Revolution at Yorktown. But neither Washington nor the colonial government had money to finance the campaign. Washington sent for Haym Solomon, who raised the needed funds and enabled the campaign that ended the Revolutionary War. Solomon lent the colonies today's equivalent of billions of dollars, a large part of which was supposedly never repaid.[9]

An interesting, but unverifiable legend concerns Washington's gratitude for Solomon's critical support to the colonies. Look at the Great Seal on the back of a one-dollar bill. Above the eagle's head you will see the thirteen stars, representing the thirteen colonies, arranged in such a way that, by connecting the peripheral straight lines, a six-pointed Star of David is created. Washington supposedly had this done out of gratitude to his, and America's, Jewish friend Haym Solomon.

Whether or not the Great Seal legend is true, the facts are that Jews were welcome in America from the beginning and have always played a role in America's prosperity greatly disproportionate to their numbers. Space prevents me from retelling the entire story of the mutual affection expressed between a Jewish congregation in Newport, Rhode Island, and the newly elected president George Washington. But after a visit to Newport, the president wrote to the congregation, "May the

Children of the Stock of Abraham, who dwell in this land, continue to merit and enjoy the good will of the other Inhabitants; while every one shall sit under his own vine and fig tree, and there shall be none to make him afraid."[10]

In truth, America's official posture toward Jews on American soil has always been positive. And the same can be said of America's initial posture toward the newly re-formed nation of Israel in her homeland in 1948 and the decades immediately following. Providence ordained that the occupant of the Oval Office at the moment of Israel's political rebirth on May 14, 1948, would be Harry S. Truman. In my 2008 book, *What in the World Is Going On?: 10 Prophetic Clues You Cannot Afford to Ignore*,[11] I tell the gripping story of the opposition President Truman faced from his top advisers over whether to recognize and affirm Israel's statehood. It was a watershed moment for U.S.-Israel relations. His decision would not only set the tone for the rest of his two terms, it would also set in motion a policy that would greatly influence his successors in the Oval Office.

Truman stood fast against his advisers and issued a press release stating that "the United States recognizes the provisional government as de facto authority of the new State of Israel."[12] Israel's chief rabbi, Isaac Halevi Herzog, later told Truman, "God put you in your mother's womb so that you would be the instrument to bring about the rebirth of Israel after two thousand years."[13]

Truman is not the only president to have made strong public statements backing Israel. I have read statements by many American presidents supporting the idea of Israel's right to someday be united in their ancient homeland. These include John Adams, John Quincy Adams, Woodrow Wilson, Warren Harding, Herbert Hoover, and Franklin

Roosevelt, to name only a few. More recent presidents—Eisenhower, Kennedy, Johnson, Nixon, Ford, Carter, Reagan—are also on record as supporters of the nation of Israel.

America has been Israel's best friend in the world, and I maintain that America has been blessed because of how we have blessed Israel. But something has changed, and I find it more than coincidental that America's prosperity, posture, and place in the world have begun to decline at the same time that our commitment to Israel has weakened. I fear that what happened to Great Britain over decades may now be happening to America.

A 2010 survey showed that 52 percent of Americans believed President Obama's administration is less friendly to Israel than former administrations.[14] But our pulling away from Israel didn't begin with him. President George H. W. Bush initiated the process that has come to be known as "land for peace"—pressuring Israel to give up more and more of her land to secure a promise of peace from her Arab neighbors. Beginning with the efforts of President Jimmy Carter, it seems every president has wanted his legacy to include solving the "Middle East problem." Each has been willing to chip away at Israel's sovereignty to satisfy the demands of Arab nations.

To further complicate our relationship with Israel, a new variable has provided more incentive for the United States to befriend the Arab states at her expense: oil. In my 2010 book, *The Coming Economic Armageddon*, I wrote this:

The desertion of Israel by the United States was once deemed unthinkable, but no longer. Increasingly, our nation is catering to the oil-producing nations whose product gives them an inordinate hold over our contemporary lifestyle. These nations have expressed hatred for Israel. As if to prove my point, in words not even used when speaking of proven enemies like Iran and North Korea, Secretary of State Hillary Clinton, with the apparent sanction of the administration, referred to Israel's proposal to build housing in its own capital city as "an insult to the United States." The [Jewish] Anti-Defamation League's president, Abraham Foxman, observed, "We cannot remember an instance when such harsh language was directed at a friend and ally of the United States."[15]

On June 4, 2009, after being in office only six months, President Obama provided further evidence of our cooling relationship with Israel. On his first major international trip, he spoke these words to a predominantly Arab-Muslim audience in Cairo, Egypt (note the portions I have italicized):

America's strong bonds with Israel are well known. This bond is unbreakable. It is based upon cultural and historical ties, and the recognition that the aspiration for a Jewish homeland is rooted in a tragic history that cannot be denied...
    On the other hand, it is also undeniable that the Palestinian people—Muslims and Christians—have suffered in pursuit of a homeland. *For more than sixty years they have endured the pain of dislocation.* Many wait in *refugee camps* in the West Bank, Gaza, and neighboring lands for a *life of peace and security that they have never been able to lead.* They endure the *daily humiliations—large and small—that come with occupation.* So

let there be no doubt: the situation for the Palestinian people is intolerable. America will not turn our backs on the legitimate Palestinian aspiration for dignity, opportunity, and a state of their own.[16]

The "more than sixty years" President Obama referred to is the time period from Israel's founding in 1948 to the day of his speech in Cairo. He was obviously saying that the Palestinians' "dislocation" for sixty-plus years is due to the establishment of Israel as a nation in 1948. Also note his claim that the Palestinians' "daily humiliations" are a result of the Jews' occupying the Palestinians' lands!

Who is occupying whose lands? God gave that land, and a lot more, to Israel as a permanent possession thousands of years ago. If there is any occupying going on, it is the opposite of what President Obama expressed: The Palestinians have for centuries been occupying the homeland of the Jewish people. That is not to say that there cannot be some measure of compromise between the two peoples. But it is to say that, in recent years, America's presidents have expected Israel, not the Arabs, to make the concessions. Why? Because the Arabs have simply stated that they want "their" land back and have proven that they will use violence or any other means to get it.

For example, President Bill Clinton initiated the signing of the Oslo Peace Accords on September 13, 1993, which were supposed to set forth a framework for peace between Israel and the Palestine Liberation Organization (PLO). But since the signing of the Peace Accords (through March 2010), Palestinian terrorist organizations have killed more than 1,600 Israelis and injured more than 11,000 in attacks.[17]

Yet, in spite of these demonstrated effects of our appeasement of Israel's enemies, President Obama on May 20, 2011, in a speech dubbed in advance as reaching out to the Muslim world, made this shocking proposal: "We believe the borders of Israel and Palestine should be based on the 1967 lines with mutually agreed swaps."[18] This is also the position endorsed by the terrorist organization Hamas, which is pledged to the destruction of Israel.

Israeli prime minister Benjamin Netanyahu, caught by surprise at the alarming proposal, expressed profound opposition to it, explaining that it would make Israel's security highly indefensible. A statement by distinguished Israeli scholar Barry Rubin expressed the shock and outrage of most Israelis: "President Barack Obama's speech on Middle East policy did more damage to U.S.-Israel relations than anything said by any previous president during the almost 40-year alliance between the two countries."[19]

President Obama's proposal takes on added significance when we look at the land he proposed that Israel give up. The territory west of the Jordan River, or the West Bank, as it is called, was originally carved out for the Palestinians after Israel's war for independence in 1949. Israel won it back in 1967 when the Arab nations attacked again, intent on destroying Israel. It is important to remember that Israel's claim to this land goes far beyond any political mandate or territorial grab. It was originally part of Judea and Samaria. So in calling for Israel to give up this territory, the Obama administration advocated taking away land that was originally included in God's promise to Abraham.

If America's leaders continue down a path of not "blessing" Israel, we should not expect God's blessing in return. That is what Genesis 12:3 plainly tells us. If Great Britain is any example, then one must ask: Do America's current troubles have anything to do with our lack of blessing toward Israel? My unsolicited advice to our leaders is this: Do not think the promises of God can be compromised or renegotiated at the bargaining table. God has spoken about Israel, and His words never fail to accomplish the purpose for which they were sent (Isaiah 55:11).

God's Program for the Church and Israel

Integrity demands that I address a point that I fear may be unknown to most Christians: Many church leaders—pastors, professors, Bible teachers, and others—are contributing to America's lack of faithfulness to Israel. They are preaching and teaching what is called "replacement theology." This view holds that the modern State of Israel, or the geographic land of Palestine that was once Israel's homeland, has no modern relevance; that Israel of the Old Testament has been replaced by the Church of the New Testament; that any unfulfilled Old Testament prophecies pertaining to the nation of Israel have found spiritual, rather than literal, fulfillment in the blessings of the Church through Jesus Christ.

If that is true, then what I'm saying in this chapter is wrong. But I don't believe replacement theology is biblical. Generally speaking, replacement theology denies a present and future role for Israel and the land promised to her. People holding this theology tend to adopt the following positions:

- They are amillennial rather than premillennial regarding eschatology. They do not hold to a literal rule of Christ on earth for a thousand years on the throne of David in Jerusalem as outlined in Revelation 20:1–6.

- They interpret the Bible from a "covenantal" rather than a "dispensational" (or mildly dispensational) framework. They hold only to a covenant of salvation for sinners and give no continuing credence to other biblical covenants such as the Abrahamic (concerning the descendants of Abraham), Palestinian (concerning the land), or Davidic (concerning kingship over Israel). They believe those covenants have all been spiritually fulfilled in Christ and will not be literally fulfilled.
- They trace their theological roots to the Reformed tradition, meaning Presbyterian, Lutheran, Anglican/Episcopal, Reformed Baptists, and others. Christians from those persuasions don't teach on this subject often because of the lack of certainty in interpretation. Biblical promises that were understood to be literal when first written are now to be interpreted nonliterally, which leads to "anybody's guess" as to what they might mean in modern geopolitical terms.

Adherents to replacement theology can have a mixed bag of views—seeming to embrace some literal and some nonliteral views concerning Israel. For instance, Chuck Colson said the following in a 2003 Breakpoint commentary:

As a Christian and believer in the Abrahamic covenant, I'm a strong supporter of Israel and the Jewish people. I take Genesis 12:3 literally. I also believe that Jesus will return and rule the earth for one thousand years from Jerusalem—a pre-millennial perspective on the second coming. I believe that God has a special plan for the Jewish people and the land of Israel.

But I think it is problematic to relate prophecy to current events unfolding in the nation-state of Israel. There may be some relationship, of course. Only God knows. But the secular state of Israel created in 1948 is not, in my understanding, identical with the Jewish people as God's chosen and called-out covenant people.

God clearly has a distinct plan for the Jewish people that the secular state of Israel helps carry out. I don't rule that out, of course. And I strongly support Israel because it is a haven for persecuted Jews—not because I think it fulfills biblical prophecy.

I also support a Palestinian state both from historical and prudential considerations. Given the state of affairs in the Middle East, a Palestinian state is the only practicable solution for peace.[20]

Chuck Colson is right about many, many issues, especially where the Bible touches modern culture. But I believe his view on Israel raises more questions than it answers. Colson's first paragraph seems to affirm what you've read in this chapter. But after that things get confusing. To whom does Genesis 12:3 apply today if one doesn't recognize the State of Israel as being the descendants of Abraham? Using phrases like "there may be some relationship" and "I don't rule that out" is not helpful in establishing an actionable theological perspective on Israel. And saying "only God knows" is equivalent to saying "God doesn't want us to know." I believe the Scriptures are given so that we *can* know. When the Bible speaks plainly, there is no reason not to interpret it plainly.

I agree with Colson that there is much about the present State of Israel that is carnal. But the same criticisms could have been applied to the church at Corinth that Paul rebuked for its lack of spiritual maturity. Would those who believe the Church replaced Israel or see no connection between the modern State of Israel and God's prophetic plans take the Genesis prophecy more seriously if there was a genuine spiritual movement happening in Israel? Would this convince them that the Jews truly are God's chosen people, whom we'd better support or suffer the consequences? Well, that day is coming:

All Israel will be saved, as it is written:

"The Deliverer will come out of Zion,
And He will turn away ungodliness from Jacob;
For this is My covenant with them,
When I take away their sins."

(Romans 11:26–27, italics added)

To say that modern Israel is only a secular state and therefore God is not at work in her would be equivalent to discounting the gradual changes we see in an individual whom God is drawing closer and closer to Himself. God has been at work for thousands of years in Israel. We need to step back from the trees and look at the forest as a whole. What has happened in Israel since 1948 is nothing short of miraculous when viewed from the perspective of AD 70 when the Jews were last in Jerusalem.

I do not deny that much of Israel's life as a nation has been characterized by carnality, proving her need for the Messiah she rejected.

The Jewish people have experienced spiritual high points, but those have been the exception rather than the rule. The Israel we see regathered in the land today—secular, self-absorbed, struggling, with religion taking a backseat to political survival—is not very different from the Israel of old. Yet it is this same Israel through which God fulfilled His promise to bless the world—primarily through the gift of the Savior and Messiah, Jesus Christ.

And it is this Israel that fits *exactly* the pattern laid out by the apostle Paul in Romans 11: They are temporarily outside God's blessing while the Gospel is delivered to the Gentiles, after which "all Israel will be saved" (Romans 11:26). Why is this true? Because "*the gifts and the calling of God are irrevocable*" (v. 29, italics added). God called Israel to Himself (Isaiah 43:1) and has called Gentiles to share in the blessings delivered to the world through her (Romans 11:11–21; 1 Peter 2:9). And that calling has not been revoked.

God told Israel through the prophet Jeremiah that there was only one condition under which Israel would cease to be a nation before Him: if the universe imploded.

Thus says the LORD,
Who gives the sun for a light by day,
The ordinances of the moon and the stars for a light by night,
Who disturbs the sea,
And its waves roar
(The LORD of hosts is His name):
"If those ordinances depart
From before Me, says the LORD,
Then the seed of Israel shall also cease

From being a nation before Me forever."
Thus says the LORD:
"If heaven above can be measured,
And the foundations of the earth searched out beneath,
I will also cast off all the seed of Israel
For all that they have done, says the LORD."
(Jeremiah 31:35–37, italics added)

Until those conditions are met, those who choose to replace Israel in their theology stand corrected by the Word of God.

God's Plan for the Peace of Israel

I began this chapter saying that Israel is the key to America's survival. I hope you now understand better why I make that claim. And I hope you have been moved to a more biblical understanding of Israel's place—in the past and in the present—in God's plans and purposes.

All the changes I have discussed in the preceding eight chapters are immeasurably important in terms of our lives, and especially the lives of our children and grandchildren. But those changes are in a different category than that of America's relationship to Israel. I do not believe that the promise of Genesis 12:3—the blessing or cursing of nations relating to Israel—is an isolated binary event. That is, I do not think God's blessing is the equivalent of an "on/off" switch in terms of America's treatment of Israel. It is not likely that if our relationship with Israel is on, He blesses us regardless of how depraved and ungodly our lives may be. Nor is it likely that if the Israel switch is off, our doom is sealed even if we are otherwise the most moral and upright people on the planet. There are obviously other areas of life that factor into our being blessed or not: America's morality, stewardship of finances, and spiritual priorities, for example. It is impossible to isolate any one factor in our national life and assign it to a given state of favor or disfavor in God's sight at any moment in time.

Yet Scripture makes it clear that to the degree America stands with, befriends, supports, and defends God's chosen people, to that degree America will enjoy the favor of God. If while supporting Israel we as a people descend into immorality and secularism, God may, in His love, chastise us and bring us to our knees in order that we may see our error and turn back to Him. Such chastisement and restoration would be a blessing much like that bestowed on Israel throughout her history. But if we make that descent into depravity and at the same time abandon Israel, we can expect to experience the same doom that has descended on Israel's enemies since the inception of that nation.

Be that as it may, this I know: Genesis 12:3 promises that God blesses those who bless Abraham's Jewish descendants. As a citizen of America, I want to enjoy the favor of God upon my nation. Were I a political leader of America, it would be incumbent on me to lead the nation in such a way as to invite His favor. So why would I knowingly diminish America's support of the one nation to which God ties His promise of blessing or cursing? The histories of nations that have abused the Jewish people provide more than enough examples of the inevitable doom brought down upon their own heads.

You and I can do two things to influence America's support of Israel: First, we can use whatever means are available to influence those who establish national policies in Washington. We can vote, write letters, or call our senators and representatives—in short, fulfill the dream of the founders who wanted our nation to be governed "by the consent of the governed." *We* are the governed who need to make our voices heard by saying, "The United States simply needs to recognize that Israeli lands belong to the Jewish people and that Jerusalem is, indeed, the capital of Israel—and has been ever since God declared it to be so."[21]

Second, we can pray, both for our leaders (1 Timothy 2:1–4) and for "the peace of Jerusalem" (Psalm 122:6). As the spiritual children of Abraham, Christians everywhere can enter into the spirit of Psalm 122, which David wrote to express his heart for the city upon which God has chosen to place His name:

When they said, "Let's go to the house of GOD,"
my heart leaped for joy.
And now we're here, O Jerusalem,
inside Jerusalem's walls!
Jerusalem, well-built city,
built as a place for worship!
The city to which the tribes ascend,
all GOD's tribes go up to worship,
To give thanks to the name of GOD—
this is what it means to be Israel.
Thrones for righteous judgment
are set there, famous David-thrones.
Pray for Jerusalem's peace!
Prosperity to all you Jerusalem-lovers!
Friendly insiders, get along!

Hostile outsiders, keep your distance!
For the sake of my family and friends,
I say it again: live in peace!
For the sake of the house of our God, [GOD],
I'll do my very best for you.

(The Message)

CHAPTER 10

When Changing Your Mind Could Save Your Life

Not infrequently these days, I will hear someone express a variation on this theme: a longing to return to the "good old days." They are thinking wistfully about a time that was happier and less stressful, simpler and less complicated.

Have you noticed that no one who longs for the good old days seems to know exactly when those days were? They were the days that came before today—days lodged vaguely somewhere in the past. The implication is, of course, that life has never been as complicated and perilous as it is today.

When someone my age refers to the good old days, it's usually a reference to the 1950s. That's the decade of my childhood, and if I can trust my memory, it was indeed different from the decade we have just completed. World War II was over, the economy was on a roll, military personnel were back home starting new families (the baby boomers were conceived in the fifties), a conservative political and cultural wind was blowing, and life was good. At least, it was a lot better than life in wartime.

Then came the 1960s, when young people rebelled against the status quo and the Vietnam War, then the seventies when the nation tried to figure out what the sixties meant, and then the eighties—the so-called Decade of Greed. By the time the 1990s arrived—the Digital Decade—the good old days appeared as a faint image in the rearview mirror of life. Then came the first decade of the twenty-first century, when society started pulling down long-standing pillars upon which our nation was built. That's when many people became alarmed and started polishing that mirror to the past, trying to recapture something they felt they had lost. The changes of the last two or three decades came so fast and furious that we began to long for a simpler, quieter, more predictable time in which to live.

The past is not always as rosy as our memories make it. I believe much of the nostalgia for the good old days stems from selective memory. Our minds tend to latch on to the good memories and filter out the rest. In reality, the fifties were not exactly a carefree decade.

It only seemed that way at first because World War II had ended. The 1940s had been a decade of a "hot war," but the 1950s were the decade of the Cold War. People tend to forget that during the 1950s, the United States and the former Soviet Union aimed enough nuclear missiles at each other to completely destroy both nations. It was the decade of nuclear-attack drills in American schools and fallout shelters in American backyards. Americans went to bed at night wondering if they would wake up to a nuclear holocaust.

My point is this: There is no such thing as the good old days! Because life seems to get more and more complicated with every passing year, we all think it would be nice to reverse the passage of time and revert to the goodness we had yesterday. And never has that been truer than now.

In 2007 I had no idea I would write four books over the next four years dealing with the crises in our world. But neither did I (nor anyone else) foresee the massive economic tsunami that swept over the shores of nations around the world. The title of my 2008 book—*What in the World Is Going On?*—said it all. Never in our lifetimes had people felt more confused and uncertain over the chaos they were witnessing. Never had they seen America experience such upheaval— the ripple effects are still being felt today. And many, including myself, believe that the worst is yet to come, as I explained in my 2010 book, *The Coming Economic Armageddon*.

The economic upheaval beginning in 2008 was, in my view, symptomatic of greater and even more dangerous changes that had occurred in the previous several decades. Financial and economic activities that led to the collapse of 2008 were in many cases deceitful and immoral—indicative of a society that had lost its moral and spiritual compass. Any nation that is drowning in debt, at war around the world, and in danger of losing her status as an example to other nations clearly has serious problems at home.

In the preceding nine chapters, I have explained some of the evidences of American disintegration that cause me great concern—things whose day I never thought I would see. This does not mean I am a pessimist; I am not. But I am a realist. You have waded through lots of statistics and historical narrative in this book by which I have documented the alarming reality of our situation as a nation. My goal has been to hold up a mirror and say, "Here's where we are—and it is not where many of us would like to be."

Though there are still plenty of secular humanists who believe man is either capable of solving his own problems or capable of surviving whatever collapse our problems produce, I am not one of them. In that respect, I am a pessimist. I am pessimistic about man's ability, independent from his Creator-God, to solve the problems he creates—especially problems of enormous scale such as those our nation and the world face today.

I am, however, an optimist about God. And it is toward Him that we must turn our attention in this final chapter. But first I must sharpen the definition of *optimism* on the whetstone of biblical realism. By optimism in God, I do not mean that I expect God to swoop down and erase our massive debts; put an end to threats of terrorism; cause a spiritual revival to sweep the nation that impacts schools, government, and commerce; and return America to the good old days. I don't think that's biblically realistic, and it's not a lack of faith that causes me to say so.

Rather, as I read my Bible I find compelling reasons to believe that the human race is on a collision course with calamity—that things are going to get worse before they get better, which will not happen until the return of Jesus Christ to earth. I believe the Bible teaches that in the last days of this age, only the return of Christ will keep humanity from destroying itself.

So what is there to be optimistic about? I am optimistic about God's ability to keep you and me from being conformed to the chaos around us. I am optimistic about God's ability to transform us—to raise us higher as the world sinks lower.

Regardless of what happens in the future, I need that protection from conformity and that power to be transformed. And I need it *today*! Even if the intensity of the storms around us doesn't increase in my lifetime or yours, they are bad enough today to make me know that I need protection and power to endure. I do not know God's timetable for America or the world. The return of Christ could be further away than I think it is, and this period of crisis that threatens us now may temporarily smooth itself out. Indeed, I hope it does. I do not wish ill upon my nation or the world.

But the truth is, even in the best of times—even in the good old days—this world is not our friend. It has been usurped by Satan, and we need to defend ourselves against being conformed to it. We need to be constantly in the transformative process of becoming more like Jesus Christ regardless of what is happening around us.

This protection from conformity and power to be transformed is the only way to find peace and joy in this life. If we allow our well-being to depend on external circumstances—our financial security, our comfort, the satisfaction of material or sensual desire, or our health, we consign ourselves to lives of anxiety over events we cannot control. We are dependent on a world that cannot offer the ultimate security and meaning we desire. The only solution is to follow a different path from that of the disintegrating world around us.

I know this is true because the apostle Paul wrote about this very protection from conformation and power for transformation nineteen hundred years ago in his letter to the Christians in Rome. Those believers were living under the hateful eye of emperors such as the demoniacal Nero, who made sport of persecuting them. And to those beleaguered believers who were no doubt already sacrificing much, Paul gave what must have sounded like the strangest advice: In order not to be conformed, and in order to be transformed, you must sacrifice yourselves.

Sacrifice yourselves? They must have wondered what in the world Paul meant. To anyone living in the first-century Mediterranean world, sacrifice was an ever-present reality. The slit throats, draining carcasses, and burning flesh of sacrificial animals were common in every city with a pagan temple. Every loyal Mediterranean Jew who made his or her way to Jerusalem for the annual celebrations to Yahweh was also familiar with the bloody ritual of sacrifice. The only redeeming aspect of sacrifice was that worshippers were glad it was the animal they contributed lying on the altar, and not themselves.

Yet Paul's words in Romans 12:1–2 changed all that. Paul told them (and he tells us) that protection against conformity and power to be transformed can happen only if we sacrifice ourselves:

> I beseech you therefore, brethren, by the mercies of God, that you present your bodies a living sacrifice, holy, acceptable to God, which is your reasonable service. And do not be conformed to this world, but be transformed by the renewing of your mind, that you may prove what is that good and acceptable and perfect will of God.

As we will see in this chapter, these two verses give us all the answers we need to be optimistic, at peace, and even filled with joy as we face the problems I've addressed in the previous nine chapters.

Those chapters were lectures on the state of our nation and the world; I want this chapter to be a conversation. Those chapters were filled with challenging facts and realities; in this chapter you will find encouragement. Those chapters brought us face-to-face with what man does; I now want you to see what God can do. And specifically, what God can do in *you* if you will heed the apostle Paul's admonition to sacrifice yourself for Him.

A New Kind of Sacrifice

Let's begin by defining the most arresting word in the passage: *sacrifice*. Romans 12:1 tells us to "present your bodies a living sacrifice." The idea of sacrifice is not readily embraced in our modern society.

To illustrate, think about the economic downturn that began in 2008. It came to light with the collapse of the housing market—the subprime housing debacle. Unscrupulous lenders provided mortgages to unqualified borrowers who could not afford the payments. Loans were so easy to get that greedy investors bought property sight unseen for the sole purpose of "flipping" it at a profit in the soaring real estate market. Investment banks bundled these worthless mortgages and sold them to investors. Other banks issued insurance policies guaranteeing the worth of the bundled mortgages. It was a greed-based house of cards built on bad credit, and it came crashing down on the country. People lost their homes and their jobs, companies laid off workers, and—like throwing gasoline on a fire—our government began printing money to stimulate the economy. The U.S. Treasury began selling bonds to the U.S. Federal Reserve bank, which paid for them with newly printed dollars—the classic case of "robbing Peter to pay Paul."

It all started because no one was willing to sacrifice—to say no to the allure of a bigger, newer home they couldn't afford; to say no to the fees generated by writing mortgages for unqualified borrowers; to say no to the fees from selling bundled mortgages; to say no to the fees from insuring those bundled mortgages. Because no one was willing to sacrifice immediate desires for the sake of long-term integrity, we ended up where we are today.

We have been trained by our culture not to believe in sacrifice—to believe instead that we can have it all. And this carries over to our spiritual lives. As Christians, we have a healthy regard for the sacrifice Jesus Christ made for us two thousand years ago by willingly laying down His life. But we think of sacrifice as "won and done"—since He won that victory by sacrificing Himself, it's not something we are called to do.

So when the twenty-first-century Church reads Paul admonishing her to "present your bodies a living sacrifice" to God, it doesn't sit too well—if for no other reason than because we're Americans. It doesn't fit the kind of life we all enjoy. We have everything we need either at our fingertips or at the nearby shopping mall, where we can get it instantly just by sliding a plastic card. We're not used to having to sacrifice for much of anything.

If *sacrifice* is such a foreign word in this land of instant abundance, maybe we'd better talk a little about just what that word really means. *Sacrifice* always means one of two things:

- Somebody has to pay.
- Somebody has to die.

If you are the one being called to sacrifice yourself—depending on the sacrifice called for—either you have to pay or you have to die.

Let's say you and your spouse bought tickets to a play, and on the way to the theater you come upon a serious accident that just happened. There are injuries, and you have had a little emergency medical training. So you stop, call 911, and render aid while awaiting the EMTs. Before it's over your good suit is dirty, you're hot and sweaty, and you've missed half the play. So you have no choice but to return home.

You have sacrificed in the sense that you had to pay. Helping another person cost you something. You paid in resources you possessed—time and skill—and you also paid the price of missing the play. You sacrificed.

Paying is one kind of sacrifice; now let's look at the other kind.

Charles Dickens's novel *A Tale of Two Cities* is set in the bloodiest days of the French Revolution when aristocrats—even innocent ones—are executed under the guillotine by the ruling mob. The hero, Sydney Carton, saves Charles Darnay, a truly noble aristocrat, by slipping into the prison where Darnay is held, drugging him, exchanging clothing, and having him slipped out of the prison. The next day Sydney Carton is executed under the guillotine. His sacrifice called for him to die.

These two stories illustrate the realistic definition of the word *sacrifice*. We pay with time, talent, or treasure, or we pay with our very lives.

Those two forms of sacrifice are easily understood, but Paul shocked his Roman readers by introducing to them (and to us) an altogether new idea—the idea of a "living sacrifice."

To be a living sacrifice actually combines the two common

meanings of *sacrifice*. The term includes the word *living*, yet we are called on to die. That's what it means to become a Christian. We die to the people we were when we lived by the power of the sinful nature we inherited from Adam. The old self is laid upon the altar and "killed." In its place, we receive the indwelling of the Holy Spirit, by which we live a new kind of life.

Living that new life involves the other definition of *sacrifice*. Since we "died" to our old selves, we are now new creatures, no longer living under the selfish power of the sinful nature. As new creatures we live a new kind of life, one directed by the power of the Holy Spirit and God's Word. That new life will be one of giving—of sacrificing our resources, our self-centered wants, our time, for the sake of the kingdom of God.

This radical concept of self-sacrifice, which is the first idea introduced in Romans 12:1–2, is a prerequisite to the second idea: the renewing of our minds. And it is the renewal of our minds that will keep us from being conformed to the world in which we live. We cannot separate the idea of sacrifice from the concept of renewal: *No one's mind will be renewed whose body has not first been given as a living sacrifice to God.*

As we can see, these two verses in Romans 12 give us a three-step process: (1) We sacrifice ourselves to God. This empties us of self so that God's Holy Spirit can step in and (2) transform us by renewing our minds. (3) This transformation will enable us to keep from being conformed to the deadly values of the world.

A Radical Decision

Needless to say, the decision to sacrifice one's self is a radical one. Dickens's Sydney Carton surely had to spend considerable time in thought before he decided to give his life for another person. Giving one's life is a pretty big deal. The martyrs for Christ who died in Roman arenas, at the stake, or under the sword could have avoided their fate simply by renouncing Christ. But they made the radical decision that their commitment to God was worth far more than their lives.

The call of Paul in Romans 12:1 to sacrifice ourselves demands this kind of radical decision. We are called to give up something—to turn our backs on our former lives and put ourselves in the hands of God, who does not guarantee that we will retain the comfort, lifestyle, or ease we've been used to having. It's a call for a radical decision.

In verse 1 when Paul calls for this decision, the first clue that he is about to say something important is the presence of the word *therefore*. We have to know what that word is "there for" in order to understand what follows. "Therefore" always connects what immediately precedes it with what immediately follows. So what did Paul say prior to Romans 12:1 that led him to call for this radical decision?

This Radical Decision Is Crucial

In chapters 9 through 11 of Romans, Paul develops a sweeping view of God's redemptive plan for Jews and Gentiles. In those three chapters, which immediately precede the word *therefore* in 12:1, the word *mercy* occurs nine times. It occurs not a single time in chapters 1 through 8. So something of critical importance is being presented in chapters 9 through 11 that has to do with mercy. Quite simply, it is that both Jews and Gentiles are saved by the mercy of God, "that He might make known the riches of His glory on the vessels of mercy, which He had prepared beforehand for glory" (Romans 9:23).

And what is mercy? It is the withholding of deserved punishment or retribution.

Mercy is not getting something bad we deserve.
Grace is getting something good we don't deserve.

The Roman Christians to whom Paul wrote (and we as well) were "vessels of mercy" on whom God chose to bestow the grace and favor of salvation. We deserved judgment because of our sin, yet God chose to have mercy upon us and save us by giving His Son to die the death we deserved.

In verse 1 of chapter 12, Paul shows the connection between God's mercy and our self-sacrifice: "I beseech you therefore, brethren, by the mercies of God, that you present your bodies a living sacrifice." In other words, in view of the mercy God has offered you, here is what you need to do in response: Sacrifice yourself to Him. Kill your old sin-infested self and open yourself to this new life He offers by His loving mercy.

That requires a decision on our part, and it's a crucial one. Will we open ourselves to the new life and mercy God offers? Or will we refuse to make the sacrifice and turn our backs on it?

The primary point of C. S. Lewis's book *The Great Divorce* is that God's mercy is free, and we must make the crucial decision to either accept it or reject it. He does not *send* anyone to eternal punishment or eternal reward. Each goes to his final destination by his own choice. Lewis's story shows that all people are offered heaven, but many choose to reject it, preferring to retain instead some pleasure, some comfort, some pet activity. They choose to sacrifice nothing. They will not make the crucial decision to accept God's mercy.

This Radical Decision Is Comprehensive

Paul asks us to present our *bodies* as a living sacrifice—not our time or talent or treasure or some other compartment of our lives, but our bodies. That's Paul's way of saying, "Present your whole self to God—all that you are and have." Paul refers to the body eleven times in Romans as a reference to the totality of who we are as persons.

We get a clear picture of what Paul means by "present your body" when we compare Romans 12:1 with a similar term used in Romans 6:13. Here Paul exhorts Christians not to "present your members as instruments of unrighteousness to sin, but present yourselves to God as being alive from the dead, and your members as instruments of righteousness to God." "Members" refers to body parts, a euphemism for one's whole self. Taking these two verses together, we can see that rather than presenting our whole selves to sin, we are to present our whole selves to God as living sacrifices.

We who live in modern societies are used to dividing our lives into a multitude of compartments. But making religion one of the subdivisions of our lives will not work at all. To have any meaning, our relationship to God must form the foundation of every facet of our lives. It must permeate every relationship, every decision, every action. That means we sacrifice our own wills in all these areas. God calls us to give everything to Him as a living sacrifice. It is a comprehensive decision.

This Radical Decision Is Costly

When a Jew selected a spotless animal from his flock to offer as a sacrifice to the Lord, there was one thing he knew for sure: He would not return home with that animal. The very definition of the word *sacrifice* means giving up something forever. Even if we sacrifice our time or talent or financial resources, what we give is gone forever. We will never get it back. Therefore, the idea of presenting ourselves to God as living sacrifices requires us to think carefully about the costs involved.

Jesus did not pull any punches when He told the crowds of the cost involved in following Him. He warned that it might cost them the love of their families; it might even cost them their lives. Because the price could be so great, He warned them not to be like a builder who doesn't count the cost of his project before beginning, or like a king who goes to battle without being sure his army is strong enough to win the victory (Luke 14:25–33). A serious commitment to Christ requires putting oneself on the sacrificial altar. And as Jesus told His disciples, He does not want quitters: "No one, having put his hand to the plow, and looking back, is fit for the kingdom of God" (Luke 9:62).

Someone once said, "The problem with living sacrifices is that they keep crawling off the altar!" That's what a quitter does, and that's why we must count the cost before presenting ourselves to God as living sacrifices. We do not know what lies ahead in our lives, the life of our nation, or the life of our world. Our faith might be tested in ways it has never before been tested. The time to count the cost and make the decision is now, before those difficult times come.

A father I know raised three daughters, all of whom married godly Christian men. When his girls began dating, the father talked to them about sexual pressure and making the right decisions: "If you wait until the moment of temptation to decide whether to stop or proceed, you've waited too long. Your aroused feelings will overpower your resolve. So, it is important that you make chastity your personal commitment before you contemplate dating any boy. A decision made in advance will be solidly in place before you need it, and it will hold you back from entering into even the first stages of 'harmless' sensual behavior."

Girls who make this decision will pay a price. Some boys will never call them for a second date. They will "miss out" on the experiences their girlfriend peers boast about at slumber parties. But what they will gain outweighs what they lose like a pot of gold outweighs a feather.

If we don't count the cost in advance and make that costly decision to follow Christ, we may find ourselves capitulating to the pressures of this world almost at the moment they arise. Without making that costly decision, we will become conformed to the world instead of transformed.

This Radical Decision Is Creative

When we make the decision to sacrifice ourselves, we are telling God that we are willing to be His personal representatives on earth, to be open to His will and to do it. But I am often asked, especially by young people, how to find the will of God for one's life. I tell them the same thing my father told me as a young man: "David, get the car moving. It's a lot easier to steer a moving car than one that's sitting still." In other words, you already know enough of the will of God to get you started in serving the Lord. The Bible is filled with it. These are things everyone is enjoined to do and not do—don't lie, don't steal, don't cheat, love your neighbor as yourself, love God—the commandments and related instructions on living a godly life.

Yet each of us has a unique role to play in reflecting the nature of God. That's why God created each of us with unique abilities. This means that within the "generic" will of God, He has a specific will for you. How you find that plan is simply to follow my father's advice: "Get the car moving." We fulfill God's will for every Christian by giving, studying, encouraging others, serving where needs exist, worshipping, and keeping ourselves unstained by the world. And in the midst of that service, God will begin to reveal new, creative directions for you personally. Make the decision to do what you know of His will, and the creative parts that apply to your particular life will begin to flow.

This Radical Decision Is Credible

Paul says that presenting yourself to God as a living sacrifice is "your reasonable service." What? You call giving up all you have and maybe even your life *reasonable*? Well, yes, considering the sacrifice Christ made for us, I'd say that what He asks in return is quite reasonable.

One thing I love about the phrase "a reasonable service" is that Paul does not discount the involvement of the mind in the process of becoming a living sacrifice. Such a commitment is reasonable. The Greek word for reasonable is *logikos*, the root of our English word *logical*. In other words, it is reasonable, logical, credible. It makes perfect sense that in light of God's mercy toward us we would present ourselves to Him as living sacrifices.

The opposite also follows logically: It is unreasonable for a Christian *not* to present his or her whole life to God as a living sacrifice. Indeed, not living wholly and sacrificially for God calls into question whether one really understands or has experienced the mercy of God at all. How could anyone receive God's mercy—that is, *not* receive God's judgment for sin—and not want to live wholly for the God who has granted that mercy?

A Rational Determination

Sacrifice is not a pretty word. It means losing something valuable— one's time, energy, resources, wants, or even one's life. Why should we make such a sacrifice? What makes it worthwhile? What is the benefit? Sacrificing one's self is too big a step to take without having a very good reason to do it. We touched briefly on the reason early in the chapter—we sacrifice ourselves in response to the mercy God offers us and to have our lives transformed. Now we want to flesh out that reason more fully.

When we lay ourselves on the altar, we open ourselves to the new life God gives us through the Holy Spirit. This means we have new power, new direction, a new goal, a new standard of behavior, a new standard for relationships. The old standard was conformity to this world, but the new standard is to "be transformed by the renewing of your mind." It is our sacrifice—our death to the old sinful self—that submits us to God so we can undergo this transformation.

This transformation, though accomplished by the power of God, does not occur automatically. God does not violate our free will, which is why a personal decision is involved. After making the radical decision to present yourself to God as a living sacrifice, you are now qualified and prepared to make a rational determination—to not be conformed to the world but to be transformed by the renewing of your mind. First, total sacrifice; then, total transformation.

This transformation is vital, for it determines your response to everything we've addressed in this book. It enables you to live through whatever comes without fear or anxiety—more than that, it enables you to live joyfully. Fail to make this transformation, and you will find yourself vulnerable in the nine arenas of life I have discussed in this book. You will be weakened and unable to stand against the conforming powers of this world. Slowly but surely you will find yourself...

- questioning the very existence of God;
- victimized by Satan in spiritual warfare;
- fearful of identifying publicly with Jesus Christ;

- questioning the necessity for entering into, or remaining in, marriage;
- lowering your moral standards;
- spending less and less time reading and studying the Bible;
- becoming disinterested in and uncommitted to your local church;
- growing fearful and confused about the rise of rogue nations like Iran;
- putting America at risk by growing complacent about the future of the Jews.

The reversals I documented in the preceding chapters are realities I never thought I would see in my life as a Christian in America. Yet these changes are fully upon us and growing more prevalent with each passing year. Only persons who make a rational determination to *not* be conformed to these trends will survive with spiritual and personal integrity intact.

That is exactly the twofold determination Paul presents: "Do not be conformed to this world, but be transformed by the renewing of your mind" (Romans 12:2). That's the choice—to be either conformed or transformed. Let's look at what these two options mean.

Do Not Be Conformed

A little study in Greek will help us here:

- "Be conformed" is from a compound Greek word, *suschematizo*, which combines *sun* (with, together with) and *schema* (figure, shape, appearance). "To be conformed," then, means "to become together with (like) another figure or shape." In the

New Testament, *suschematizo* appears only in Romans 12:2 and 1 Peter 1:14, where the word refers to conformity to the world (Romans) and conformity to the lusts of the world and flesh (1 Peter).

• In both Romans and 1 Peter, the word appears in the passive voice. That means pressure to conform comes from a source outside ourselves. We do not "conform"; we are "conformed" by outside pressure.

Paul commands the believers in Rome not to allow the world to conform them to its agenda, values, culture, norms, priorities, or expectations. The force pushing at us from the culture to "be conformed" is powerful and unrelenting, like the massive flood of water pouring over Niagara Falls. Water is thundering over the edge of that waterfall at this very moment. It will be thundering tonight, tomorrow, next week, next month, and next year. It is loud and powerful and unstoppable. No individual in his own strength can do a single thing to stop the force of that natural flood.

That is why Paul used the passive voice. It would do no good to tell us not to conform, as if we could resist this force by our own power. He tells us instead not to be conformed, which indicates that in spite of our own inability to resist, there is a way to avoid being swept away by this unrelenting force. More about that in a moment.

Perhaps the most vivid translation of Romans 12:2 is in the paraphrase by the late English bishop J. B. Phillips, *The New Testament in Modern English*: "Don't let the world around you squeeze you into its own mould." That is a perfect picture of the pressure that the world applies constantly to every person on the planet—including Christians.

Eugene Peterson's paraphrase from *The Message* gives us another helpful slant: "Don't become so well-adjusted to your culture that you fit into it without even thinking." I find the phrase "without even thinking" extremely helpful. The pressure is so constant, so ongoing, so pervasive that it becomes part of the environment and we no longer notice it. I've heard that the malodorous reek of old tanners' shops was so strong it would make visitors sick. But the tanners who worked within the shops did not notice the smell at all. They had grown accustomed to the odor and thought nothing about it.

How many of us are guilty of fitting in better in the kingdom of this world than in the kingdom of God because we have stopped thinking about the difference?

But Be Transformed

If, as we have noted, we do not have the power to resist the world's unrelenting pressure to conform us to its mind-set, how can we respond to Paul's admonition not to be conformed? He provides the answer in the very next phrase of Romans 12:2: "but be transformed."

To get the full picture of what that means, let's go back to Greek grammar school for a moment:

- "Be transformed" is translated from the word *metamorphoo*, which is a compound made up of *meta* (together with, accompanied by) and *morphoo* (to form). Literally, it means "be formed with"; or in our English, "transformed." From this compound word comes our word *metamorphosis*, which, as we all learned in school, is the name of the process whereby a caterpillar turns into a butterfly.

- In its four uses in the New Testament, *metamorphoo* is always rendered in the passive voice. That means no one transforms himself, but he is transformed by a process initiated by a power outside himself.

In this verse God has given us two commands. Obeying the second command gives us the power to obey the first:

- DO NOT be conformed by the power of the world around you. That power comes from Satan.
- DO submit to the process of transformation. The power to do that comes from God and His Word.

Before we go on, let's pause and connect the links we have forged so far. Our overarching need is to learn how we can live positive, optimistic lives concerning our future while living in a disintegrating society that threatens to take us down with it. The first step is to give ourselves over to God by sacrificing our lives to Him. This submission to Him makes us available for His power and His Word to come into our lives and transform us into a new kind of creature with a new way of thinking. This transformation enables us to resist the growing tide of culture and live by a higher standard that promises peace and joy in spite of all the turmoil about us.

Now we have one more step to make the process complete. What are the means by which this transformation is accomplished?

A Rigorous Discipline

In the phrase following Paul's admonition to be transformed, he tells us how this is to be done: "Be transformed by the renewing of your mind" (Romans 12:2). Just what does it mean to renew one's mind?

A friend of mine in North Carolina was once driving through the mountains in search of an old farmhouse to purchase and renovate. He came around a bend in the road and there it was, standing in a beautiful field directly in front of him. Actually, it was nothing but two tall, stately brick chimneys standing like sentinels keeping guard over the patch of charred ashes on the ground between them. What had once been a large, probably beautiful two-story farmhouse had been reduced to ashes. Indeed, for the *This Old House* crowd, that was certainly the ultimate fixer-upper! It's like saying you're going to patch up an old shirt when there's nothing left of it but a button.

When Paul speaks of the renewing of our minds, he doesn't mean this kind of renovation. He doesn't mean that God is willing to leave certain solid parts standing and rebuild from there. If your mind was that old fixer-upper house in North Carolina, those two chimneys would have to be knocked down and the charred foundation scraped away. Why? Because what the apostle Paul wrote of himself is true of all of us: "I know that in me (that is, in my flesh) nothing good dwells" (Romans 7:18)—not even in the chimneys and foundations.

God is not interested in renewing most of your mind—not even 99 percent of your mind. He wants to renew it all. He wants to pull down every remnant of your pre-Christian "house" and fill your mind with His agenda, values, culture, norms, priorities, and expectations. If He leaves intact any remnant at all of the old mind, that one little part, like a bad apple, can infect the rest. He wants to renew our minds completely through the renewing work of the Word of God as employed by the Holy Spirit.

Two Agents: The Holy Spirit and the Word of God

The apostle Paul obviously liked the picture of the believer's mind being renewed by the Holy Spirit. Look how often he repeated it:

- 2 Corinthians 4:16: "The inward man is being renewed day by day."
- Ephesians 4:23: "Be renewed in the spirit of your mind."
- Colossians 3:10: "Put on the new man who is renewed in knowledge according to the image of Him who created him."
- Titus 3:5: "He saved us, through the washing of regeneration and renewing of the Holy Spirit."

And in 2 Corinthians 10:5, Paul speaks of "bringing every thought into captivity to the obedience of Christ."

All these terms—"the mind"... "the inward man"... "renewed in knowledge"... "renewing of the Holy Spirit"... "taking thoughts captive"—refer to the same jewel of truth that Paul holds up to the light so we can see it from a number of different angles. It is clear that our transformation—which is our defense against worldly conformation—takes place as our minds are renewed by the Holy Spirit; as our minds are filled with new knowledge and new truth about life and this world. To use Paul's metaphor from Ephesians 6:17, we fight off the forces of conformity by using the "sword of the Spirit, which is the word of God."

When I underwent cancer treatment in the 1990s, part of the protocol in preparation for a stem cell transplant was a process called *pheresis*. First, I was given a drug to increase my white blood cell count. Then my blood was removed through one arm, run through a machine that separated out the white blood cells, and returned to my body through the other arm. That's a bit like what happens when the Holy Spirit floods your mind with the Word of God. There is a replacing, a renewing, that takes place as truth replaces the lies and distortions that filled your mind before.

A well-known Christian psychiatrist, the late Dr. John White, described the renewing result the Word of God had in his life:

> Bible study has torn my life apart and remade it. That is to say that God, through his Word, has done so...If I could write poetry about it I would. If I could sing through paper, I would flood your soul with the glorious melodies that express what I have found. I cannot exaggerate for there are no expressions majestic enough to tell of the glory I have seen, or of the wonder of finding that I, a neurotic, unstable, middle-aged man have my feet firmly planted in eternity and breathe the air of heaven. And all this has come to me through a careful study of Scripture.[1]

There are many areas in which the world pressures us to conform to its perspective—especially when it comes to fear and anxiety about what life on Planet Earth might be like in the not-too-distant future. Prolonged fear and anxiety are sins. The only way to avoid them is to follow the path of the psalmist: "Your word I have hidden in my heart, that I might not sin against You" (Psalm 119:11).

What we learn from God's Word and submission to Him does not change anything about our external circumstances. The world may still deteriorate; we may be persecuted or otherwise suffer. But what will change is our minds, and that makes all the difference. The apostle Paul was one of the most abused, persecuted, and oft-imprisoned men who ever lived. Yet he was also one of the most joyful. His joy came from his renewed mind and its strong connection to God.

Two Actions: External and Internal

Did you know it's possible for a person to listen to biblical preaching and teaching, and even read the Bible himself, yet have it make very little difference in his life? I say that being fully aware that God's Word never returns void (Isaiah 55:11) and that it is alive, penetrating into our deepest thoughts (Hebrews 4:12).

My point is this: It takes more than just the mechanical exposure to the Bible to accomplish the renewing of the mind. It takes a receptive heart that is eager to receive the Word—a mind that desires to be renewed. Jesus and His half brother James both touched on this reality. Jesus compared the heart to soil in varying degrees of cultivation. Only the heart that is made ready to receive the Word will produce fruit (Matthew 13:1–23). James must have remembered Jesus' illustration when he expanded the metaphor, saying that only the implanted word "is able to save your souls" (James 1:21).

So the external dimension of renewing the mind is exposure to the Word of God, which is necessary but does not alone guarantee success. What is required is the internal dimension, which is a cultivated heart and mind that *want* to be renewed. This doesn't happen automatically. Remember the image of the water thundering over

Niagara Falls with millions of tons of pressure? That's the pressure that's working against you, urging you to maintain the status quo; urging you not to do anything radical or rigorous in your life; forcing you to be squeezed into the mold of this world.

Renewing the mind is your only defense against this force, and so it's not surprising that it pushes hard—propelled by Satan himself—against the process of renewal. It takes daily discipline of the kind described by famous basketball coach Bobby Knight: "Discipline is doing what needs to be done, doing it when it needs to be done, doing it the best it can be done, and doing it that way every time you do it."

If collegiate basketball players can exercise discipline to gain a "perishable crown," how much more should we be willing to exercise discipline in order to gain an "imperishable crown" (1 Corinthians 9:25)? Just as the never-ending force of water over a cliff eventually wears away the face of the fall, so the never-ending pressure of the world will wear down our spiritual defenses and cause us to conform—if we are not involved daily in the discipline of renewing our minds with the Word of God.

Two Attitudes: Serious and Submissive

Someone once said to me, "The problem with the Christian life is that it is so *daily*." I laughed at that expression; I knew exactly what my friend meant. Does the world ever stop its relentless attempts to squeeze you into its mold? No. We never get a break. The Christian life is "so daily" because the world's attempts to conform us are so daily. Which is why the renewing of our minds must be just as daily. In the original language, the word "be transformed" in Romans 12:2 is in the present tense. In another reference to renewal Paul says, "The inward man is being renewed day by day" (2 Corinthians 4:16).

Again he uses a present-tense verb, showing that renewal is a continuing, ever-present, never-ending reality that requires our ongoing "day-by-day" diligence.

Being transformed by the renewing of the mind is serious business, as anything that never ends must be. But it is also a submissive business. Remember that the Greek term "be transformed" is rendered in the passive voice. This is not something we do. We are the old, burned-out house that submits to the process of renewal. It is the Holy Spirit who does the work in us. We each submit to His rebuilding and renewing work by offering up a heart and a mind that are receptive to the Spirit's chief tool, the Word of God. In other words, by offering ourselves as living sacrifices.

A Real Demonstration

How can we know whether we're being conformed to the world or being transformed by a renewed mind? Paul gives us the evidence: "You may prove what is that good and acceptable and perfect will of God" (Romans 12:2).

The nine categories of cultural and international decline I have written about in this book are areas in which God has a will for His people. He wants us to be committed to marriage, to the Bible, to the lordship of Christ, to understanding the rise of rogue powers on the world stage, to supporting His chosen people, the Jews, and so on.

Now I urge you to demonstrate the "good and acceptable and perfect will of God" in each of these areas by the way you live your own life. If you are not sure what that will of God is in one or more of these areas, you can discover it by giving the Holy Spirit free access to reveal the Word of God to you. You can move from being confused and complacent about these critical areas to being committed and consecrated in each. By this way of thinking and living, you can know that you are being transformed by the renewing of your mind.

A Christian who is thus transformed will *learn* the will of God, *live* the will of God, and *love* the will of God. That person will not fear the chaos and collapse he sees around him. He will stand like an immovable beacon of light, life, and hope to all who are tired of being squeezed into the mold of this world.

I wish I could announce to you that the decline I have noted in these nine areas is going to undergo a major reversal by such and such a date. But I cannot. No one knows the future. America is at a delicate tipping point in her national life, and only God knows which way she will tip. As I have stated earlier, I do not believe the world will get a permanent reprieve from chaos and confusion until the return of the Lord Jesus Christ. So whether or not we get a temporary reprieve from our nation's downward course, the Church of Jesus Christ has to prepare herself for the long-term indications of Scripture.

There is no middle ground in which to stand. Jesus Himself said, "He who is not with Me is against me, and he who does not gather with Me scatters" (Luke 11:23). Either a person will be transformed by the renewing of his mind or he will be conformed to the beliefs of this world system—a system that is continually degenerating and will pass into oblivion. The apostle John wrote, "The world is passing away, and the lust of it; but he who does the will of God abides forever" (1 John 2:17). How do we know the "good and acceptable and perfect will of God"? By being transformed by the renewing of our minds as the Holy Spirit fills us with the Word of God.

Romans 12:1–2 and this chapter are both about making a choice between two words: *conformed* or *transformed*—conformed to this world or transformed into the image of Christ to do the will of God. May you and I decide, determine, and discipline ourselves to make the right choice: to be living demonstrations, day after day, of His will.

NOTES

Introduction: A Slow Drift in the Wrong Direction

1. The three books are: *What in the World Is Going On?* (2008), *Living Confidently in a Chaotic World* (2009), and *The Coming Economic Armageddon* (2010).

Chapter 1: When Atheists Would Be Angry

1. Christopher Hitchens, interview by Anderson Cooper, *Anderson Cooper 360*, CNN, May 15, 2007, accessed April 19, 2011, http://transcripts.cnn.com/TRAN SCRIPTS/0705/15/acd.01.html.
2. Dinesh D'Souza, *What's So Great About Christianity* (Washington, DC: Regnery, 2007), xiv.
3. Richard Dawkins, *The God Delusion* (New York: Houghton Mifflin, 2006), 51.
4. "The New Intolerance: Fear Mongering Among Elite Atheists Is Not a Pretty Sight," *Christianity Today* editorial, January 25, 2007, accessed April 21, 2011, http://www.christianitytoday.com/ct/2007/february/17.24.html.
5. Antony Flew with Roy A. Varghese, *There Is a God: How the World's Most Notorious Atheist Changed His Mind* (New York: HarperCollins, 2007), xvi.
6. Joe Carter, "When Atheists Are Angry at God," First Things, January 12, 2011, accessed April 19, 2011, http://www.firstthings.com/onthesquare/2011/01/when-atheists-are-angry-at-god.
7. Gary Wolf, "The Church of the Non-Believers: A Band of Intellectual Brothers Is Mounting a Crusade Against Belief in God. Are They Winning Converts, or Merely Preaching to the Choir?" *Wired* 14, no. 11 (2006), accessed April 21, 2011, http://www.wired.com/wired/archive/14.11/atheism.html.
8. Flew, *There Is a God*, xvi.
9. Martin A. Coleman, ed., *The Essential Santayana: Selected Writings* (Bloomington: Indiana University Press, 2009), 288.
10. The word *evangelistic* actually means "proclamation of good news." I use it here only to denote the new atheists' passion for spreading their doctrine—not the

doctrine they are spreading—because there is no equivalent word that means "proclamation of bad news," which is what atheism is.

11. Quoted in Gayle Trotter, "Intimidating Intelligence Dims the Brights," *Evangel*, March 28, 2010, accessed April 19, 2011, http://firstthings.com/blogs/evangel/2010/03/intimidating-intelligence.

12. Daniel C. Dennet, "The Bright Stuff," *New York Times*, July 12, 2003, accessed April 21, 2011, http://www.nytimes.com/2003/07/12/opinion/the-bright-stuff.html?scp=1&sq=dennett%20the%20bright%20stuff&st=cse; see also http://www.the-brights.net/.

13. Richard Dawkins, "The Future Looks Bright," guardian.co.uk, June 21, 2003, accessed April 19, 2011, http://www.guardian.co.uk/books/2003/jun/21/society.richarddawkins.

14. Steven Waldman, "NPR Commentary by Steven Waldman September 4, 2003," The Brights, accessed April 19, 2011, http://www.the-brights.net/vision/essays/waldman_futrell_geisert_npr.html.

15. D'Souza, *What's So Great About Christianity*, 178.

16. Antony Flew, "Theology and Falsification: A Golden Jubilee Celebration (2000)," Secular Web, http://www.infidels.org/library/modern/antony_flew/theologyandfalsification.html (accessed April 21, 2011).

17. Associated Press, "Famous Atheist Now Believes in God," *Free Republic*, December 9, 2004, accessed April 21, 2011, http://www.freerepublic.com/focus/f-news/1298098/posts.

18. James A. Beverly, "Thinking Straighter: Why the World's Most Famous Atheist Now Believes in God," *Christianity Today*, April 8 2005, accessed April 21, 2011, http://www.christianitytoday.com/ct/2005/april/29.80.html.

19. These descriptions of Flew's book were adapted from the back cover of the trade paper edition.

20. A. N. Wilson, "Can You Love God and Agree with Darwin?" *NewStatesman*, April 2, 2009, accessed April 19, 2011, http://www.newstatesman.com/religion/2009/04/returning-to-religion.

21. Janie B. Cheaney, "Lost and Found: Doctrine Brings a Famous Atheist Back to Faith," *World*, June 6, 2009, accessed April 19, 2011, http://www.worldmag.com/articles/15410.

22. Wilson, "Can You Love God and Agree with Darwin?"

23. Matthew Parris, "As an Atheist, I Truly Believe Africa Needs God: Missionaries, Not Aid Money, Are the Solution to Africa's Biggest Problem—The Crushing Passivity of the People's Mindset," *Sunday Times*, December 27, 2008, accessed April 19, 2011, http://www.timesonline.co.uk/tol/comment/columnists/matthew_parris/article5400568.ece.

24. Peter Hitchens, *The Rage Against God: How Atheism Led Me to Faith* (Grand Rapids, MI: Zondervan, 2010), 82–83.

25. Ibid., 86–87.

26. Alister E. McGrath, *The Passionate Intellect: Christian Faith and the Discipleship of the Mind* (Downers Grove, IL: InterVarsity Press, 2010), 159.

27. Hitchens, *The Rage Against God*, 110.

28. Ibid.

29. McGrath, *The Passionate Intellect*, 147.

30. Steven Pinker, *How the Mind Works* (New York: W. W. Norton, 1997), 555.

31. D'Souza, *What's So Great About Christianity*, 206.

32. Ibid.

33. Ibid., 206–7.

34. Ibid., 207.

35. Christopher Hitchens and Douglas Wilson, *Is Christianity Good for the World?* (Moscow, ID: Canon Press, 2008), 28.

36. Flew, *There Is a God*, 76.

37. Ibid., 77.

38. C. S. Lewis, "The Funeral of a Great Myth," *Christian Reflections* (Grand Rapids, MI: Eerdmans, 1967), 86.

39. Richard Lewontin, "Billions and Billions of Demons," *New York Times Book Review*, January 9, 1997, accessed April 25, 2011, http://www.drjbloom.com/Public%20files/Lewontin_Review.htm.

40. Dawkins, *The God Delusion*, 309, 315.

41. Alister E. McGrath, *Surprised by Meaning: Science, Faith, and How We Make Sense of Things* (Louisville, KY: Westminster John Knox Press), 86.

42. D'Souza, *What's So Great About Christianity*, 214, 221.

43. McGrath, *The Passionate Intellect*, 168.

44. "Alister E. McGrath: Biography," from the official Alister E. McGrath website, accessed April 20, 2011, http://users.ox.ac.uk/~mcgrath/biography.html.

45. Alister E. McGrath, "The Twilight of Atheism," *Christianity Today*, February 28, 2005, accessed April 20, 2011, http://www.christianitytoday.com/ct/2005/march/21.36.html.

46. "The New Intolerance," *Christianity Today*.

47. D'Souza, *What's So Great About Christianity*, 1.

48. Ibid., 11.

49. Tony Snow, "New Atheists Are Not Great," *Christianity Today*, March 13, 2008, accessed April 20, 2011, http://www.ctlibrary.com/ct/2008/march/25.79.html.

50. George Weigel, "Christian Number-Crunching," First Things, February 9, 2011, accessed April 20, 2011, http://www.firstthings.com/onthesquare/2011/02/christian-number-crunching.

51. C. S. Lewis, *Surprised by Joy* (New York: Harcourt, Brace, 1955), 224.

52. Quoted in Rob Moll, "Saved by an Atheist," *Christianity Today*, August 25, 2010, accessed April 20, 2011, http://www.christianitytoday.com/ct/2010/august/28.40.html.

53. Katharine Tait, *My Father, Bertrand Russell* (New York: Harcourt Brace Jovanovich, 1975), 189. Cited by Roy A. Varghese in the preface to Flew, *There Is a God*, xx–xxi.
54. Bertrand Russell, *The Autobiography of Bertrand Russell* (London: Allen and Unwin, 1967), 146. Cited by Roy A. Varghese in the preface to Flew, *There Is a God*, xxi.
55. John D. Steinrucken, "Secularism's Ongoing Debt to Christianity," *American Thinker*, March 25, 2010, accessed April 20, 2011, http://www.americanthinker.com/2010/03/secularisms_ongoing_debt_to_ch.html.
56. Ibid.
57. Ibid.
58. George MacDonald, "The Golden Key," in *The Gifts of the Child Christ* (Grand Rapids, MI: Eerdmans, 1973), 171.

Chapter 2: When Christians Wouldn't Know They Were in a War

1. William Slim, *Defeat into Victory* (London: Pan, 2009), 550–51.
2. Scott Wilson and Al Kamen, "'Global War on Terror' Is Given New Name," *Washington Post*, March 25, 2009, accessed April 26, 2011, http://www.washingtonpost.com/wp-dyn/content/article/2009/03/24/AR2009032402818.html.
3. Mark Phillips, "Exorcisms May Be on the Rise," *CBS News*, February 26, 2008, accessed December 12, 2010, http://www.cbsnews.com/stories/2008/02/26/earlyshow/main3877560.shtml.
4. Ibid.
5. Laurie Goodstein, "For Catholics, Interest in Exorcism Is Revived," *New York Times*, November 12, 2010, accessed December 13, 2010, http://www.nytimes.com/2010/11/13/us/13exorcism.html.
6. Sun Tzu, *The Art of War* (Hollywood, FL: Simon and Brown, 2010), 11.
7. John Phillips, *Exploring Ephesians and Philippians: An Expository Commentary* (Grand Rapids, MI: Kregel, 1995), 187.
8. R. Kent Hughes, *Ephesians: The Mystery of the Body of Christ* (Wheaton, IL: Crossway, 1990), 217.
9. Barna Group, "Most American Christians Do Not Believe That Satan or the Holy Spirit Exist," April 10, 2009, accessed January 24, 2010, http://www.barna.org/barna-update/article/12-faithspirituality/260-most-american-christians-do-not-believe-that-satan-or-the-holy-spirit-exis.
10. J. C. Ryle, *Holiness* (Chicago: Moody, 2010), 118.
11. A. W. Tozer, *This World: Playground or Battleground?* (Camp Hill, PA: Christian Publications, 1989), chap. 1.
12. Paul G. Hiebert, "The Flaw of the Excluded Middle," *Missiology* 10: 35–47, January 1982. Reprinted in Ralph D. Winter and Steven C. Hawthorne, eds., *Perspectives on the World Christian Movement: A Reader*, 3rd ed. (Pasadena, CA: William Carey Library, 1999), 414–21.

13. Ibid.
14. Craig Brian Larson and *Leadership Journal, 750 Engaging Illustrations for Preachers, Teachers, and Writers* (Grand Rapids, MI: Baker Books, 2002), 70.
15. Ibid.
16. Bob Gass, *The Word for You Today,* September/October/November 2010 (Alphareta, GA: Bob Gass Ministries), 21.
17. Ibid.
18. Randy Alcorn, *If God Is Good: Faith in the Midst of Suffering and Evil* (Colorado Springs: Multnomah, 2009), 51.
19. Albert Mohler, "On Exorcism and Exorcists: An Evangelical View," November 15, 2010, accessed December 13, 2010, http://www.albertmohler.com/2010/11/15/on-exorcism-and-exorcists-an-evangelical-view/.
20. J. C. Ryle, *Holiness* (Chicago: Moody, 2010), 115.
21. Jack R. Taylor, *Prayer: Life's Limitless Reach* (Kent: Sovereign World, 2004), 127–28.
22. Ibid.
23. C. Mark Corts, *The Truth About Spiritual Warfare: Your Place in the Battle Between God and Satan* (Nashville: B&H, 2006), 151.

Chapter 3: When Jesus Would Be So Profaned

1. "The Colbert Report," Colbert Nation, January 13, 2011, accessed February 11, 2011, http://www.colbertnation.com/the-colbert-report-videos/371019/january-13-2011/thought-for-food—fruit-pouch—doritos-ad—super-big-gulp.
2. Dotson Rader, "Elton John: 'There's a Lot of Hate in the World,'" *Parade*, February 17, 2010, accessed May 4, 2011, http://www.parade.com/celebrity/celebrity-parade/2010/elton-john-web-exclusive.html.
3. Richard Dawkins, "Atheists for Jesus," Richard Dawkins Foundation for Reason and Science, April 10, 2006, accessed May 4, 2011, http://richarddawkins.net/articles/20-atheists-for-jesus.
4. Ibid.
5. Jesus Seminar, accessed February 19, 2011, http://jesusseminar.com/Mission/mission.html.
6. See critiques by scholars like N. T. Wright, Ben Witherington III, Darrell Bock, Luke Timothy Johnson, Craig Blomberg, Craig Evans, and William L. Craig.
7. N. T. Wright, "Abandon Studying the Historical Jesus? No, We Need History: A Response to 'The Jesus We'll Never Know,'" *Christianity Today*, April 9, 2010, accessed February 17, 2011, http://www.christianitytoday.com/ct/2010/april/16.27.html.
8. R. Kent Hughes, *Hebrews: An Anchor for the Soul*, vol. 1 (Wheaton, IL: Crossway Books, 1993), 22.
9. Thomas Jefferson and Cyrus Adler, *The Jefferson Bible* (Stilwell, KS: Digireads .com Publishing, 2005), 12.

10. Christopher Hitchens, "Jefferson's Quran: What the Founder Really Thought About Islam," *Slate,* January 9, 2007, accessed May 8, 2011, http://www.slate.com/id/2157314/.

11. Marilyn Mellowes, "Thomas Jefferson and his Bible," *Frontline,* April 1998, accessed February 17, 2011, http://www.pbs.org/wgbh/pages/frontline/shows/religion/jesus/jefferson.html.

12. Scot McKnight, "The Jesus We'll Never Know: Why Scholarly Attempts to Discover the 'Real' Jesus Have Failed. And Why That's a Good Thing," *Christianity Today,* April 19, 2010, accessed February 17, 2011, http://www.christianitytoday.com/ct/2010/april/15.22.html.

13. Darrell L. Bock and Daniel B. Wallace, *Dethroning Jesus: Exposing Popular Culture's Quest to Unseat the Biblical Christ* (Nashville: Thomas Nelson, 2007), 4–5.

14. Raymond Brown, *The Message of Hebrews* (Downers Grove, IL: InterVarsity Press, 1982), 56.

15. C. S. Lewis, *Mere Christianity* (New York: Macmillan, 1952), 124–25.

16. Dwight L. Moody and James S. Bell, *The D. L. Moody Collection: The Highlights of His Writings, Sermons, Anecdotes, and Life Story* (Chicago: Moody Bible Institute, 1997), 54–55.

17. Lee Strobel, *The Case for the Real Jesus: A Journalist Investigates Current Attacks on the Identity of Christ* (Grand Rapids, MI: Zondervan, 2007), 268–69.

Chapter 4: When Marriage Would Be Obsolete

1. "Royal Shack-Up: Kate and William Moved in Months Ago," MSNBC, November 28, 2010, accessed March 2, 2011, http://today.msnbc.msn.com/id/40253368/ns/today-today_people.

2. Ibid.

3. "Canons of the Church of England," Church of England, accessed March 24, 2010, http://www.churchofengland.org/about-us/structure/churchlawlegis/canons.aspx.

4. Pew Social Trends staff, "The Decline of Marriage and Rise of New Families," Pew Research Center, November 18, 2010, accessed December 9, 2010, http://pewresearch.org/pubs/1802/decline-marriage-rise-new-families.

5. Ibid.

6. Quoted in C. S. Lewis, *Surprised by Joy: The Shape of My Early Life* (New York: Harcourt Brace), 205.

7. Lisa Miller, "What the Bible Really Says About Sex," *Newsweek,* February 6, 2011, accessed March 10, 2011, http://www.newsweek.com/2011/02/06/what-the-bible-really-says-about-sex.html.

8. Sharon Jayson, "More View Cohabitation as Acceptable Choice," *USA Today,* June 9, 2010, accessed January 12, 2011, http://www.usatoday.com/news/nation/2008-06-08-cohabitation-study_N.htm.

9. Ibid.
10. CBS News/ *The New York Times*, "American Public Opinion: 30 Years Ago," July 11–15, 2009
11. "Royal Shack-Up."
12. Sharon Jayson, "Census Reports More Unmarried Couples Living Together," *USA Today*, July 28, 2008, accessed March 3, 2011, http://www.usatoday.com/news/nation/census/2008-07-28-cohabitation-census_N.htm.
13. Bonnie Eslinger, "Yes to Love, No to Marriage," *Newsweek*, January 5, 2008, accessed March 10, 2011, http://www.newsweek.com/2008/01/05/yes-to-love-no-to-marriage.html.
14. Ibid.
15. Ibid.
16. Larry King, "Interview with Art Linkletter," CNN, July 26, 2002, accessed May 4, 2011, http://www-cgi.cnn.com/TRANSCRIPTS/0207/26/lkl.00.html.
17. Bertrand Russell, *Russell Autobiography* (New York: Routledge, 2010), 138
18. Paul Strathern, *Bertrand Russell in 90 Minutes* (Chicago: Ivan R. Dee, 2001), 41.
19. Caitlin Flanagan, "Is There Hope for the American Marriage?" *Time*, July 2, 2009, accessed December 27, 2010, http://www.time.com/time/nation/article/0,8599,1908243,00.html.
20. Dan Hurley, "Divorce Rate: It's Not as High as You Think," *New York Times*, April 19, 2005, accessed May 4, 2011, http://www.nytimes.com/2005/04/19/health/19divo.html.
21. The traditional calculation has been to compare the marriage rate per 1,000 people in the population with the divorce rate for the same population. In 2003, that meant 7.5 marriages per 1,000 compared to 3.8 divorces per 1,000, leading to a 7.5:3.8 ratio—or 1.97:1, or 2:1, or roughly 50 percent. The problem with the method is that the "one" person divorcing every year is not one of the "two" people getting married—it's comparing apples with oranges.
22. Hurley, "Divorce Rate."
23. Glenn T. Stanton, "First-Person: The Christian Divorce Rate Myth (What You've Heard Is Wrong)," Baptist Press, February 15, 2011, accessed March 8, 2011, http://www.bpnews.net/BPnews.asp?ID=34656.
24. Ibid.
25. Steven E. Rhoads, *Taking Sex Differences Seriously* (San Francisco: Encounter Books, 2004), 248.
26. Maggie Gallagher, transcribed from a lecture at Southern Evangelical Seminary's Veritas Lecture Series "Marriage: Why It Can and Must Be Saved," Charlotte, NC, April 1, 2010, accessed March 11, 2011, http://www.youtube.com/watch?v=wAOrdMJAbAQ.
27. Robert P. George and Jean Bethke Elshtain, eds., *The Meaning of Marriage: Family, State, Market, and Morals* (Dallas: Spence Publishing, 2006).
28. Robert P. George, transcribed from a lecture at Southern Evangelical Seminary's Veritas Lecture Series "Marriage: Why It Can and Must Be Saved," Charlotte, NC, April 1, 2010, accessed March 11, 2011.

29. Elton Trueblood, *Foundations for Reconstruction* (New York: Harper and Brothers, 1946), 78.
30. Andreas J. Köstenberger and David W. Jones, *God, Marriage, and Family: Rebuilding the Biblical Foundation* (Wheaton, IL: Crossway, 2010), 80.
31. Pew, "The Decline of Marriage."
32. Dinesh D'Souza, "Redefining Marriage?" To the Source, August 7 2003, accessed March 10, 2011, http://www.tothesource.org/8_7_2003/8_7_2003.htm.
33. Trueblood, *Foundations for Reconstruction*, 76.
34. W. Bradford Wilcox, ed., *The State of Our Unions, Marriage in America 2010: When Marriage Disappears: The New Middle America*, xi, 52, December 2010, accessed January 11, 2011, http://www.stateofourunions.org/2010/SOOU2010.pdf.
35. Köstenberger and Jones, *God, Marriage, and Family: Rebuilding the Biblical Foundation*, 25–26.
36. "Royal Wedding: Transcript of Marriage Service," BBC, April 28, 2011, accessed May 4, 2011, http://www.bbc.co.uk/news/uk-13220173.
37. Ibid.

Chapter 5: When Morality Would Be in Free Fall

1. Pat Forde, "BYU Puts Principle Over Performance," ESPN, March 2, 2011, accessed March 3, 2011, http://sports.espn.go.com/espn/print?id=6175251&type=story#.
2. Quoted in Brad Knickerbocker, "BYU Basketball Player Suspended: Sports World Shocked—And Impressed," *Christian Science Monitor*, March 3, 2011, accessed April 1, 2011, http://www.csmonitor.com/USA/Sports/2011/0303/BYU-basketball-player-suspended-sports-world-shocked-and-impressed.
3. *Brigham Young University Undergraduate Catalog, 2010–2011*, accessed April 1, 2011, http://saas.byu.edu/catalog/2010-2011ucat/GeneralInfo/HonorCode.php.
4. Vanderbilt University, accessed April 1, 2011, http://admissions.vanderbilt.edu/insidedores/2011/03/honor-council/.
5. C. S. Lewis, *Mere Christianity* (New York: Macmillan, 1952), 57.
6. George Dohrmann and Jeff Benedict, "Rap Sheets, Recruits and Repercussions," *Sports Illustrated*, March 7, 2011, accessed April 4, 2011, http://sportsillustrated.cnn.com/vault/article/magazine/MAG1182621/index.htm.
7. Ibid.
8. Lesley Stahl, "Slot Machines: The Big Gamble," *60 Minutes*, January 9, 2011, accessed February 23, 2011, http://www.cbsnews.com/video/watch/?id=7228424n&tag=contentMain;contentBody.
9. *Merriam-Webster's Collegiate Dictionary*, 11th ed., s.v. "decent," accessed May 10, 2011, http://www.merriam-webster.com/dictionary/decent.
10. *Wikipedia*, s.v. "Gambling in the United States," http://en.wikipedia.org/wiki/Gambling_in_the_United_States#1931.E2.80.93present.

11. Associated Press, "Idea to Tax Prostitution Dies in Committee," *Arizona Central,* April 9, 2009, accessed March 7, 2011, http://www.azcentral.com/offbeat/articles/2009/04/09/20090409ODDprostitution-tax0409-ON.html.
12. Jeffrey M. Jones, "Nurses Top Honesty and Ethics List for 11th Year," Gallup, December 3, 2010, accessed March 3, 2011, http://www.gallup.com/poll/145043/Nurses-Top-Honesty-Ethics-List-11-Year.aspx.
13. Linda A. Smith, Samantha Healy Vardaman, Melissa A. Snow, *The National Report on Domestic Minor Sex Trafficking: America's Prostituted Children,* Shared Hope International, May 2009, 11, accessed March 7, 2011, http://www.sharedhope.org/Resources/TheNationalReport.aspx.
14. Bob Herbert, "Young, Cold and for Sale," *New York Times,* October 19, 2006, accessed October 19, 2006, http://select.nytimes.com/2006/10/19/opinion/19herbert.html?_r=1.
15. Katelyn Beaty, "Christians Launch Anti-Slavery Efforts for Super Bowl XLV," *Christianity Today,* January 25, 2011, accessed January 25, 2011, http://blog.christianitytoday.com/women/2011/01/christians_launch_antitraffick.html.
16. Tresa Baldas, "Child Pornography Prosecutors: Victims Are Getting Younger, Acts More Vile," Detroit Free Press, January 31, 2011, accessed March 7, 2011, http://www.ongo.com/v/322070/-1/DF7576B52DEB982C/child-pornography-prosecutors-victims-are-getting-younger-acts-are-more-vile.
17. U.S. Department of Justice, *The National Strategy for Child Exploitation Prevention and Interdiction: A Report to Congress,* August 2010, accessed March 7, 2011, http://www.projectsafechildhood.gov/docs/natstrategyreport.pdf.
18. U.S. Department of Justice, accessed April 3, 2011, http://bjs.ojp.usdoj.gov/content/glance/corr2.cfm.
19. Jeffrey M. Jones, "U.S. Satisfaction with Gov't, Morality, Economy Down Since '08," Gallup, January 24, 2011, accessed January 25, 2011, http://www.gallup.com/poll/145760/Satisfaction-Gov-Morality-Economy-Down.aspx.
20. Jeffrey M. Jones, "Americans' Outlook for U.S. Morality Remains Bleak," Gallup, May 17, 2010, accessed March 3, 2011, http://www.gallup.com/poll/128042/americans-outlook-morality-remains-bleak.aspx.
21. "What Has Happened to Morality in the United States?" University of Chicago News Office, May 8, 1998, http://www-news.uchicago.edu/releases/98/980508.civil.society.shtml.
22. "A New Generation of Adults Bends Moral and Sexual Rules to Their Liking," Barna Group, October 31, 2006, accessed October 31, 2006, http://www.barna.org/barna-update/article/13-culture/144-a-new-generation-of-adults-bends-moral-and-sexual-rules-to-their-liking.
23. Ibid.
24. Ibid.
25. Douglas D. Webster, *The Easy Yoke* (Colorado Springs, CO: NavPress, 1995), 91.

26. Michael J. Wilkins, *The NIV Application Commentary: Matthew: From Biblical Text to Contemporary Life* (Grand Rapids, MI: Zondervan, 2004), 256.

27. Ibid.

28. "Clinton Denies Sexual Relations with Lewinsky," BBC News, January 27, 1998, accessed April 5, 2011, http://newsrss.bbc.co.uk/1/hi/world/17301.stm.

Chapter 6: When the Bible Would Be Marginalized

1. "Publisher's Note," in *The New-England Primer: Improved for the More Easy Attaining the True Reading of English. To Which Is Added the Assembly of Divines, and Mr. Cotton's Catechism* (Boston, 1777; repr., San Antonio, TX: Vision Forum, 2002–2010).

2. William H. McGuffey, *McGuffey's Eclectic Primer* (Cincinnati: Truman and Smith, 1836; repr., Fenton, MI: Mott Media, 1982), 57–59.

3. *Wikipedia*, s.v. "McGuffey Readers," accessed March 18, 2011, http://en.wikipedia.org/wiki/McGuffey%27s_Readers.

4. William H. McGuffey, *McGuffey's Eclectic Primer*, rev. ed. (New York: American Book Company, 1896), 23.

5. James Neill, "John Dewey, the Modern Father of Experiential Education," Wilderdom, January 26, 2005, accessed May 5, 2011, http://wilderdom.com/experiential/ExperientialDewey.html.

6. John Robinson, *The Works of John Robinson* (London: John Snow, 1851), xliv.

7. *The American Heritage Dictionary of the English Language*, 4th ed., digital version, s.v. "marginalize."

8. Tony Lane, "A Man for All People: Introducing William Tyndale," *Christian History* 6 (16): 7.

9. "Did You Know…?" *Christian History* 6 (16): 4.

10. Lane, "A Man for All People," 9.

11. See Brother Andrew and John and Elizabeth Sherrill, *God's Smuggler* (Grand Rapids, MI: Chosen Books, 2001).

12. Simon Hooper, "The Rise of the 'New Atheists,'" CNN World, November 8, 2006, http://articles.cnn.com/2006-11-08/world/atheism.feature_1_new-atheists-new-atheism-religion?_s=PM:WORLD.

13. Quoted in ibid.

14. Joseph L. Mangina, *Karl Barth: Theologian of Christian Witness* (Louisville, KY: Westminster John Knox Press, 2004), 9.

15. Frank Newport, "Near-Record High See Religion Losing Influence in America," Gallup, December 29, 2010, accessed March 20, 2011, http://www.gallup.com/poll/145409/Near-Record-High-Religion-Losing-Influence-America.aspx.

16. "New Research Explores How Different Generations View and Use the Bible," Barna Group, October 19, 2009, accessed November 1, 2010, http://www.barna

.org/barna-update/article/12-faithspirituality/317-new-research-explores-how-different-generations-view-and-use-the-bible.

17. Ibid.
18. Ibid.
19. Ibid.
20. Ibid.
21. Marty Cooper, "2010: The Year of the Bible?" American Family News Network, May 26, 2009, accessed November 15, 2010, http://www.onenewsnow.com/Politics/Default.aspx?id=540182.
22. Mark A. Noll, "The Bible and American Culture," Houston Baptist University, July 16, 2007, accessed November 15, 2010, http://www.hbu.edu/hbu/The_Bible_and_American_Culture_by_Mark_Noll.asp?SnID=2.
23. Nicholas D. Kristof, "Test Your Savvy on Religion," New York Times, October 9, 2010, accessed November 16, 2010, http://www.nytimes.com/2010/10/10/opinion/10kristof.html.
24. Ruby Scott, Jungle Harvest (Golden, CO: Conservative Baptist Home Mission Society, 1988), 99.
25. Ibid.

Chapter 7: When the Church Would Be Irrelevant

1. Leonard Sweet, Learn to Dance the SoulSalsa: 17 Surprising Steps for Godly Living in the 21st Century (Grand Rapids, MI: Zondervan, 2002), 71.
2. Chuck Swindoll, "The Problem with Pizzazz: Has Entertainment Replaced Scripture as the Center of Our Worship?" Christianity Today, May 2, 2011, accessed May 31, 2011, http://www.christianitytoday.com/le/2011/spring/problempizzazz.html.
3. D. Martyn Lloyd-Jones, Studies in the Sermon on the Mount (Grand Rapids, MI: Eerdmans, 1959–60), 28.
4. The capitalization distinction I'm using here is not universal. You will find that some authors I've quoted in this chapter and others do not make this distinction in their writing. But the distinction between the two concepts—building and people—exists in their writings just as it does in mine. And I believe context will make their usage clear.
5. To see the four churches, go to http://tinyurl.com/c674ea and use the map controls to zoom in, then "Street View" to pan around the intersection of Main and Canandagua Streets in the heart of downtown Palmyra.
6. Charles Colson and Ellen Vaughn, Being the Body (Nashville, TN: W Publishing, 2003), 307–8.
7. "Americans Say Serving the Needy Is Christianity's Biggest Contribution to Society," Barna Group, October 25, 2010, accessed April 8, 2011, http://www.barna.org/faith-spirituality/440-americans-describe-christianity-contributions.

312   Notes

8. Justin Martyr, from *The First Apology of Justin*, Christian History Timeline, accessed May 25, 2011, http://www.christianhistorytimeline.com/GLIMPSEF/Glimpses/glmps155.shtml.

9. From *The Epistle to Diognetes*, Christian History Timeline, accessed May 25, 2011, http://www.christianhistorytimeline.com/GLIMPSEF/Glimpses/glmps155.shtml.

10. Ibid.

11. Rodney Stark, *The Rise of Christianity: How the Obscure, Marginal Jesus Movement Became the Dominant Religious Force in the Western World in a Few Centuries* (New York: HarperOne, 1997), 161–62.

12. Ram A. Cnaan, Tuomi Forrest, Joseph Carlsmith, and Kelsey Karsh, *Valuing Urban Congregations: A Pilot Study*, http://www.philanthropy.iupui.edu/events/docs/WIMPS_2011/CnaanPaper.pdf. See the summary at *Christianity Today*, accessed April 7, 2011, http://www.christianitytoday.com/ct/special/pdf/110331spot_church economicworth.pdf.

13. Matthew Petrillo, "Putting a Price on Your Church's Services: A New Study Calculates the Economic Value of Those Contributions," Voice of America, April 7, 2011, accessed April 7, 2011, http://www.voanews.com/english/news/usa/Putting-a-Price-on-Your-Churchs-Services-117583204.html.

14. For a startling picture of what the world might have been like without the Christian Gospel, read D. James Kennedy and Jerry Newcombe, *What If Jesus Had Never Been Born?* (Nashville, TN: Thomas Nelson, 1994).

15. Ferdinand S. Schenck, *Christian Evidences and Ethics* (New York: Young Men's Christian Association Press, 1910), 85, quoted in Kennedy and Newcombe, *What If Jesus Had Never Been Born?*, 237–38.

16. Christina Woodside, "Those Charming Steeples Aren't So Quaint Anymore," *New York Times*, July 29, 2001, sec. 14CN, 1.

17. Scott Gabrielson, "Here's the Church, Here's the Steeple: A Primer on Choosing the Right One for You," *Christianity Today*, May 1, 2001, accessed May 31, 2011, http://www.christianitytoday.com/cbg/2001/mayjun/5.33.html.

18. Ibid.

19. Brett McCracken, *Hipster Christianity: When Church and Cool Collide* (Grand Rapids, MI: Baker, 2010), 233, 234; italics in original.

20. J. Sidlow Baxter, *Explore the Book*, vol. 5 (Grand Rapids, MI: Zondervan, 1960), 308.

21. Michael Horton, *Christless Christianity: The Alternative Gospel of the American Church* (Grand Rapids, MI: Baker, 2008), 22.

22. Michael Horton, *The Gospel Commission: Recovering God's Strategy for Making Disciples* (Grand Rapids, MI: Baker, 2011).

23. David Ferguson, *The Great Commandment Principle* (Wheaton, IL: Tyndale, 1998), 1–2.

24. Steven J. Lawson, "The Priority of Biblical Preaching: An Expository Study of Acts 2:42–47," *Bibliotheca Sacra* 158 (April–June 2001), 198–99, quoted in Charles R. Swindoll, *The Church Awakening: An Urgent Call for Renewal* (New York: FaithWords, 2010), 239–40.

Chapter 8: When a Muslim State Could Intimidate the World

1. Mahmoud Ahmadinejad (prayer before the Sixty-fifth Session of the United Nations General Assembly, September 23, 2010, accessed September 27, 2010). For a transcript of Ahmadinejad's prayer and speech, visit: http://www.un-iran.org/index.php?option=com_content&view=article&id=876:address-by-he-dr-mahmoud-ahmadinejad-president-of-the-islamic-republic-of-iran-before-the-65th-session-of-the-united-nations-general-assembly-new-york-23-september-2010&catid=41:general-assembly&Itemid=54.

2. William Kern, "Ahmadinejad Announces Iranian Plans to 'Administer the World': Die Welt, Germany," Moderate Voice, December 15, 2009, accessed December 18, 2009, http://themoderatevoice.com/56031/ahmadinejad-announces-iranian-plans-to-administer-the-world-die-welt-germany/.

3. Mohammad Mohaddessin, *Islamic Fundamentalism* (Washington, DC: Seven Locks Press, 1993), 83.

4. Ibid., 35.

5. "Ahmadinejad: U.S. Blocking Savior's Return," UPI, December 8, 2009, accessed December 18, 2009, http://www.upi.com/Top_News/US/2009/12/08/Ahmadinejad-US-blocking-saviors-return/UPI-86901260290829/.

6. Abbas Djavadi, "The Apocalypse, Messianism Define Ahmadinejad's Policies," Radio Free Europe/Radio Liberty, December 9, 2009, accessed December 18, 2009, http://www.rferl.org/content/The_Apocalypse_Messianism_Define_Ahmadinejads_Policies/1899060.html.

7. Karl Vick, "Iran's President Calls Holocaust 'Myth' in Latest Assault on Jews," *Washington Post*, December 15, 2005, accessed February 3, 2011, http://www.washingtonpost.com/wp-dyn/content/article/2005/12/14/AR2005121402403.html.

8. Ahmadinejad speech, see endnote 1 above.

9. "Iranian Leader: Wipe Out Israel," CNN, October 27, 2005, accessed February 3, 2011, http://edition.cnn.com/2005/WORLD/meast/10/26/ahmadinejad/.

10. Dudi Cohen, "Iran Says It Can Destroy Israel in Week," YNET News, May 20, 2010, accessed September 29, 2010, http://www.ynetnews.com/articles/0,7340,L-3891781,00.html.

11. Djavadi, "The Apocalypse."

12. Mohaddessin, *Islamic Fundamentalism*, 17.

13. Ibid., 23.

14. Ibid., 28.

15. Jeffrey Goldberg, "The Point of No Return," *Atlantic*, September 2010, accessed September 29, 2010, http://www.theatlantic.com/magazine/archive/2010/09/the -point-of-no-return/8186.

16. Ibid.

17. Ibid.

18. Adele Berlin and Marc Zvi Brettler, eds., *The Jewish Study Bible* (New York: Oxford University Press, 2004), 1666–67.

19. Bernard Lewis, "Roots of Muslim Rage," *Atlantic*, September 1990.

20. Georges Sada, *Saddam's Secrets: How an Iraqi General Defied and Survived Saddam Hussein* (Brentwood, TN: Integrity, 2006), 286.

21. Ibid., 289.

22. David Jeremiah, "The New Axis of Evil," in *What in the World Is Going On?: 10 Prophetic Clues You Cannot Afford to Ignore* (Nashville: Thomas Nelson, 2008).

23. Joel C. Rosenberg, *Inside the Revolution: How the Followers of Jihad, Jefferson and Jesus Are Battling to Dominate the Middle East and Transform the World* (Wheaton, IL: Tyndale, 2009), 379.

24. Ibid., 382.

25. Ibid., 385.

26. Ibid., 387.

27. For a helpful discussion of these issues, see J. D. Greear, *Breaking the Islam Code: Understanding the Soul Questions of Every Muslim* (Eugene, OR: Harvest House, 2010).

28. Philip Yancey, *What Good Is God?: In Search of a Faith That Matters* (Nashville: FaithWords, 2010), 204.

Chapter 9: When America Would Turn Her Back on Israel

1. Thanks to Middle East expert Mike Evans for his succinct statement of this truth: "I believe Israel is the key to America's survival." Mike Evans, *Betrayed: The Conspiracy to Divide Jerusalem* (Phoenix, AZ: TimeWorthy Books, 2010), 59.

2. Thomas Newton, *Dissertations on the Prophecies* (London: Longman, 1832), 93, 104.

3. George Santayana's (1863–1952) original statement was, "Those who cannot remember the past are condemned to repeat it," in *The Life of Reason* (Amherst, NY: Prometheus Books, 1998), 82.

4. Jennifer Rosenberg, "Balfour Declaration," http://history1900s.about.com/cs/holocaust/p/balfourdeclare.htm.

5. *Exodus*, ©1960 Metro-Goldwyn-Mayer Studios, Inc. All rights reserved.

6. Peter Grose, *Israel in the Mind of America* (New York: Knopf, 1983), 134.

7. "Forget the Great in Britain," *Newsweek*, August 1, 2009, accessed June 23, 2011, http://www.newsweek.com/2009/07/31/forget-the-great-in-britain.html.

8. Jerry Klinger, "The Canary in the Coal Mine? American Jewry 1654–1770," *Jewish Magazine*, accessed May 10, 2011, http://www.jewishmag.com/79mag/usahistory2/usahistory2.htm.

9. *Wikipedia*, s.v. "Haym Solomon," accessed May 5, 2011, http://en.wikipedia.org/wiki/Hayim_solomon.

10. "To Bigotry No Sanction, to Persecution No Assistance," Jewish Virtual Library, accessed May 5, 2011, http://www.jewishvirtuallibrary.org/jsource/US-Israel/bigotry.html.

11. David Jeremiah, *What in the World Is Going On?: 10 Prophetic Clues You Cannot Afford to Ignore* (Nashville, TN: Thomas Nelson, 2008), 19–22.

12. Ibid., 22.

13. Ibid.

14. McLaughlin and Associates, "National Survey October 5, 2010," Committee for Israel, accessed October 12, 2010, http://www.committeeforisrael.com/wp-content/uploads/2010/10/ECI-National-Poll-October.pdf.

15. David Jeremiah, *The Coming Economic Armageddon* (New York: FaithWords, 2010), 171–72.

16. "Text: Obama's Speech in Cairo," *New York Times*, June 4, 2009, accessed May 5, 2011, http://www.nytimes.com/2009/06/04/us/politics/04obama.text.html?pagewanted=1&adxnnlx=1304006424-qJNyzY0YUQPF6d7kZqJW7w.

17. Wm. Robert Johnston, "The Chronology of Terrorist Attacks in Israel Part XI: 2007–2011," Johnston Archive, January 30, 2011, accessed May 5, 2011, http://www.johnstonsarchive.net/terrorism/terrisrael-11.html. Cited in Evans, *Betrayed*, 169.

18. Tony Blankley, "Blankley: Obama's Israeli Border Brouhaha: Who Knows What the President Really Meant," *Washington Times*, May 23, 2011, accessed May 24, 2011, http://www.washingtontimes.com/news/2011/may/23/obamas-israeli-border-brouhaha/.

19. Ibid.

20. Chuck Colson, "Covenant and Conflict: Israel's Place in the World Today," BreakPoint, February 18, 2003, accessed May 5, 2011, http://www.breakpoint.org/commentaries/3320-covenant-and-conflict.

21. Evans, *Betrayed*, 168.

Chapter 10: When Changing Your Mind Could Save Your Life

1. Quoted in Derek Tidball, *The Message of Holiness: The Bible Speaks Today* (Downers Grove, IL: InterVarsity Press, 2010), 216–17.

STAY CONNECTED
to the
TEACHING SERIES
of
DR. DAVID JEREMIAH

PUBLISHING · RADIO · TELEVISION · ONLINE

FURTHER YOUR STUDY OF THIS BOOK

Incorporate these correlating
I Never Thought I'd See the Day! Study Materials

To enhance your study on this important topic, we recommend the correlating study guide, audio message album, and DVD messages from the *I Never Thought I'd See the Day!* series.

Audio Message Album
Ten CD Messages

The material found in this book originated from messages presented by Dr. David Jeremiah at the Shadow Mountain Community Church where he serves as Senior Pastor. These ten messages are conveniently packaged in one audio album.

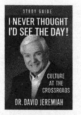

Study Guide

This 128-page study guide resource correlates with the *I Never Thought I'd See the Day!* messages by Dr. Jeremiah. Each lesson provides an outline, overview, and application questions for each topic. Topical charts and maps are included in this study guide.

DVD Message Presentations
Ten DVD Messages

Watch Dr. Jeremiah deliver the ten *I Never Thought I'd See the Day!* original messages in this special DVD collection.

New York Times Best Seller book
The Coming Economic Armageddon
by Dr. David Jeremiah

"COULD WE BE STANDING TODAY on the edge of a recession from which no one economy, no one nation, no one union will be able to extricate the world? The Bible predicts that such an era is coming. Fueled by the world's economic convulsions, the only answer will seem to be the unification of the nations under one economic system and one world ruler."

In *The Coming Economic Armageddon,* **Dr. David Jeremiah examines the current financial events and how they might be pointing to the "end times"** **as prophesied in the Bible.** Meticulously researched and clearly presented, Dr. Jeremiah believes it is possible to interpret these events as steps toward the ultimate collapse of the global economy and the development of a one-world monetary and governmental system—events the Bible says are signs of the "end of the age."

Rejecting the fear and discouragement usually accompanying the subject of biblical prophesy, Dr. Jeremiah presents the hope given by a loving and sovereign God. This is a real hope—one not dependent on the ups and downs of stock portfolios, monetary value fluctuations, or risky-future trading. Instead, it is a hope, a future, based on His eternal Word. We can trust God for our well-being because he has given us sound financial principles that can stabilize our personal finances and get us through tough times.

New York Times Best Seller book

What in the World Is Going On?
by Dr. David Jeremiah

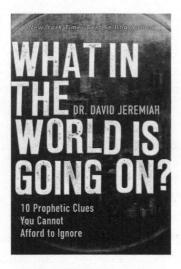

IS THE TURBULENT ECONOMIC AND POLITICAL STATE of this world actually prophesied in the Bible? If so, what are we to do about it? It is hard to piece together all this information in a way that gives a comprehensive picture of what the "end times" will look like. That's why so many theories abound. And that's why Dr. David Jeremiah has written *What in the World Is Going On?*, a unique book that cuts through the hundreds of books and numerous theories to **identify the ten essential biblical prophecies that are affecting our world today.**

There is no other book like this. You'll find it is the ultimate study tool for understanding the future. You'll have a greater sense of comfort that, even in these turbulent times, God is indeed in control. If Bible prophecy has always been a mystery to you, Dr. Jeremiah's book will help you solve the mystery. At last, Bible prophecy can make sense, and make a difference. It's never been more important. *What in the World Is Going On?* is shocking and eye-opening but essential reading in these turbulent days.

WHAT IN THE WORLD IS GOING ON?
BRINGS BIBLE PROPHECY TO LIGHT ON:

The oil crisis • The resurgence of Russia • The new axis of evil
The importance of Israel • The new powers of the European Union

---

DR. JEREMIAH *on* RADIO

Dr. Jeremiah's English Radio program, *Turning Point*, was launched in 1982 and is now transmitted over 1,300 stations, with over 2,000 daily broadcasts heard in the United States, Canada, the Caribbean, Central America, the South Pacific, Europe, and Africa. The thirty-minute radio programs are also available worldwide via the Internet.

In addition, *Turning Point*'s Spanish programming, *Momento Decisivo*, reaches all 23 Spanish-speaking countries with nearly 50 translated series. On any given day there are more than 799 programs airing from 573 transmitters around the world, 79 of which are in the United States.

As of March 2011, *Turning Point* is also broadcasting through China potentially reaching 780 million Mandarin Chinese speakers. Turning Point is currently working toward translating and transmitting radio programs into ten other languages including Punjabi, Tagalog, and Farsi, seeking to deliver biblical truth to people around the world.

For more information, and to find a station in your area that carries *Turning Point*, visit the Turning Point website at www.DavidJeremiah.org/radio.

DR. JEREMIAH *on* TELEVISION

Dr. Jeremiah's ministry, *Turning Point*, also features weekly television programming. Senior Pastor at Shadow Mountain Community Church, Dr. Jeremiah's Sunday sermons are recorded live and adapted for hour- and half hour-long telecasts.

Launched in 29 cities in April of 2000, *Turning Point* telecasts can now potentially be viewed from every household in America. *Turning Point* Television is carried by ION TV, Trinity Broadcasting Network, FamilyNet, DayStar, Faith TV, and Inspirational Network in the U.S., Vision TV in Canada, Trinity Broadcasting in Europe and the United Kingdom, Shine TV in New Zealand and Australia, and METV in the Middle East. Arabic translations are also available in the Middle East via Kingdom Satellite.

Turning Point Television continues to grow and expand, reaching more local stations in cities across the United States in order to minister more directly to receiving communities.

For more information on *Turning Point* Television, go to www.DavidJeremiah.org/Television.

 **DR. JEREMIAH ONLINE**

Dr. Jeremiah's website offers up-to-date information on ministry happenings including current television and radio series, available resources, upcoming live events, and articles by Dr. Jeremiah. You can also read daily devotionals, learn about Turning Point's global outreach, and shop at the online bookstore.

From the Turning Point bookstore you can purchase all resources offered through Turning Point, including books by Dr. Jeremiah, teaching series on CD and DVD, pamphlets, study guides, and many other resources.

Shop today at www.DavidJeremiah.org/Shop.

STAY CONNECTED

to the teaching of Dr. David Jeremiah

Take advantage of two great ways to let Dr. David Jeremiah give you spiritual direction every day! Both are absolutely FREE!

Turning Points Magazine and Devotional

Receive Dr. David Jeremiah's monthly magazine, *Turning Points*, each month:

- Monthly Study Focus
- 52 pages of life-changing reading
- Relevant Articles
- Special Features
- Humor Section
- Family Section
- Daily devotional readings for each day of the month!
- Bible study resource offers!
- Live Event Schedule
- Radio & Television Information

Your Daily Turning Point E-Devotional

Start your day off right! Find words of inspiration and spiritual motivation waiting for you on your computer every morning! You can receive a daily e-devotion communication from David Jeremiah that will strengthen your walk with God and encourage you to live the authentic Christian life.

Sign up for these two free services by visiting us online at www.DavidJeremiah.org. Click on DEVOTIONALS to sign up for your monthly copy of *Turning Points* and your Daily Turning Point.